LISA HELEN GRAY
MASON
A CARTERS BROTHER NOVEL BOOK TWO

Mason

©2015 Lisa Helen Grey

Copy rights reserved

All rights reserved

No part of this publication may be reproduced or transmitted in any form or by any means, electronic or mechanical, including photocopy, recording, or any information storage and retrieval system without the prior written consent from the publisher, except in the instance of quotes for reviews. No part of this book may be scanned, uploaded, or distrusted via the internet without the publishers permission and is a violation of the international copyright law, which subjects the violator to severe fines and imprisonment.

This book is licensed for your enjoyment. EBook copies may not be resold or given away to other people. If you would like to share with a friend, please buy an extra copy, and thank you for respecting the author's work.

DEDICATION

All our dreams can come true,
if we have the courage to pursue them
-*Walt Disney*

MASON

PROLOGUE

Giving my room one more glance over, I make sure I haven't forgotten anything, and sadness engulfs me. With the last of my bags packed and my Nan downstairs there isn't anything else keeping me here.

My parents don't want me, *he* doesn't want me and I'm pretty sure this is how my life is going to be for the rest of my life.

For eighteen years now I've tried to make my parents be proud of me, but nothing I ever did was good enough. My news yesterday only confirmed what a disappointment I really am to them. It's why I'm leaving with my Nan to live miles away.

My life really sucks.

"Are you ready Denny?" Nan asks sneaking up on me.

"Is it okay if I go say goodbye to my friends before we leave?"

"Of course you can. I'm going to go see an old friend then, so why don't you call me once you've finished and I'll come pick you up."

"Sounds great," I lie.

She leads me down the stairs to where my parents are. My mother is standing by the grand fireplace looking beet red in the face speaking in a low tone to my father. He's sitting down in the armchair like a school boy getting told off by the teacher. That's the thing about my dad; he doesn't have a backbone where my mother is concerned. She says jump, he asks how high. It's always been the same. God forbid he ever has an opinion.

"We're off Charles. Denny is going to say goodbye to her friends, so I'll go visit with Deborah."

"That sounds. . . . ," my father starts.

". . . like a bad idea. After all, those friends of yours are to blame for corrupting you. You will do no such thing," my mother interrupts, her face stone cold, void of any sort of emotion.

"Well then Vivian, it's a good job she isn't in your care anymore then isn't it?" my Nan answers back. My lips twitch, knowing my Nan hates mom as much as I do.

We live in what people call the richest part of town, where the houses are bigger and the people are stuck up. Most of them are anyway. My mother just seems to be the worst and heaven forbid someone answer her back. Seeing my Nan talk back to her is pretty funny.

"Charles and I can see this being a bad idea. Maybe it will be best if Denny finds her own way. After all, living with you, Mary doesn't seem like a good enough punishment."

"Well *Vivian*, you don't get to decide. Denny turned eighteen last week, and legally, she is free to do as she pleases."

My Nan really does kick ass when she gets going!

"Don't be absurd. She doesn't turn eighteen until next week. I should know, I did give birth to her," she says, twisting her face up in disgust.

"Yes, you should know," Nan replies bitterly.

Mom opens her mouth to speak, but I interrupt her wanting to go see Harlow before I leave. I texted her on my way down the stairs asking if it was okay if I went over and she replied with a 'hell yes.'

"It was last week mom. You would know if you ever paid any attention to me," I snap, feeling brave. I'm just so angry at them, more so at my dad for not speaking up for me when mom was laying into me.

"Don't talk back to me young lady. You're still young enough to get a spanking. Just get out of my house now. Get out! I'll not have you insulting me in my own home," she yells.

"Goodbye dad," I tell him quietly.

He looks up at me with sad eyes and for a minute a spark of hope hits me, hoping he'll stand up to my mother and stand by my side for once. He opens his mouth, but my mom steps next to him squeezing his shoulders. My Nan tuts in disgust before helping me carry the last of my luggage to the car. I couldn't leave anything to chance knowing my mother will have my room emptied the second the door is shut, so I packed pretty much everything that is important to me.

LYING DOWN ON Harlow's bed, her phone rings startling me. I still haven't managed to tell her what's going on. I guess I feel like if I tell her then it will all be real, and I'm not ready for that.

It doesn't help my head is still next door. I'd braved it and gone to speak to Mason, but he was occupying some other woman, so I didn't want to embarrass myself any further. It's not like I haven't done enough of that when it comes to him.

"Malik?" I grin and she nods her head with an eye roll.

I listen to their conversation in envy. I wish I had that. Malik, Harlow's boyfriend, has stood by her side since the whole Davis thing happened. I'm jealous she has him. He hasn't left her side until tonight which is something I'm so desperate to have. I want someone to hold me in their arms and tell me it's okay, to tell me that they're there for me and that they love me.

I catch the last part of their conversation and my ears pick up. I know I can't put off saying anything any longer. My Nan texted me not long ago saying no more than an hour because we had a three hour drive to make.

"What are we doing?"

"I need to go meet Malik, are you coming? He wants to show me something. Mr. Gunner said he's found a way to help me move on," she says sheepishly.

"Well, I'm intrigued. I can only stay for a little bit, but I have to leave in . . . " I frown pretending to look at my watch, hoping that miraculously I'll get more time. "In less than an hour."

"Is everything okay, Denny? You said you needed to talk, but you've avoided any conversation since you got here."

"Yeah, I do, but can I tell you after?" I plead, hoping she doesn't notice my eyes watering.

"Okay," she agrees reluctantly.

We pull up to where Malik stands waiting at the edge of the lane, his face sporting the biggest grin ever. Whatever it is he needs to show is obviously important. The lad hardly smiles. The one time when he did, I thought his face was going to crack.

"This better be good," Harlow warns him nervously.

"You'll be fine, babe. I wouldn't bring you out here if I didn't think this may do you some good," he grins.

"Is that smoke?" I gasp from behind them. The smell of smoke is strong in the air. I walk towards the old house and grin. They're burning down the old Gunner house. I can hear Harlow asking Malik if he did this when a man I recognise as Chris's dad marches over looking grim.

Uh-oh.

As soon as I hear that this wasn't all Malik and that Chris's dad is the one who decided to burn the house down, I take a step back, wanting to get out of the way. One, I'm pretty sure inhaling all this smoke isn't good for me or the . . . see? I can't even say it.

Another texted message flashes on my phone asking me where I am. I reply with the address and where to wait for me. When I look back up from my phone Hannah is talking to Harlow. The bitch really has a nerve. I'm about to step in and give her another punch to the face like I did a few weeks back, when I notice Mason over by the fence talking to the rest of the Carter brothers, a girl hanging off his arm. It's not even the same girl I saw him with earlier when I went to try and talk to him.

Fucking typical.

His eyes reach mine, and I swear he can reach inside my soul with just one look. His eyes are a chocolate brown colour, but when he's turned on or angry, they mould into the darkest brown you'll ever see.

Shivers rake through my body, his stare captivating me, making it hard for me to look away. The spell is soon broken when the girl he's with steps in front of him, rubbing her boobs up his chest. My eyes start to water and I have to look away, but giving him one last glance I see him giving me those soft puppy dog eyes, the same eyes that got me into bed.

I don't think my feelings for him will ever change. All I know is that I'll never let another boy like Mason walk all over me.

Time is passing too quickly and before I know it, my Nan has texted telling me she's here and to say goodbye.

My eyes water, tears spilling down my cheeks as I walk over to where Harlow is, cuddled in Malik's arms. Half of me doesn't want to interrupt them, they look so peaceful together. I could just walk away quietly and they'll never know I had gone.

I tap her on the shoulder, knowing I need to get this out, I need to say goodbye. She gives me one look before worry etches across her face. Malik gives me the same look, but instead of lingering which I was worried he'd do, he gives Harlow a kiss then leaves us to it.

As soon as he's out of earshot she's pulling me into her arms. It makes me cry harder, no noise leaving my mouth. I just hold her, never wanting to let go, but I do when she asks me to tell her what's wrong.

"He told me so many lies. Told me he had wanted me for years that he never met anyone like me before. I believed everything he ever said to me. Then that night, I gave myself to him. I gave him everything and he doesn't even realise just how much he's taken from me," I sob and for the first time I feel myself becoming angry. I loved him, I think I did anyway. We'd been texting each other off and on from the first moment we met each other. At first it was just light 'how are you?' texts and getting to know each other. Then it turned to much more and I became connected to him. I honestly thought he felt the same way, but I was nothing more than someone to stick his dick into.

"Hey, everything's going to be okay. What is wrong? Things will get better in time Denny, you'll be crying over some other dickhead in a few months, I bet ya." Her enthusiasm isn't lost on me. She just doesn't realise how wrong her comment truly is. Nothing will ever be the same again.

"That's the thing Harlow; I don't have time," I cry, shoving my face into my hands, not able to look at her.

"What do you mean?"

"I'm leaving," I blurt out, pulling away from her.

"What . . . like going home?" she asks, confused, her eyes watering too, which makes this even harder to do.

"No. My parents kicked me out. My Nan has offered to let me live with her, so I'm moving to Wales."

"You can stay with us. Gram's wouldn't mind and she has a spare room," she pleads.

"You don't understand Harlow. It's not that simple. I *can't* stay here."

"Make me understand. What is it you're not telling me Denny?" she pleads sounding desperate.

"I'm pregnant."

My hand covers my mouth in shock, not believing I had just said that out loud. I wasn't ready for anyone to know. I told my parents last night. Hence the reason I'm being kicked out, but as for everyone else, I just wasn't ready.

Her face is a mixture of shock and confusion. Her head snaps over to Mason, who is still standing over by the fence, his eyes clearly fixed on us and if I'm not mistaken, worry etched across his face.

"Mason," she says, and I nod my head as a cry leaves my mouth.

Another texted message alerts me that I need to go. "I have to go," I whisper, but her hand shooting out stops me from moving.

"Wait here. We can sort this out, let me go get Mason. You don't need to leave," she says quickly, her mind obviously going over every scenario.

My mouth opens to stop her, but I snap it shut and give her a tight nod. Once she starts to walk away, I turn, and move towards the gate where I can see my Nan's car waiting for me.

I'm just by the car when I hear her shout my name, along with a voice that still sends shivers down my spine and makes my skin break out in goose bumps. I don't bother turning around. I open the car door and put on my belt.

"Please drive," I cry, my voice barely a whisper.

My Nan looks out the window and for a second I'm ready to scream at her to drive, but before I can open my mouth, she slowly peels out of her spot and drives off.

I lean my head on the window, looking out into the dark field whilst tears stream down my face.

"Everything is going to be okay," Nan says, placing her hand on my thigh.

I don't bother correcting her. Nothing is going to be okay. I can feel my heart breaking into thousands of little pieces the further we get away from the one person who could make this all better.

ONE

MASON

Two and a half months later

DIFFERENT DAY, same shit!

That seems to be the new motto in my life ever since the day I found out Denny Smith was pregnant with my baby.

I spent months, if not more trying to push the girl away, when all along I should have been winning her over. It's not just about the baby. I wanted her before I found out she was even pregnant, but I told myself I didn't deserve her. I'd let my past define my present, and that is something I promised myself I wouldn't do.

My dad cheated on my mother left, right and centre when we were kids. He also hit her constantly. Can you see where I'm going with this? What if the apple doesn't fall far from the tree? What if I turned out just like him and destroyed Denny? She's everything I'm not and I didn't want to take the risk of destroying her like my dad did my mother. No way. I care for her way too much to even contemplate it.

Then the rules changed.

I found out she was pregnant five minutes after watching her drive out of my life. At the time I thought it was for good, that I'll never see her again, until earlier this week when I overheard Harlow telling Malik, my brother, that Denny had been summoned to court. She arrives back in town tomorrow evening and I've been working my ass off trying to get everything together for when she returns.

I've tried getting Harlow to send me Denny's new number, even asked for her address, but Harlow wouldn't let up on the information, so I've spent the past two and a half months going stir crazy.

I've kept busy with the last bits to the renovations to the house Maverick and I *were* moving into. Now, he's given Denny and I full rein to move in, and even changed it so it's now a three bed with an en-suite instead of a four bedroom house. The only room that's incomplete decoration wise, is the nursery. I'm not sure whether the baby is a girl or a boy, so I've left it blank until I find out. Then I'll deck it out and give the baby and Denny the best nursery ever.

I scrub my hands down my face groaning. Denny probably won't even want to speak to me, let alone move in with me. I can't let her raise our baby miles away without me. This is karma coming back to bite me in the ass, something Harlow warned me about the day after sleeping with Denny.

Fuck! That night had been one of the best nights of my life. I've fucked a lot of girls in my years, but never, and I mean never, have I ever felt connected to one like I did with Denny. We were both so caught up in the moment that it had taken me until the morning to realise she was a virgin. That's when everything went to shit. I flipped out, got scared and ruined the best thing to ever have happened to me.

When she told me she had been a virgin, I looked up into her big, vulnerable, dark green emerald eyes and froze. All I could see was this vulnerable, perfect, young, beautiful woman in my bed and I had already tainted her by taking her virginity. I didn't romance her, buy her flowers, or take her out on a date and it made me realise just how alike my dad and I are. He would most likely have done the same. So instead of apologising and treating her the way that she should be treated by taking her out on a date, I pushed her away. I pushed and I pushed, to the point I think it may be too late for me to take it all back. I made her believe I slept with all those women that I threw in her face, when in truth, I could never keep my mind away from Denny long enough to fake it with another girl. I just wanted *her,* but I didn't want to ruin her life. She's perfect in every sense of the word and she deserves more than I'll ever be able to give her.

Now, though, the rules have changed. We have a baby on the way. If that isn't proof enough that pushing her away was the worst thing I could ever have done, the ache in my chest since the day she drove off would pretty much do it. I don't even want to explain the feeling I had the morning I kicked her out of my bed, that was hard enough for me to handle, but her leaving, that nearly killed me.

A touch startles me from my thoughts and I frown at the woman standing next to me.

"So . . . ?" she huffs and I realise she must have been speaking to me while I drifted off into my own head. Maverick made me come into work telling me I'll need some time off if I ever want to make things right with Denny again. So I came into work under the impression I'd be working nonstop, only to find out that I had put a few extra people on staff tonight, so I'm not really needed. Hence the reason I'm sitting down on a stool at the end of the bar, nursing a beer with some woman trying to grab my attention.

"Are you even listening?" Her voice is high pitched and I can tell she really wants to scream at me right now, but doesn't want to show her true colours just yet, so instead, she's trying to sound seductive. I imagine to her own ears she sounds just that, but to mine? It just sounds like sharp nails scratching down a chalkboard.

"No, sorry I'm not," I deadpan, keeping my eyes locked into my beer. My mind wanders back to Denny, and tomorrow, when all of a sudden a plan comes to mind and I grin to myself. The woman still standing next to me must take that as a sign to rub her breasts against my arm. I turn to her shaking my head in disgust.

"Look love, I'm gay and although you do have manly features, I prefer dick."

With that, I grab my jacket from off the bar and head over to the offices downstairs. I need to work out a plan with everyone and hopefully we can get Harlow to agree. I know she's looking out for her friend, but sometimes that girl can be stubborn as shit. She kind of reminds me of her Nan.

If it all works out I could have Denny living with me by the end of the week. Hopefully by the end of tomorrow, but I'm not going to get myself too psyched up over it just to be let down again.

TWO

DENNY

"Nan, I'm fine, honestly," I assure her, rubbing a hand over my ever-growing bump. I'm only twenty one weeks gone, but my Nan says I look like I'm further along with how large my bump is. I've only had one scan since finding out about the baby, and I'm due for another one any day now, but for some unknown reason I've been putting it off for three weeks now.

"Are you sure? Have you spoken to Evan yet?" My Nan is driving me insane with all her smothering. Don't get me wrong, I love that she cares, but sometimes it all becomes too much. As for my brother, he hasn't contacted me since I called him a week ago asking to crash at his place after I got my summons letter from the courts.

"Yes, Nan, he texted me earlier to let me know he's waiting for me outside the train station," I lie. She's been so worried about me travelling alone from Wales to Coldenshire that she's been on my back most of the way here. I didn't want to tell her that Harlow is picking me up because I'll know she'll flip out when she finds out I'll be that much closer to Mason. And now that he knows about the baby, I have no idea how he's going to react.

With the long journey back to Coldenshire, I downloaded a new romance novel I found on Amazon yesterday to read, but with her constantly calling me every twenty minutes I've not been able to pass the first page.

"Thank goodness Denny. That boy really needs to answer that mobile phone of his. Call me when you arrive and if Evan isn't there to pick you up...."

"I promise, so stop worrying," I plead interrupting, fanning myself with the newspaper that some guy had left a few stops back. The mid-August heat is overbearing and I can't wait to get off this hot stuffy train. My silent prayers are answered when the intercom announces the next stop. "Nan, I'm the next stop. I need to get my stuff together, I don't want to get trampled on."

"Of course, you go on now. Don't forget to call me. And make sure you drink plenty of water and remember to take those vitamins. I packed a spare packet in your suitcase."

Rolling my eyes, I thank her, ending the call and putting my phone in my handbag. I quickly grab my hand luggage and suitcase, and then start to make my way towards the exit.

Taking my phone back out of my pocket I text Harlow to make sure she's still okay to pick me up and to let her know I've arrived. I'm starting to worry she's forgotten when my phone beeps alerting me of a text.

Harlow: Out in the parking lot. X H

I shake my head, excited to see her for the first time since I told her about the baby. We've spoken to each other over the phone occasionally, but for the first month of staying with my Nan I ignored most of her calls, especially when she brought up *his* name. It hurts too much when I let myself think about him, let alone someone reminding me of him.

The doors open and I delight in the cool breeze for a moment before everyone starts to shuffle past me in a hurry off the train. I'm stunned for a second, in total shock at how rude people are.

"Hello? Pregnant woman here and carrying two bags, assholes," I snap when another business man knocks past me.

I'm just about to go sumo wrestler on the asshole who takes my luggage from my hands, but before I can even blink or process what is going on, he's back. I'm startled when his two strong, muscled hands grab me from under my arms and lift me off the train, safely onto the platform.

I'm in two minds about what to do. Shall I scream and shout? Or shall I gracefully thank him like nothing had happened?

"Hello Denny." His voice is still deep and raspy, and much to my disappointment it still covers my skin in goose bumps, sending shivers down the back of my spine. How can he still have such a powerful effect on me after everything he's put me through? I don't get it. It's like I'm glutton for punishment or something.

"Hello Mason."

We stand staring at each other for what seems like hours. I'm actually thankful now that I put on my white sundress that ends just above my knees. Not that I have many options lately on what to wear. But the thought of our first encounter being in sweats and a baggy t-shirt gives me the heebie-geebies.

Mason's hair looks longer than it did a few months back. His eyes are lined with dark circles and he looks like he hasn't shaved since the last time I saw him. Even his bright, sparkly brown eyes look different. They seem duller, full of sadness, pain and regret, and it hurts my heart to see him like this.

My eyes water not knowing what to do, so I do the only thing I can do, I run away. Not literally, I'd never make it a step without being out of breath, but I walk away, not knowing what to say to him.

"Why didn't you tell me?" he blurts out, sounding between angry and sad about it as he reaches out to stop me. His touch has me stopping short, standing there frozen and contemplating what to do. He's occupied my thoughts for so long that you would think I would know what to do right now, what to say, but the truth is, I don't.

"I never had the chance," I whisper feeling really bad. It's obvious Harlow told him about the baby, she made it no secret, but she never came right out and said she told him. It's not like I told her it was a secret, so I can't really be mad at her for it either. In fact, I'm madder at myself more than anything. I just wish we didn't have to have this conversation right now. I'm hot, I'm hungry, and I'm also so freaking tired I could fall asleep standing up right now. And okay, yes, I'd been hoping to avoid seeing him the whole time I was here. I'm just not ready for this confrontation yet. Is that bad of me?

"You didn't? Didn't it occur to you when you were around me and my brothers to tell me or even one of them? I deserved to fucking know Denny. I deserved to be there for you and our baby."

My head snaps up to him, my blood pressure rising. I'd like to blame it on the pregnancy hormones, but no, this is all me. How dare he push all the blame onto me.

"I'm sorry. When I tried to text you to talk to you, you would never even gift me with a reply and then, not long after, you blocked my number. Oh . . . oh . . . maybe I should have told you when you started to avoid me? Better yet, when I actually saw you with one of your hook-ups, maybe I should have told you then. Mason, I tried to fucking tell you over and over again, but you were the one always too fucking busy avoiding *me*. I'm the one that had to go through this on my own. I'm a fucking teenager for fuck's sake and I had to do it on my own. Oh . . . wait . . . the best part, the first people I do finally find the courage to tell disown me and kick me out.

"Yes I agree I should have told you, but you never gave me the time of day, Mason." I'm yelling and crying so hard that we've gathered the attention from the other passengers around us.

"I'm sorry. I'm sorry for everything I did after I slept with you. I just . . . I . . . come on, the others are waiting," he says, looking deflated, and just like that he grabs my bags and walks towards the exit.

I follow behind at a slower pace, my mind reeling over him being here, with me. I've been trying so hard to move on from him that I didn't expect for my old feelings to resurface the moment I laid eyes on him again. I want to kick my body and thump my heart so bad right now; why can't they get in check with my head?

"Welcome home," is shouted and I'm immediately stunned, standing frozen, staring at everyone in front of me with wide eyes. All of the Carter brothers are there with their Granddad and so is Harlow with her Gram's. I didn't think anyone would want to speak to me again after I upped and left the way I did, pregnant and all.

"What are you guys doing here?" I ask completely shocked, the tears again falling from my eyes.

Harlow is the first one to step out from the gang and rush over to me, bringing me into a tight hug.

God, I've missed the crazy girl!

"Oh my God, you look stunning Denny. I can't believe how big your belly is," she gushes making me smile and feeling a little self-conscious.

"Yeah babe, what are you packing under that dress?" Max flirts coming up to give me a hug. Pulling away his eyes drift down towards my cleavage, which is pretty impressive I must say. Another perk that comes to being pregnant.

"Move your eyes, dickhead," Mason growls making me jump. I hadn't noticed that he had moved to stand so close beside me and now that I'm fully aware, I can feel my body heat, and it's not because of the sun.

"Sorry," Max says not sounding sorry before he's shoved out of the way by Myles.

"It's good to have you back. The gang has been so lost without you," he mutters before giving me a hug.

"Thanks," I whisper, feeling overwhelmed. I hid my pregnancy from all of them, yet they're all here welcoming me back with open arms.

Malik gives me a head nod, and it makes me smile. It seems some things don't change around here. Harlow grins up at him from where she's leaning against him, and it makes my heart swell and a lump to form in my throat.

"Welcome home Denny sweetie," Harlow's Gram's, Joan, tells me before giving me a hug. Mark, Mason's Granddad does the same before moving back to Joan's side. Harlow mentioned the two had gotten together and were officially living together now, but seeing them together like this . . . they look so cute.

Maverick, the eldest of the Carter sibling's steps forward last, his eyes warm and soft as he approaches me. We haven't really spoken to each other in the past, so it's surprising to see him here with everyone else.

"Welcome to the family, Darlin.'" His words shock me, but when he brings me in for a hug it completely baffles me.

"Thank you," I whisper back once I've found my voice.

"We've cleaned out Malik's old room over at Mark's for you to stay in, sweetie. Don't worry, it's only until the boys finish off the painting in the new house, then you can stay there," Joan says and once again I'm completely frozen and left speechless. What are they on about? What house? What paint? I look at Mason for answers, but he's looking at me like he's trying to gauge my reaction.

"I'm sorry? I'm confused."

"Well, you can't live in a house full of boys with a new baby on the way silly girl. With Mark and Malik living with us now there is only Max, Maverick and Myles living there, but even still, you, Mason and the baby need your own space."

My head whips to Mason in shock. I'm getting whiplash with all this new information. Why didn't know one tell me any of this? My eyes narrow at Mason while I try to process everything. This is not how I saw my welcoming home.

Am I hearing this right? Is she telling me I'm moving in with Mason? The same Mason who has done nothing but break my heart for the past few months? Does she really believe I could live with someone who will have a long line of women in his bedroom each night?

"I'm sorry, but I'm not staying long and definitely not with Mason. I'm going to crash at my brothers until the court case is over then I'm going back to live with my Nan."

Everyone goes quiet sneaking glances at Mason, like they're waiting for him to contradict me or something. I do the same, wondering what the hell I'm missing, only to find him glaring down at me.

"Like fuck you are, Denny," he snaps.

"Excuse me?" I snap back, placing my fists on my hips.

"Why? What did you do?" he snaps sarcastically.

"What the hell is your problem, Mason?"

"You are. You're not moving back to your Nan's, Denny. We're having a baby together for Christ sake."

"News flash Mason, *I'm* having a baby. Not you. You didn't want anything to do with me before you found out. Now all of a sudden you expect me to come running back to you, obey your demands . . . yeah, I don't bloody think so."

"Yes, actually I do. Maybe if you had told me in the first place we wouldn't be in this mess."

"Are you telling me I should have had an abortion?" I yell, feeling my stomach turn. This was one of my biggest fears when I realised I would need to tell him. "Get lost you prick. I'm not asking you to be a part of this baby's life, or to be with me. I wouldn't want to tie you down, or God forbid, make you do something you don't want to do."

With that I grab my suitcase and carry on towards the taxi rank, ignoring his and everyone else's shocked faces. Tears are streaming fluidly down my face, and my heart is pumping so hard I worry about passing out. I can't believe he said that. I rub on my chest with my free hand trying to get rid of the dull ache when I hear the distinct sound of crunching of boots from behind me.

"Wait." His voice sounds urgent and I pause not wanting to cause another scene in front of loads of people. He pauses for a second before walking up in front of me, his face full of sorrow and pain. "I'm sorry. I should have asked you about it first, and I know we have a lot to sort out, but I want to be with you."

"Why now? Because of the baby?" I croak out, and for the first time I'm jealous of my baby. How childish is that? The fact the love of my life wants me now has me wanting to laugh out loud in hysterics. Typical! Unlucky for him though because I'm not one of those girls who settle.

"What? Huh? No. That isn't why... yes it's a reason, but it's not why. I wanted to be with you before you wanted to be with me, Denny. Look, we have loads to talk about and I have some explaining to do, but can we get you home first? It's getting late and I bet you're hungry."

As if the baby could understand his words my belly grumbles, loud enough for Mason to hear and send me a knowing smirk.

A lot doesn't add up. He's either playing me again or he generally means what he said. I just can't trust him after everything he put me through.

"Yes to food, but no to staying with you guys, I promised my brother I'd be there to look after his house," I lie, not really knowing whether my brother will be there or not.

"Well, don't get used to it Denny. One way or another you're coming to live with me. I'm not letting you go this time."

I roll my eyes not believing his idol threat and move to grab my bags, but Mason swoops in and grabs them from me.

We all ended up going for a meal together. Maverick and the twins were the first to bail. Maverick had to get to work, and Max and Myles went to meet some girls from school. Harlow and Malik left not long after to watch a movie at the cinema, and Mark took Joan home, leaving me alone with Mason to take me home.

"There aren't any lights on. Are you sure you don't want to stay with me at mine?" Mason asks looking over to my brother's bungalow that looks pretty deserted. I've tried calling him a few times, but it's gone straight to voicemail, and now I'm panicking I have to actually sleep over at Mason's house and that isn't something I want to do.

When I found out I needed to come back for the court hearing I never believed I'd come back to this welcoming. I thought everyone would hate me, or worse, Mason asking me to abort the baby. I knew from the start that it was something I could never consider.

Truth is, I think that was the main reason I never told him about the baby. I was scared of him asking me to abort the baby. To have him here asking me to make a go of things with him is just making my already jumbled mind worse.

"Yeah I'm sure. Maybe he fell asleep waiting for me? I did tell him I'd be here over two hours ago," I shrug, another lie.

"I'll get your bags while you go and knock on the door," he says sceptically, his eyes scanning the area. It's not one of the best neighbourhoods to live in, but around here it's one with the lowest crime rate.

Walking up the path I knock on the door, and then ring the doorbell after noticing it for the first time. When no one answers and I hear Mason walking up behind me, I can feel myself starting to sweat and it isn't because of the muggy night.

"I don't think he's hear Tink." Gah, that freaking nickname! I hate it, yet completely love it all at the same time. I look nothing like her now, not that I did before, but with my pixie haircut, my white blond hair and my short height, I can see why he would see the resemblance between me and the Disney fairy.

"Hey, hi, I'm Lexi, Evan's next door neighbour," a beautiful brunette around twenty five calls, jogging across from the garden next to us. I'm stunned for a minute, so I take the time to take in her short shorts, and her tiny strap top. I look down at my large stomach and feel like crying. My eyes start to water and I look up to see if Mason is checking her out. After all, she looks just like his type. Not that he has a type, I think . . . When I look up, I'm surprised to find his eyes on mine, freezing me in place. His big chocolate brown eyes bore into mine and I try hardest not to melt in his arms right there.

". . . Here you go," the woman, Lexi, speaks up and I shake my mind wondering what I missed. Mason gives me a smirk and I give him a glare before turning back to the woman, my cheeks reddening when I realise I'd been standing gawking at Mason.

"I'm sorry, what?" I ask, feeling embarrassed.

"It's fine. I'm friends with your brother, we're neighbours, and he came by yesterday to let me know he had to go out of town on a job, and asked me to give you the keys when you arrived. I've been waiting for you to get here for hours. I had started to think you weren't coming until I heard a car pull up."

"Thank you," I smile, taking the keys from out of her hand. "I'm Denny by the way."

"Yeah, he's told me all about you. I've done your room and cleaned it up a bit. I knew he wouldn't have touched the place and I was right. The only room I wouldn't tackle was his bedroom," she blushes, scrunching up her nose. It makes me giggle because I seriously don't blame her. When my brother lived with us he would leave all his dirty washing around his bedroom floor, and have food shoved under his bed, it was gross. If he still lives like that then I feel deeply sorry for the woman standing in front of me.

"That bad, huh?"

"Something like that," she laughs. "He didn't know what you'd need, so I went round last night before he left and took a look. He left some money with me to get what you needed for the house, so I got you new bed sheets, towels, blankets and a new mattress. The change is on the kitchen counter. He thought you'd sleep in his bed," she scrunches her nose up again and it makes her look adorable.

"Sounds like him. Thank you for doing that, you didn't need to."

"Trust me, I did. I'll leave you to get settled in, but if you need anything please let me know, I only live next door . . . I said that already didn't I?"

I chuckle, rubbing my rounded belly, until my chuckle turns into a yawn. Mason chuckles and the woman smiles, waving goodbye to us.

Turning around I open my mouth to say goodbye and thank Mason for dropping me off when he interrupts.

"I don't think you should stay here by yourself. It doesn't feel right you bein' in this place alone when you could stay at our place," he says.

"We've talked about this already, Mason. I'm not ready. You spent months pushing me away and then all of a sudden I'm back and you want me to move in, it's all too soon."

"I didn't want to push you away, I thought I was . . . look, we can talk about this tomorrow. Let's get you inside. Do you want me to stay the night until your brother gets back?"

"It's fine. I'm a big girl, plus, I need some time to myself. I've had my Nan spoiling me rotten back home, so I need the space."

"That's not your home," he growls, his shoulders tensing.

"Huh?"

"Here is your home, well not here, here, but with me here."

Another yawn leaves my mouth making him chuckle. I smile tiredly up at him, before locating the right key to the door.

"Can I come see you tomorrow?" he asks as he places my luggage by one of the front room chairs.

Unsure on what to do or say, I wait a couple of seconds before agreeing, "Just don't expect too much from me."

"The only thing I want to know before I leave is, are we having a boy or a girl?"

"It's fifty, fifty at the moment."

"What do you mean?" he asks scratching the back of his neck, his arm muscles tightening under his tight t-shirt.

"I have an appointment Friday at the hospital. I missed the last two because it didn't feel right going. I guess it felt wrong not sharing it with you or anyone," I shrug, tears springing to my eyes again. Jeezus, if I cry one more time today, I'm going to eat a large chocolate cake. By myself.

"Oh . . . can, um . . . can I come?" he asks nervously, his eyes on my rounded stomach.

"I'd really like that," I tell him honestly.

"Okay. Good. Yeah," he grins big, as he heads back to the front door. I follow behind him, standing in the open door as he leaves. He turns around looking at me, his eyes shinier than they were earlier. My stomach flips with how intense he is looking at me, like I've just given him the world, or a day pass at the playboy mansion.

"See you tomorrow," I smile, waving as he walks down the path to his car.

"See you beautiful," he winks, jumping back into the car.

A shadow to the left catches my eye, making me jump. When Mason's car pulls away from the curb, chills run up my arms and down my back. When I look back over to the shadowed figure it's gone, and I quickly shut the door, double bolting it before checking the rest of the house.

By the time I'm finished, I'm completely exhausted. My legs and back ache so badly that I can't think of doing anything but sleeping. I'm out before my head hits the pillow.

Tomorrow I will worry about Mason, the baby, the court case and my friendship with Harlow. Tomorrow I will fully inspect my brothers little pad, but until then, I'm to the land of the fairies.

THREE

LIGHT STREAMS THROUGH the window and I groan, rolling to my side, trying to block it out. When I hear banging on the door, I turn and scream into the pillow, muffling the sound.

Urgh!

One thing I dislike about being pregnant is not being able to lie down on my stomach. I won't even attempt to do it, but the urge is never too far from my mind when I'm lying in bed. Especially when it's the best position to be in when you want to block out unwanted noises, like someone knocking on your door at God knows what time in the morning.

Sliding my legs off the side of the bed, I look down at my crinkled dress I didn't bother to change out of last night and silently curse. When I look in the mirror at my wild blonde hair, I try to tame it down as much as I can before heading towards the door. On the way the knocking gets louder, so picking up my speed I end up stubbing my toe on the corner of the sofa.

"Argh, fuck! Owe," I cry out, really wanting to jump up and down in pain, but my large stomach prevents me from doing anything, so instead I have to grit my teeth and wait for it to subside. I try until the banging continues to become much louder.

"Alright, alright," I shout through the locked door.

Opening the door, I'm surprised to find Harlow on my doorstep looking nervous.

"Hey," she waves, her bottom lip trembling.

"Hey, what's wrong?" I ask looking behind her for Malik. Since the attack a few months back Malik hasn't left her side from what she's said on the phone. When I went to live with my Nan we spoke a few times over email and text, but for the most part I distanced myself from her and everyone else linked to Mason, scared of how much harder it would be for me to hear that he had moved on.

"We need to talk."

"Okay, come in. I'm sorry it took me a while, I've only just got up."

"I'm sorry, did I wake you?" she asks taking a seat on the sofa.

"Nah," I lie. "Would you like a cup of tea?"

"Sure."

After making a cup of tea and a piece of toast for myself I head back into the front room and sit on the comfy, thick armchair, pulling my feet under me.

"What's wrong?" I ask after taking a bite of my toast.

"Gram's has been asking why the court case has been taking so long to go to trial. We found out today after the police finally released the information that the case is still on-going."

"What do you mean on-going?" I ask her confused. The case should be straight forward. Davis drugged her, took her against her will and was going to rape her. Not to mention the physical scars she will carry for the rest of her life.

"Can you remember the day you left?"

"Yeah." Like I could forget the day I left. I never thought I'd be able to breathe again when Nan and I drove away.

"Hannah left that night getting into a car . . . "

"Yeah, with some woman wearing scrubs," I finish, wondering where this is going. I hate talking about that bitch and what she originally planned to do to Harlow. I should have beaten her ass harder when I had the chance. Hannah has always been the school bitch, but what she was going to do to Harlow went far beyond 'bitch.'

"That's it. I couldn't remember . . . ," she says trailing off. The look on her face has me worrying. She's paler than normal and is hesitant to talk to me about whatever is bothering her, which just makes me all the more curious.

"Harlow, please just tell me what is wrong, you're worrying me now."

"She's disappeared. Her mom said she got dropped off at home before she went to work and no one has seen her since. At first her mom thought she went to stay with her dad in London, she's been known to do that during the Holidays, but when she called Hannah she never answered."

"She's probably hiding because she's ashamed of what she did. She's going to get in trouble and she knows it."

"That's what I said, but then . . . then the solicitor called this morning telling us why the trial has been postponed for so long and it's because she was one of the main witnesses to the case. They found a bloody jacket, the same one she'd been wearing the night her mom dropped her off. So the investigation is now linked to the case," she says, her eyes watering.

"They think it's because of the case? How? Davis is in custody until the hearing, so I don't understand."

"Me either, but what if he got someone else to do it, to hurt her like he was going to hurt me? Denny, I don't think I could live with myself. I feel like this is all my fault," she cries, and that's when I realise why it's eating up at her. Harlow has a heart of gold, and by God she's the purist of them all. Only she could feel like this towards the person who had a hand in getting her nearly raped. Me . . . I'd most likely do a happy dance. Okay, I'm totally lying, but you get the gist.

"Harlow, this has nothing to do with you and everything to do with those two. If something bad has happened to Hannah then that isn't on you, that's on her getting mixed up with Davis in the first place. Both of them need to take responsibility for their own actions. They only have themselves to blame, Hun."

"I just feel so bad. Her mom came by to see us once the investigation went public. They wanted to keep it quiet so it didn't scare whoever is involved with her disappearance off their tail. She's so torn up. She said it was her and Hannah's dad's fault for the reason she was the way she was. Apparently they didn't have a good marriage and Hannah got caught up in the middle of that. Even still, it doesn't excuse what her daughter did, but seeing her like that really got to me. Then the fact I asked myself what would happen now she isn't here to get up on that stand and give her statement makes me feel more quilt. Will Davis get to walk free?"

Her tears are streaming down her face and I go to stand up to comfort her, but my big belly keeps me glued to the sofa. The cushions are that soft that as soon as I sat down I felt lost in the armchair. Turning a little to my side, I use the arm of the chair as leverage to help me up, but it's no use, my belly gets in the way and I become sweaty and tired.

"Need some help?" Harlow giggles, wiping her eyes.

"I'm supposed to be the one helping you out here, not the other way around," I groan holding my hand out to her.

"It's the thought that counts," she smiles, her smile not reaching her eyes.

Once I'm up I bring her into a hug, okay I press my belly into her. "Everything is going to be okay. You'll see. She'll turn up in no time and everything will be okay."

Pulling away she wipes at her eyes just as the front door knocks. I look over confused wondering who the hell it is. Did someone place an ad in the local paper about my arrival and where I'd be staying?

"That should be Malik and Mason with food," she grins.

"Mason's here? With Malik, and food?" I squeak, looking down at my wrinkled clothes.

"Yeah, it's midday, I thought you'd be up already."

"Crap! I'm just going to have a quick shower and change clothes," I rush out, walking at a fast pace out of the room. I'm scared to run in case I piss myself. It wouldn't be the first time that happened to me.

Half an hour later I'm walking back into the front room wearing another sundress. This was the first and only maternity item I was willing to buy. The coral sundress has crossover cleavage with silver embellishment stylish shoulder straps and a high back. And although it has elastic around the bust and back, the dress is perfect for my ever-growing baby bump. It fits comfortably and if I could wear this all the time I would.

"Wow!" is what snaps my attention back to the present and my eyes collide with Mason's. I suddenly feel self-conscious knowing what he's seeing and I twiddle with the end of the dress. My boobs are bigger and so is my stomach, and I've let my hair down to dry by itself. With the heat it shouldn't take long.

"Hey," I wave dumbly.

"We got you a burger and stuff. I didn't know what you wanted so I got you a bit of everything. The woman at the counter said you're not allowed to eat raw eggs and another bunch of stuff whilst pregnant and you can't drink coffee. I found that out myself. I'd hate to be the woman who craved caffeine when they were pregnant," he chuckles making me smile. I love it when he chuckles, especially when he's unsure if what he's laughing at is funny or not. It comes out husky and deep and guaranteed it always makes my belly do summersaults.

"Yeah, raw fish is another too and other stuff. Kind of stupid," I giggle nervously, not knowing what to say. "My Nan told me once her friend had a craving for sucking bath water out of a sponge. Do not ask how she started that craving. I asked myself what she was doing with the sponge in her mouth in the first place, but my Nan wouldn't answer. I'm just glad I don't have any," I ramble feeling my face heat.

"A sponge? Really?" he asks disbelieving.

"She's right. My mom told me she had a craving for my dad's aftershave. She said when he wasn't around for her to smell it, it would drive her crazy, but when he was around her and she could, she felt high as a kite," Harlow butts in giving me a wink.

"Why didn't she just buy his aftershave?" Malik asks, taking a bite from a burger. Even though I've not long had some toast my mouth waters from the smell, so I pick up the bag Mason pointed to earlier and grab the burger.

"She said it was never the same. They tried it the once when he had to go to work and she ended up having a breakdown crying over the phone to my dad. Apparently it wasn't just about the aftershave, but about his scent too. It's kind of romantic when you think about it. I'd love it when they would talk about things like that," she murmurs, her eyes distant and I know she's thinking about them. She lost them a few months before she came to live with her Gram's, so it's all still so raw for her. Malik, bless his heart, grabs her waist and lifts her up into his lap. She tries to squirm away at first until she ends up giggling. I watch the two, envious of their close relationship.

Feeling eyes on me, I turn my head to Mason to find him watching me with an intense expression. I'm about to open my mouth when Malik interrupts. "We thought we'd go out for the day. We need to meet Maverick and Max at the club."

"The club?" I question shocked. It's the one place Mason and Malik would never take me and Harlow. At first it didn't bother me, but then I felt paranoid, like Mason was hiding something. "I thought we weren't allowed in there?"

"You're eighteen Angel, you can go in there whenever you like . . . but you're not."

"Says who? You just said I'm eighteen and can go when I like." I send Mason a glare, taunting him to continue. How dare he tell me where I can and can't go!

"It gets packed in there on nights and weekends, there is no way I'm going to risk you getting bumped into by someone in there."

I feel my face soften. He has a point. One knock could do the world of damage and my baby's life is something I'd rather not take a gamble with.

"Okay, so what are we going to do?" I ask, ignoring Malik whispering what must be dirty words to Harlow, if her red face and giggles are anything to go by.

"It's a surprise, but we should get going," Mason says smiling at me.

I smile shyly back, loving this side of Mason, the side I had all the time before we slept together. Harlow's phone ringing startles me and I look away from Mason.

"Hello . . . Hi Max. Yeah we're on our way. We had to stop off to get food . . . I'll buy you something when we get there . . . Okay, see you in a bit," she says before ending the call. "Max is getting impatient, grab your stuff," she says to me.

"I'll just grab my phone and bag and I'll be ready," I tell her, then rush back into my bedroom. My bag is already on the bed where I left it last night before crashing and my phone is on the bedside table. Grabbing my suitcase, I open the compartment where I stuffed all my sandals and grab my coral ones with the coral flower on the top. They go perfectly with the sundress I'm wearing. Slipping them on, I notice my white cardigan on top of the pile of clothes in my case and grab it, tucking it over my arm before heading out.

***

AFTER PICKING UP Max and Maverick we drove for thirty minutes before coming to a stop outside one of the biggest parks around our area. It's beautiful. There's a huge stage where live bands play and I guess today is one of those days. There is a mini fair towards the back of the park, where I can hear the screams of kids on rides. The arcades are not too far away from the rides and I smile widely when I see a candyfloss stand in the distance.

"Can we go get some candyfloss please?" I squeal, delighted.

"Why don't you go find somewhere to sit, and make sure there is shade," he says looking at Maverick before giving me a look. I don't have time to figure out what the look meant because Mason grabs my hand. I try to pull away, but he just holds on tighter, sending delicious tingles up my arm.

"Can you get me a pic-a-mix and a bottle of Pepsi?" Harlow asks giddily, looking around the place. It's the first time she's come to one of our town carnivals I realise, and I gasp in surprise horror.

"You cannot drink Pepsi. You need to try this amazing slush puppy, it's to die for. The one year I got brain freeze, and then it started pissing it down with rain," I shrug, and then laugh inside when I realise it's the first time it hasn't rained at one of these events. Usually the weather is so bad they have to cancel for another day.

"I'll have both," she giggles.

My giddy smile drops when Mason squeezes my hands tighter and I look up to him to find his jaw tense and his posture rigid. His eyes are stormy brown, staring at something in the distance. I follow his sight to see who has him shooting death glares and feel my own body growing tight and rigid. It's my turn to squeeze his hand and step closer to him.

My parents are standing not far from where we're all standing, throwing me a disgusted look, well my mother is anyway, my dad doesn't know where to look.

Oh no! Please not here!

"Fuck," I mumble when they start over here, my dad looking like he wants to run, but instead follows like the good dog he is.

"What are you doing here?" my mother hisses grabbing my arm so tight I wince.

"Let her go, now," Mason growls shoving my mother's hand from off my arm.

"Don't talk to me, you filthy scumbag," she hisses at him and I look around mortified. Maverick's jaw is hard, Malik looks bored, Harlow looks shocked, and Max looks like he's two seconds away from pissing himself laughing. "I'll ask again young lady, what are you doing here?"

"I'm staying here. Evan let me sleep at his house until I am finished with court and I can go back to Nan's."

"Thank God for that. Now go back to Evan's. I don't need people knowing what a hussy I have for a daughter," she snaps and Mason growls from beside me, his hand loosening, but only to go around my shoulder.

"Your daughter isn't going anywhere and she isn't going to be going back to her Nan's. She will be living with me."

"Well, no wonder you're pregnant if you sleep with riff raff like that," she sneers, looking Mason up and down with disgust.

"Are you going to let her talk to your daughter like that?" Mason snaps at my dad. I'm in complete shock and I can feel tears spring to my eyes.

"Come on Vivian, let's go meet Robert and Darla," my dad answers, his expression grim.

Max laughs shaking his head and my mother turns her scowl over to him, looking at him with the same expression she did with Mason.

"Something funny?" she snarls.

"Yeah you. You have a brilliant daughter right in front of you. She got good grades; she's polite as fuck to everyone and hardly ever swears. She lost her virginity to my brother and got up the duff. Worse things could have happened ya know. She could have come back with an STD or on drugs. If you're going to stand there looking disgusted, go direct it in a mirror. That's where the disgust should be aimed."

"How dare you!" she gasps horrified. "Charles, dear, are you going to let him talk to me like that?"

"Boy, watch your mouth around the lady. Come on Vivian, I can see Darla and Robert over there."

My mother's head whips up so fast to look around her. She gives me one more disgruntled look before walking off with my father again in tow. I'm still frozen and kind of shocked.

"Your parents seem really . . . nice," Harlow says once they're out of earshot. The comment breaks the awkward silence and I burst into a fit of laughter, looking at her as if to say 'no shit.'

"Your mom's a bitch. Now can you go get me food, you guys owe me for eating without me. Oh grab some mayo and chips if they have any," Max says before walking off.

"Are you okay?" Mason asks, the same time Maverick walks over to us.

"Don't let her get to you. She might come around . . . ,"

I snort, "Or not."

"Or not," he chuckles.

"Let's go get some food," Mason mumbles, his posture still tense and rigid, his eyes focused back to where my parent's just left.

"Yeah," I whisper, feeling my eyes water. I pray like hell he doesn't notice them or that they fall. I never imagined bumping into my parents when I found out about coming back. To be honest, they never crossed my mind. Nan said she called up my father a few times, but it was always my mom to answer the phone. She said if she could get him on his own, he may be able to speak for himself.

Seeing them here is a complete surprise and another reminder of why I can't stay around here. It hurts too much to know my own parents kicked me out when I needed them the most. I just wanted my dad to cuddle me and my mom to tell me everything was going to be okay. Unlucky for me, my parents have never been those kind of parents. They were always too busy with their image they had to uphold than to worry about their daughter.

I was the mistake. I was the one they didn't want, so all my life I had to watch my brother get everything and anything while I suffered through my mother's continuous criticism where she belittled me every chance she got.

FOUR

After grabbing some food Mason and I head over to where the group said they'd be. Mason carried both the trays while I carried the bag of drinks and a tub of pink candyfloss.

"Good, I'd started to think I'd have to go make the food myself for a second," Max mumbles unhappily.

"Wouldn't want you to do something that productive now would we," Maverick sarcastically replies making us all chuckle.

"Not when you're buying it from robbing idiots. Hot dog, seriously, four ninety nine with small fries and a can. I can get a tin of hotdogs that have eight in a tin, a pack of eight hotdog buns and a bottle of ketchup with a large bottle of pop for less than that."

"But then you'd have to cook it yourself," Malik replies looking amused at his younger brother.

"Which is exactly why I'm okay with Mason buying it for me," he chuckles earning a glare from Mason.

"Well I'll be hungry in an hour so I hope you got some money on you Max because the next round is on you," I smile gently, rubbing my rounded stomach.

"Trust me, I don't think there's enough food here to fill that," he says pointing at my stomach.

"Cheeky fucker," I giggle rubbing my stomach affectionately.

Feeling eyes on me as I look to the floor where they've laid blankets down on the grass, I look up. Mason is staring at me with a soft expression and a soft smile on his face. His eyes are focused on my stomach and the look in his eyes has me pausing my hand movements on my stomach. He. . . . he looks happy. I know it's so premature to say such a thing, I mean, the novelty of having a baby could wear off within a few days, but something about the look he giving my rounded stomach, tells me every emotion he's feeling. He's happy about the baby. Not that I've had time to talk to him about it.

"You going to sit down or what? You're making the place look untidy," Max pipes up again amused. He obviously saw the little stare down I was giving Mason which has me blushing.

"Yeah . . . Um . . . I'll just," I trail off, looking around the park for a bench or something, but they're packed with families.

"What's wrong?" Mason asks standing back up next to me.

"If I do manage to get down there, I don't think I'll be able to get back up," I tell him slightly embarrassed.

He chuckles, "Come here." He holds his hands out to me and I take them and use his strength to sit down on the blanket. Once I'm sitting on the blanket, I can already tell it's going to be a nightmare when I need to get up every two minutes for the loo.

"Ladies and gentlemen, today we have a local tribute band up first called Mini Mix. . . . ," a man booms over the microphone. I look over to the stage just as five girls around fifteen come out on stage, going straight into *Little Mix's* song 'Wings.' I flipping love that band. I spent thirty quid the night of the X-Factor finals for them to win. My favourite has to be 'Little Me,' it is so soulful, so truthful, and so beautiful.

"I love this song," I cry out, hearing amused chuckles around me.

"You love all songs," Max fires back.

"Hey, 'Living on a prayer' is the tune, my man," I tut scowling at him. He's also had it out for me when it comes to the music I listen to. The one time I was singing, 'I Need a Hero' by Bonnie Tyler and Max literally laughed in my face over my choice in music.

"You said the same thing about Miley Cyrus's song 'Wrecking ball' until you watched the video for it and said it put you off the song," Mason pipes in.

I turn to him, shocked that he remembered that which is really sweet. I'm about to say something sassy back now I'm starting to feel comfortable around them, but just then, the girls on stage go straight into the next song 'Move' and I squeal loudly, clapping my hands and wiggling my hips.

A sharp kick to my stomach has me groaning and bending forward.

Shit that one hurt little man.

"Are you okay? What's wrong? Is it the baby? Are you okay?" Mason rushes out next to me just as another kick lands in my stomach.

Seems like someone's awake.

Wanting to give him a reassuring smile I turn towards him, trying to sit up straighter, but I'm taken back when I find everyone looking at me with concerned expressions and Mason looking pale as a ghost.

Still short of breath from the kicking I'm enduring, I grab Mason's hand, trying my hardest to ignore the spark that zaps through me when I touch him. I place his hand low on my stomach just in time for the baby to give me another powerful kick.

Mason's head snaps up, looking at me bewildered and in complete awe. I give him a smile knowing exactly how it feels to feel it for the first time.

"Does it hurt?" he whispers, his eyes drifting away from where his hand is resting on my stomach to my face. When his eyes reach mine they're brimmed with tears and it takes everything in me to stop myself from crawling into his lap.

"No," I whisper back, too lost in the moment. Too lost, that when I hear Maverick's voice sounding rather close to me, I jump.

"Can I feel?" he asks hesitantly.

Maverick is the largest out of the brothers, he's also the oldest, so him asking to do such a thing as to feel my baby kick is making me want to cry. He hardly talks and when I first met him I thought it was rude, but once I came to know them all better I realised he just carries a lot of responsibility on his shoulders and a whole world of pain.

I nod my head 'yes' and grab his hand. I know Mason heard the conversation, I felt his body tense when Maverick asked to touch, but he hasn't moved his hand from my stomach.

"Mason, Maverick wants to feel," I whisper, melting at his behaviour. Tough, rugged, man whore Mason is whipped by an unborn baby and it melts my heart to see him like this.

"Not for long," he says gently, but gives his brother a warning glare before reluctantly removing his hand.

Placing Maverick's hand on my bump, I smile at encouragingly. He gasps when the baby kicks my stomach hard, making me wince for a second.

"Definitely a boy. Feels like he's playing football in there," Maverick gushes, looking like the proud uncle.

"I wouldn't know, you're hogging the belly," Mason grumbles making me chuckle.

"I need to feel this," Harlow says crawling over the blankets to us. Mason grunts beside me not sounding very impressed, but I just roll my eyes at him and nod my head at Harlow.

Her reaction is the same as Maverick's, except her eyes water as she tells me how incredible it feels.

"Malik, you need to feel this," she gushes, but he shakes his head 'no' looking horrified. "Don't be a baby," she snaps teasingly, and grabs a hold of his hand.

"Holy fucking hell. It didn't seem real until this moment. There really is a baby inside there." Malik's face is priceless. He has the same expression as Maverick, but looks more in awe than anything.

"What, did you think I'd just gotten fat or something?" I ask, pretending to be hurt.

"Shut up idiot," Mason snaps at his younger brother.

The only person who hasn't felt him move is Max and he's been quieter than usual, so I take a look over at him to find his eyes firmly fixed on my belly. Or my chest, it could be either.

"Want to feel?" I ask him.

"I don't think Mason would appreciate me feeling his girlfriend up in public," he winks. The word girlfriend has me tensing before I remind myself not to get worked up over it. Mason growls and curses at him under his breath.

"Come here you pleb-head," I tell him, reaching out for his hand.

When he moves forward, he places his hand over the same place the others did, and nothing happens.

"I don't feel anything," he says sounding disappointed.

"Hold on." I poke my stomach, waking the baby back up when all of a sudden he turns and Max flies backwards, his face pale as he stares at my stomach with a horrified expression.

"She's giving birth to an alien. I knew it would be half alien anyway coming from my brother and all, but holy shit that felt really weird. Did that hurt? Was that a kick? I saw your stomach move doing the Mexican wave," Max rambles, his voice high pitched.

"No that was definitely not a kick, he moved position."

"Doesn't that hurt?" Mason asks and I shake my head 'no.' The only time it really hurts is when I'm startled by a kick or get a kick to the bladder, the rest just feels foreign to me.

"That was amazing," Harlow announces. "Hey, I need to get some new photos, say cheese," she says looking towards me, Mason and Maverick. Both lads pull in close to me, obviously used to Harlow's photo fetish. Before I have the chance to smile or say cheese she snaps the photo taking me off guard.

Great! I'm going to look like one of the hillbillies off 'The Hills Have Eyes' while Mason and Maverick are going to look like something out of 'Magic Mike.' It's unfair.

We spend the rest of the afternoon watching different acts up on the stage. There have been some really good acts, then some horrible ones, but even those were still entertaining.

The best part of the day has been spending time with everyone. Over the past two and a half months I've missed them like crazy and never imagined that we'd have this easy friendship again because of my betrayal. But they've all welcomed me back and not once has there been any tension or a time when I've felt uncomfortable being with them.

It's coming to the end of the show and we're all heading back soon, as the place seems to be getting more crowded now everyone is getting off work. The heat is already getting to me even though Mason moved us into some shade. The shade only lasted twenty minutes before it had moved on. After the fourth time of moving I gave up and said I was okay. I'm really hot, and probably look like a sweaty whale right now. Not that I've ever met a sweaty whale, but if I did, it would look like I do right now.

Fanning myself with the leaflet some pizza guy left with us, I lean against the tree Maverick stacked with the spare blanket. They've all been like this, sweet and attentive. It's actually been nice and nothing like how I pictured they would react to me when I came back.

"Are you hungry again?" Max moans when he sees me rub my belly.

Seriously, I ate four times since we've gotten here. Two of those times were just to get Max to spend his money after his comment about Mason buying him expensive food. I almost laugh at his shocked face.

"Believe it or not Max, no I'm not," I laugh.

"Thank the Lord. I'm down to my last tenner," he groans.

"Oh, so you've got enough to get me some more candyfloss before we go?" I half joke, really wanting to eat another tub.

Max opens his mouth, but it's not his voice I hear. "Don't you think you had enough food?" A sweet, bitter voice giggles.

A group of girls I remember from school are all standing around us, ogling the Carter brothers.

"Nah, I could totally go to KFC and I'd still probably enjoy a Subway after," I reply sweetly.

"Okayyy," she replies rolling her eyes before her beady little eyes land on Mason and her smile spreads into a seductive grin. "Hi Mason."

Her seductive voice grates through me and my hand clenches into a fist ready to strike Mason if he says hello back to her in front of me. My heart couldn't take another rejection by him or my pride. When he grunts his acknowledgement I give her a triumphant smirk. She returns my smirk with a glare and I feel like doing a happy dance, especially when Mason moves closer towards me.

"A few of us are going to Heaven tonight, you should come. We can go back to mine after . . . ," she says suggestively and I want to gag right now. He just completely ignored her and moved closer towards me like he was staking his claim. Well it was either that or he wanted to show her he was taken.

"Sorry, he's going to be busy with me," I tell her sweetly, throwing in a wink to piss her off.

The girl stomps her foot and her friends take her queue and send me glares of their own. I just smile sweetly then nearly choke when I hear Harlow mutter under her breath.

"Somebody give her a brain."

Malik chuckles loudly, not caring about expressing his amusement. When the girls glower down at him he shoves his head into the crook of Harlow's neck, howling with laughter.

"Girls, as boring as it's been seeing you, you're blocking the last bit of the light," Max says, shooing them away with his hand, nearly making me choke.

"Call me if you change your mind. My number is . . . "

"Seriously bitch, back the fuck off. You can see he's not interested by the lack of conversation. So run along with your friends and leave us alone," I snap, ready to wobble to my feet and kick some ass.

"Whatever bitch," she sneers, and then huffs when Mason doesn't turn his head in her direction. When it's clear he isn't going to talk to her, she storms off with her friends trailing behind her.

As soon as they're out of sight Mason's shoulders slump, his body relaxed. He looks at me with a sad smile, his eyes full of remorse.

"Please tell me you've never been with her?" I question, hoping like hell he says no.

"What? No. She comes into the club on occasion. I know my reputation isn't clean cut, but I do have some standards," he grumbles looking embarrassed.

"Of course you do," I patronize sarcastically tapping his shoulder. "You slept with me."

His head snaps to me, a slow smirk curving his lips as he shakes his head. Maverick gets up wiping the grass from off his hands. He'd been leaning back on his hands enjoying the show.

"I need to get going guys. Does anyone need a lift?" He asks looking at Malik and Max.

"I'm going to get me some pussy. I'll see you guys later. Denny . . . it's good to have you back," Max says holding his hand up for a high five. I slap his hand grinning like a fool. That is until he opens his mouth again ruining it. "Let me know when you're ready to tell Mason the kid is mine," he winks before storming off.

Mason growls looking ready to run after him. Thankfully he doesn't. "Prick," he grunts.

"We will get a lift from you. We need to get back," Malik answers, and I turn to look at Harlow, her face is flushed and immediately I know why they need to get back and I roll my eyes. Maverick must clue in too, because he, the same as I, rolls his eyes at the loved up couple.

Mason helps me to my feet, refusing to let me help clear the stuff away or even carry something back to the car. The only reason he let me carry the pop earlier was because he didn't want to drop the food.

Lexi is standing outside my brother's front door when we return. She's dressed in a maxi dress; the purple material clinging to her curves in all the right places. It makes me wonder again if there is more to her and my brother than just neighbours.

"Thank you for today. I had a really good day," I smile turning to Mason. I lose my smile when he shuts off the car and undoes his seatbelt. "What are you doing?"

"I'm coming in for a bit. We need to talk and we've not had a chance to yet. We've got the scan on Friday, that's two days away. I don't want things to be hanging in the air when I get to see our baby for the first time," he says smiling softly at me.

"Okay," I squeak.

Opening the door, I exit the car and search my bag for the keys. I'm starting to lose faith I'll find them just as my fingers touch a key. I refrain myself from fist pumping the air and shouting 'got them.'

Lexi notices us walking up the path and her pacing outside the door stops.

"Hey Lexi," I wave.

"Hey Denny, can I talk to you for a second? Alone?" her eyes flicker to Mason briefly before locking them back onto me.

"Sure," I tell her then turn to Mason holding out the keys. "Why don't you go put the kettle on? I'm not sure what we have though."

"Okay," he says looking to Lexi then back to me. His face looks pensive, unsure whether to leave me or not. He looks to be at war and it seems I won out because he sighs, his shoulders slumping before he heads inside.

"What's up?" I ask once Mason closes the door behind him.

"Have you spoken with Evan at all?"

"No, why?" I ask, concerned by the slight hitch in her voice.

"He usually calls by now and he hasn't. I thought it was him walking up the path earlier, not long after you left actually, but it wasn't. It was some lad dropping off a letter or something. I walked out as he started back to his truck and realised it wasn't your brother. I'm just worried," she rambles, all her words mixing together and not making complete sense.

"I'm confused. Is there something about you and my brother that I don't know about? He'll be fine. He's probably just busy," I assure her, not really wanting to tell her he's the biggest manwhore known to man and she shouldn't waste her time on him. Not that I don't love my brother because I do, it's just where women are concerned he has no shame or morals.

"What? God no! I just . . . I um," she stutters chewing on her bottom lip looking unsure and slightly frightened to tell me what she needs to say.

"It's okay, I don't mind."

"No it's not that. We're not a couple or anything or having any kind of sexual relationship. I'm positive you don't know about me, so please, what I'm about to tell you I'd rather you kept to yourself," she says with her eyes pleading with me to agree. I nod my head 'yes' letting her finish with what she wants to say. "Your brother saved me from an abusive relationship. If it wasn't for him I would be dead right now. He let me move in next door for free. He offered to keep me safe. He's the only real friend I've got. I'm probably just being silly and he's just too busy to call."

"I'm sure he'll call once he has a chance. I'll try calling him later to see if he answers, but to be honest I'm not so sure he will answer to me."

"Thank you. I'm sorry if I've worried you. It's just not like him," she smiles and I genuinely feel sorry for her. She cares for my brother and from what she's saying he cares for her too. It's kind of sweet really. "I'll let you get in."

"Okay. Hope he calls back," I smile take two steps to the door, knocking.

"Me too," she whispers before waving her goodbye.

Mason is standing in the doorway, his large muscled arms crossed over his large sculpted chest, his beady eyes narrowing on the woman next door.

"What did she want?" he growls.

"Jesus, gossip much."

"She basically just dismissed me like I don't have feelings. That really hurt my feelings, Angel."

I laugh at his lame attempt to look miserable. His eyes droop and his lips pull down into a sad pout.

"Poor Mason. She was just asking if I had any spare tampons left, but . . . ," I say pointing down at my huge belly, and smile inside when Mason's face turns pale. "I'm kidding."

"Yeah. I knew that," he says shaking his head. He moves over to the sofa gesturing for me to sit down next to him. Not wanting to torture myself any longer than I have to, I move over to the sofa and sit down next to him, my body getting lost in the fluffy pillows.

"We need to talk about things," he says looking at me intensely. "I really think you should move in with me Denny. I know I've been a jerk, but I can make this right. This baby deserves us to try."

"No. I've grown up in a cold, lonely home Mason. I don't want that for our baby. It's one of the reasons why I never told you in the first place. If I had told you back then would you have asked me to get rid of him?"

"Her!"

"Her?" I question confused.

"Yes, her. The baby is going to be a she. If you had told me back then I'd be saying the same things now. I want to give us a try."

"Mason, you couldn't stand the sight of me. Now you want something to do with me *because* of the baby. I don't want that Mason. I want someone to love me, to cherish me and believe it or not, be happy to be with me. I don't want you to feel forced into a relationship you clearly didn't want a few months ago," I tell him sadly, feeling my eyes water as old feelings resurface.

"You really don't get it do you? I've wanted you for years. I know I'm older, but I liked you when you started high school."

"You kicking me out the morning after the night we slept together tells me differently," I snap lightly, a slight quiver in my voice.

"That night was the best night of my life, Denny. When I woke up you were sleeping, looking so peaceful and innocent with your ruby red lips, your flushed cheeks, and your blonde hair fanning the pillow. My chest hurt just watching you. Then I went to get into bed and noticed the blood and it all hit me. I'd just taken your innocence. I felt like I was turning into my dad and I couldn't do that to you. That night we didn't make any promises to each other, but I felt everything was said with our actions, and then everything . . . everything went to shit. I honestly thought pushing you away was what was best for you at the time. I didn't want you to end up with a waste of space like me," he frowns, and I can tell by the look in his eyes he's being sincere.

"So why break my heart the way you did, throwing all those girls you slept with in my face, Mason? You watched me suffering and you did nothing. You hurt me with those words you spoke that morning and they continued to hurt me each night in my dreams, haunting me."

I'm not even trying to hide my tears from Mason; it wouldn't help anyway. They fall heavily down my face.

"I didn't sleep with them," he whispers, looking ashamed as he casts his head down.

"Don't lie to me Mason. I saw you with more than one girl. I even came to tell you the day I left to live with my Nan that I was pregnant, but with another girl walking out of your house, I didn't want to interrupt. You looked really close," I tell him, my voice heated. One thing I hate more than cheats and bullies, and that's liars. Why people feel the need to lie just to get their way is beyond me. If you're selfish enough to throw a good thing away, or do something that ends up with you needing to lie then you need to grow up and face the music and take responsibility for your actions.

"What you saw was what you wanted to see, what I needed you to see. If you had tried to talk to me, or beg me to take a chance on you just once, I would have surrendered and done anything you wanted. I never slept with any of those girls."

"What? I . . . I don't . . . what?" I shake my head, not believing what I'm hearing. It all feels too much and I rub at my chest above my heart, trying to ease the ache there in my heart.

"I made it look like I was sleeping around. All of them tried, I even went so far to try with one. I got so far, but I just couldn't do it. I'd wanted you for so long, dreamed about you, and then when I had you I couldn't forget you. No other girl could ever compare to you. I'm so sorry for what I did. You'll never realise how much."

"I feel so lost right now. How am I supposed to believe you never slept with any of them? What about the girl at the race track? The one Davis blackmailed to sleep with you?"

"She was the only one I got close to sleeping with Denny and believe me, I only did it because when I looked at you, when I saw how much you hated me, I couldn't handle it. I needed to erase it from my mind. I got drunk; but it wore off as soon as her mouth got around my cock."

"I don't want to know specifics Mason. Christ!" I cry, standing up.

"Shit! Sorry. I just needed you to understand Denny. I never did that to you."

"But I felt everything like you *did* do it to me, Mason. I had no one to talk to about the baby. No one I could confide in enough to trust. After the night we shared, and the way you treated me like a little kid after made everything harder. I had all sorts of scenarios playing through my mind. Like what if I told you and you told me to get rid of it, or that you blamed me for trapping you. I don't want that for you, Mason. You had hurt me enough. Then when Harlow texted me telling me she had told you, I panicked and changed my number. Do you know that when I got the letter summoning me to court to testify I had a panic attack? Yeah, all because I was worried you and your family would hate me, that they'd make me go get an abortion," I cry, tears falling from my eyes as I cover my stomach protectively.

"Denny," he calls standing up. He grabs my shoulders stopping me from pacing. "I would never have asked you to abort the baby. If anything I spent the whole two and a half months worried I'd never see you again or you would abort the baby. I would never have had any way of stopping you doing it either. We're in this together. I know it was shit from the start, but we can get through this."

"What if we can't? What if you change your mind and I wake up only to have my heart ripped apart?"

"Then move in with me. Let me show you how wrong you are; let me show you how good we are together and how sorry I am. I never meant to hurt you. I was trying to prevent that from happening," he grunts, his hands shaking as he places them over my large bump. The baby takes that moment to kick at Mason's hand and he chuckles, looking down at my stomach in wonder and love.

"I don't know what to do," I whisper honestly, scared out of my mind that he will hurt me again. He's all I've ever wanted and not to sound creepy, but I even saved my virginity just for him. I wanted him to be the one who owned me, who I remembered for the rest of my life. It's why I always told people I'd never say no to him, even if it was for one night. I'd take anything I could get from him. I guess I never expected that one night to be as beautiful and amazing as it was. Nothing could ever compare to the night we shared together.

"Will you at least think about it?" he asks sadly, his eyes full of sorrow.

I nod my head, yes and feel the loss from him as soon as he moves his hands away from my belly. I nearly protest and reach out for his hands to place them back, loving the feel of his warm hands touching my skin.

"I'm going to get going and let you get some rest, it's getting late. Ring me if you need me and please Denny, please think about it."

"I will, I promise."

With that we say our goodbyes and I lock up behind him for the night. Not having had chance to unpack and too tired again to do it now, I head to the bathroom to wash up.

When I get into the bedroom I grab my pyjamas and walk over to the curtains in just my towel. I'm about to shut them for privacy when a dark figure across the street startles me, making me jump. Nearly losing my towel I squeal, then straighten it and look back out of the window to where I saw the shadow, but there's nothing there. Sighing, I rub my eyes; knowing the long day is catching up with me and making me see things that aren't there.

With that I shut the curtains, feeling tingles shoot up my neck like someone's watching me and carefully pull my pyjamas on, careful not to drop the towel until I'm completely covered.

FIVE

For the next two days I unpack, hang out with Harlow and sometimes Max at my brother's place. The heat has been too hot for me to go anywhere and my feet have swelled to the point they have gone up three shoe sizes.

I called the doctor when I remembered an article I read on the dangers during pregnancy. Swollen feet were on that list, but they assured me to elevate my feet and all will be fine.

My Nan has called every day, three times a day and has questioned me over and over about Mason. I told her everything he told me the other day and she seems to think I should give him a chance. I asked if she was trying to get rid of me, but she laughed saying 'never' and admitted that she wanted to keep me as a kid. I wish she did. It would have been better than growing up in a cold, unloving home with parents who only cared about their reputation. The only reason my mother cared about what I did in and out of school was so she could either brag about what a good, clever girl I was and show me off to all her friends, or control me so I don't embarrass her when I'm out. Any other time she couldn't wait to get rid of me.

The door knocks snapping me out of my daydream. Today's the day I find out the sex of the baby. Not just that, but according to the nurse I spoke to on the phone, I'll have measurements taken to see how the baby is developing, and

I'll need some blood work taken. I'll also get to hear the baby's heart beat again. It was the first time I actually felt guilty for *not* going to the appointment. I never realised just how important the twenty week mark scan was. Now I'm twenty two weeks gone and only just attending the check-up.

"Hey," I smile when I open the door to see Mason standing there, in a pair of cargo shorts, a white short sleeved t-shirt and a cap that he's wearing backwards. He looks so freaking hot right now with his tanned skin, bulging muscles and sexy as sin grin.

"You ready? We've got about twenty minutes to get there."

"Yep, let me just go grab my bag," I tell him and rush down to the room I'm staying in. Walking in the window is open, the cool air breezing through the room. I'm pretty sure I didn't open that. Lexi came around the day after we all went out to the park to watch the live bands and told me the fan in the room doesn't work when the window is open, so for it to work they needed to be shut. I've pretty much kept it shut since arriving here. Not just because of what she said, but because I have a phobia of moths. I hate them. They aren't scared to land right on the tip of your nose in the middle of the night, fluttering their tiny little wings and making themselves known with the little buzzing sounds they make. Gah, I hate them. I shiver rushing over to the window and sliding it shut before pushing the latch over to lock it.

My eyes lift and I look over to where I saw the shadow two nights ago seeing nothing, but it still feels like someone has been watching me. Knowing I'm being paranoid I turn, trying to shake off the uneasy feeling inside my stomach that's been there for a few days now.

"You okay?" Mason asks watching me with interest when I walk back into the room.

"Yeah. The window was open and I'm pretty sure I didn't open it. I can't be sure though," I shrug, still feeling unsettled over it.

"I hate you staying here on your own. Have you thought anymore about moving in to the new place? Joan and Harlow helped decorate it. They seemed to know what you'd like, so the only room left to do is the baby's room, but I wanted to confirm she's a girl."

"Optimistic aren't you," I half tease as he opens the passenger door to his car.

"Yep, I've already got the pink paint in the shed ready for when we get back," he winks, shutting the door once I'm seated.

When he's in the car, I wait for him to pull his seatbelt on before speaking. "I was talking about me moving in there."

"I know. I just didn't want to make you mad by going on about it. It needs to be your decision, not mine. I'd never force you into something you didn't want, just like you wouldn't do it to me. I really want this with you Denny; I don't want to fuck it up by being controlling."

Damn him and his easy charm. My belly does a little flip and butterflies swarm my belly and it's not from the baby moving. I really want to take this step with him, but I'm so scared of my past fears that I'm stalling the inevitable. We've got a baby on the way together, for Christ sakes. You can't get any more committed than that. We drive the rest of the way in silence, both of us left to our own thoughts.

We arrive at the hospital on time. We sign in and take a seat in the waiting area ready for our name to be called by the nurse. We're only waiting a few minutes when the nurse walks out and calls my name. She's a small framed lady with red hair and soft features.

"Denny Smith?"

"That's me," I smile standing up and grabbing my bag. Mason stands with me, looking from the nurse before looking back over to me with nervous movements. "Come on, you can come with."

"Yeah. Sure. That's really good," he smiles, nearly tripping over the wooden table with all the pregnancy magazines piled on.

We walk into a room with an ultrasound machine, a bed and other equipment. The room is surrounded in dim lighting, giving it a warm feeling.

"Lay down on the bed, use this to cover your bottom half and lift your dress up over your bump. I tell all the ladies who come in here to tuck the paper towel inside the waist band of their knickers. It helps prevent the gel from getting them all sticky," she smiles.

Doing as she says, I lye back and relax and watch as she types a couple of things into the computer before walking back over to us. Mason has taken the seat to my left, looking nervous as hell. His leg is jittering, the motion and tapping becoming annoying.

"You'll have Mr. Harris performing the scan today. He should be here . . ." she doesn't get to finish as the door opens and a burly man with a large stomach wearing large blue scrubs walks in, pulling his glasses back over his eyes. He looks up when he notices us already in the room and smiles.

"Hi, I'm Mr. Harris. I'll be doing your scan today. We just received your notes from your midwife. Can you give me your name, date of birth, and address please?"

He takes the seat next to me, listening as I answer his questions and a few more. Mason stays seated in his chair, listening intently to what the doctor is telling us. When he presses a few buttons on the ultrasound, I start to become restless and nervous. What if something's wrong? What if I risked our baby's life by not seeing a doctor sooner?

Oh no, I feel sick, which is not good when my bladder is screaming at me to go relieve myself. I even asked if there was another way to have the scan without drinking two pints of water an hour before attending the appointment. It's worse because when you know you can't do something it only makes you want to do it that little bit more.

"Are you ready to see your baby?" he smiles encouragingly. Mason gulps next to me and out of instinct I reach for his hand. He doesn't miss a beat, holding my hand in his, squeezing gently when the doctor reaches out with a tube of gel.

"This may be cold, so be prepared," he warns and I inwardly groan. Just another thing my bladder needs right now, me tensing up. I'm seriously going to empty my bladder all over the floor. In front of Mason out of all people.

The cold gel hits my stomach and to my own relief, I tense without wetting myself.

My relief is short lived when he presses the handheld machine onto my belly, right under my bump where it presses down onto my bladder.

Yep, I think I'm losing fluid. Great! This is just great!

I wiggle feeling uncomfortable, my bladder screaming to be released. The doctor or whatever he's called in his line of work notices and gives me a reassuring smile.

"I'll just take the measurements and what I need as quickly as I can. Then the bathroom is right through there," he smiles and Mason turns to give me a confused look.

"What? Huh?"

"I think I drank too much water and I'm kinda struggling not to pee myself," I giggle, then immediately wish I never had.

"Oh," is all he replies then his mouth falls open, his eyes fixated on something behind me. His eyes start to glass over and with a panicking breath, I turn my head to see what's wrong. What I see when I turn is the most beautiful picture I'll ever get to see apart from when I get to see it in the flesh of course. Harris has the screen tilted towards us while he takes measurements, pointing out the different body parts, although most are clear to see.

My eyes glass over. I don't think I'll be able to forget this moment. With Mason's hand clutching mine tightly and seeing our baby for the first time, it's unbelievable. A lone tear runs down my face, but I'm too riveted on the screen in front of me to wipe it away.

The babies hand is in its mouth, its one leg resting up at a weird angle and for a second I worry something is wrong. Then Harris assures us it's normal. He takes measurements and gives us the estimated weight of the baby.

"Eight pounds? Eight pounds? Oh my God, I'm going to be torn in two," I panic, my eyes never flickering away from the screen. Mason chuckles beside me and I turn for the first time to get his reaction. His eyes are fastened to the screen like mine were, glassed over and filled with emotion. My heart warms seeing just how much he does care for this baby.

Another hard press to my stomach and I'm tightening my lower parts to stop myself from pissing myself everywhere. It's uncomfortable, but totally worth it as I look back up at the screen. The baby moves, kicking out making Mason and I chuckle.

"Would you like to know the sex of the baby?" he asks us and Mason and I look at each other and nod our heads. We discussed this already. He wants to have a little girl, he said he grew up in a house full of boys, but it wasn't the only reason. He wanted a little girl just like me. I think in that moment I fell for him a little bit more, even though my head is screaming at me to not be fooled or to let myself forgive him so easily.

"You are having. . . . oh there we are, it's very clear. You are having a. . . . girl," he congratulates, giving us warm smiles. "I'll print some pictures off here and you can collect and pay for them at the reception. I just need to make up your next appointment, so I'll leave you to get cleaned up and I will be back shortly. Do you have any questions before I leave?"

Too lost for words, my eyes transfixed on the screen, I shake my head.

A girl!

We're going to have a girl!

The door shutting startles me and I turn to Mason with a watery smile, his own expression mirroring mine.

"We're having a girl," he whispers huskily, the emotion raw in his voice.

"Yes, we are," I croak out, my head filled with so much happiness it's overwhelming.

"We're having a girl," he repeats, his eyes still glued to the screen where the last picture Mr. Harris captured of the baby is still there. He stays like that for a few more seconds before looking back down at me grinning. "We're having a fucking girl," he shouts grinning like a fool. I grin back, loving that he's as excited as I am.

"We are," I tell him softly, then watch in amazement as his face softens and tears fall from his eyes. The first one hits his lap before he realises that he's even crying and when he does he grabs my face in his rough palms and leans forward. The movement catches me so off guard that I'm not prepared when he leans in and kisses me. It's soft and slow at first, and I will admit I'm a little hesitant, but when I feel his tongue at the seam of my lips, I give in and start kissing him back.

I feel the kiss all the way down to my toes, his touch setting my whole body on fire and I moan in pleasure as his tongue massages sensually against mine.

God he tastes good!

His body shifts off the chair, leaning over me. His one hand is resting on my cheek still while the other roams down the side of my body. As soon as he touches my stomach I gasp. The baby kicks at his touch and in the process pushes down on my bladder.

"You okay?" he says pulling back, a worried look marring his face.

"I need to piss," I shoot out, sitting up in bed making him move away from me. I want to protest and scream at my bladder to give me five more minutes kissing him, but when you gotta go, you gotta go.

He chuckles watching me as I rush to clean the gel off my stomach, pull my dress down, slide off the bed and run to the toilet off to the side in the room. I open the door and lock it behind me, ignoring his chuckling.

By the time I come out the doctor is back and talking to Mason who is standing waiting for me.

"So she has one more scan, then has a check-up with the midwife every so often?" he asks Harris, the doctor.

"Yes. Her midwife will take regular measurements to make sure the baby is growing nicely and will check the heartbeat with every appointment. Denny will also need more blood work taken at the end of next month due to low blood pressure, but it's just a precaution."

"So everything is okay?"

"Yes," he chuckles then notices me. "Feel better?"

"Much. Please tell me I won't need to drink that much again for my next scan?" I ask, not remembering it being this uncomfortable at my first scan. Not that there was a lot to see on my first scan. It just looked like a black blob to me.

"We'll expect you to drink some fluid, but not as much as today."

"Thank God," I breathe feeling relieved.

"I've written your next appointment down and given the slip to dad here. If you'd like to collect the pictures at the front desk they will be ready," he smiles.

We both thank him and leave the room to grab the scan photos.

We both end up walking to the car in a daze, both of us looking down at the scan pictures in awe.

"Have you decided on names?" Mason asks as we drive home.

"Honestly, no. When I was at Nan's and she'd ask me the same thing. I always put it off, not knowing, but then seeing you today in that scan room has made me realise why. You needed to be there to have some input on what we should call her. I still can't believe we're having a girl. It seems too unreal."

"I know what you mean. I'm still reeling over the fact that our girl is inside you, growing each day. It's mind blowing," he says. He's quiet for a few moments until I feel his eyes flicker over to me before turning back to the road. "Thank you . . . thank you for letting me share today with you. After everything I've put you through I would not have blamed you to tell me to fuck off, but you didn't, so thank you."

"Would you have listened to me if I did tell you to fuck off?"

"I dunno. I'd want to grant your wishes, but I'd also want to see my baby. It's a hard choice. Now I have two girls to think about, to worry about, to . . . to look after."

My damn eyes water again and I wish I could stop him from saying all these beautiful things to me, but secretly, I love hearing him talk to me like that.

Mason's phone rings cutting through the silence. He puts it on loud speaker answering it.

"So . . . you gonna tell me the good news or what?" Max shouts excitedly through the phone.

"No," Mason deadpans, his face a mixture of annoyance and amusement.

"Ahhhh, it's not yours is it. Look bro, I should have told you before. Denny and I, we have this amazing chemistry . . . ."

"Fuck off Max," Mason growls and I giggle. He shoots me a warning glare and I make a motion of zipping my lips, my grin spreading across my face.

"Oh come on bro. You wanna be an uncle, I get that, but I'm the daddy . . . ."

"I'm cutting you off asshole."

"Who's the daddy?" Max sings through the phone. "I'm the mother fucking daddy."

Mason glares at the phone and I giggle again, this time ignoring his murderous glare. "Is there something you fucking wanted Max other than to piss me off?"

"That's no way to speak to your lovers baby daddy is it Mason. Nah, I'm fucking around, keep ya knickers on. We're all heading over to the Manor, want to meet us there for lunch and give us the good news?"

"We'll be there," he growls. "Oh and I'm kicking your ass," Mason snaps before shutting his phone off. "Don't even start."

I hold my hands up in surrender, the grin spreading across my face hurting, "Wouldn't dream of it *daddy*." My voice is full of amusement and I watch as Mason tries hard to keep a straight face, but before I turn my attention back out the window his lips twitch into a smile.

We turn up at the restaurant twenty minutes later with all the gang outside waiting for us. Harlow is the first one to run over to us, running into my arms and giving me a tight hug.

"So? What are we expecting, a niece or a nephew?" Maverick calls with a grin, making his way over to us.

"I'm the daddy, I should find out first," Max teases, giving me a wink.

My heart melts and I can feel tears fill my eyes as I take in everyone. They are all here to support me. I spoke with my Nan on the way here, wanting her to be the first to know. She congratulated me and told me having a girl is one of the most precious gifts I'll ever receive. I did reply what if it was a boy and she laughed saying she'd wish me all the luck in the world. I knew she was only joking. My Nan knew any child brought into this world was a gift. Not everyone could carry that gift so they were to be cherished in every possible way. I had to agree. Carrying a child is the best gift I could ever receive and I know I'll spend the rest of my life cherishing her.

"We are having a . . . ," I smile, before turning to Mason, gesturing to him to tell them the good news.

"We're having a girl," he shouts in triumph, pulling me to his side and oddly enough it's comforting being there. Everyone hollers out their own congratulations, giving us both hugs. It's only when Mark, Mason's granddad comes over to give me his blessings that things get emotional.

"Girl, you'll never know how pleased I am to see my first grandbaby coming into the world and that you've brought in the second girl this family-on my side anyway- has ever been blessed with," he says choked up, his eyes watering. I want to argue and don't think Mason's mom is someone you can call being blessed with. From what I know and from little of what Harlow has mentioned, their mom is a piece of work. She never once looked after the boys and ran off leaving them with a complete bastard of a father.

I wipe my eyes, feeling tears fall. Feeling Mason coming up beside me I try to compose myself, but it's too late.

"You upsetting my girl, Granddad?" he teases Mark.

My girl! He called me his girl. Everything looks like rainbows and ponies.

I'm doing a happy dance inside hearing him call me his girl. I've never thought I'd hear him say those things, and to be honest, it's doing funny things to my stomach.

"No son. Just letting her know how pleased I am she's a part of this family, and for giving me a granddaughter," he tells him, looking at me adoringly.

"Thank you," I whisper, feeling myself becoming choked up.

He steps forward bracing his arms out for a hug and I step the last bit of space between us and step into his arms, breathing in his musky, detergent scent. It reminds me of my granddad when he was alive. It's comforting to know as I wrap my arms tightly around him.

"You're good for him girl," he whispers once Maverick pulls Mason away from us. "He never meant to hurt you. It killed him doing it. I watched the life draining from that boy every time he hurt you more. I'm glad you're back and he has you," he says pulling away.

Not able to hold it in and I'm totally blaming the pregnancy hormones, I burst into tears. Not just silent tears that run down my face, but gut wrenching sobs that tear from my mouth and I throw myself back in his arms.

"Thank you for wanting me here," I manage to choke out.

I'm removed gently from his arms and placed into another set of warm ones. Although I could feel who it was, like my body was accustomed to him; it's his smell that gave him away. His woodsy, outdoorsy aroma, with a hint of something rare, something Mason, something only he could pull off. I've never been able to put my finger on it, I just know he very rarely uses his cologne and when he does it just makes his scent more potent.

"You okay?" he asks me in a hushed tone making me shiver and sniffle at the same time.

"Yeah, I'm just being silly. I'm not used to this," I tell him pulling away. I'm ready to point to his family so he understands, but they are nowhere to be seen. "Where did everybody go?"

"Inside, to give us some privacy. Now, are you sure you're okay?"

"Honestly, I'm just being stupid. If it hasn't escaped your notice my family isn't really close like yours. I never had what you had. Only when I was around my Nan and Granddad or brother, but my Granddad is dead and my brother hasn't spoken to me in weeks. Even when we did he wasn't that happy about me being pregnant. I know he'll help me and support my decision; he always told me as much, but it's not the same when he's not here. Your family have not only been supportive for you, but they have for me, even after everything I did. They should hate me for running away to live miles away and not telling you. It's just overwhelming I guess."

"Angel, you are our family now. It isn't just you anymore. You've just taken on another family by agreeing to have our baby. You're not going anywhere and I promise I'm going to make up for all the shit I put you through to get you to stay where you belong," he promises.

I should really tell him I'm already staying, that there was no way I could take our girl away from her family and away from him, but something holds me back, stopping me from telling him. I guess half of me wants to see what he's willing to do to prove to me he's sorry.

"Come on let's eat," I smile and on queue my stomach grumbles causing us to laugh.

"Come on before you waste away," he laughs, curling me into his arms, leading me into the restaurant.

SIX

"SO . . . DATE NIGHT HUH?" Harlow teases lying on my bed at my brothers. Speaking of, my brother still hasn't called me back and I've been here three weeks now. I had hoped he would be back in time to come to court with me, but Lexi said he checked in with her and told her to tell me he was sorry he couldn't make it. I'd love to know what he does for a job that it keeps him away from the phone for so many days and then, he only gets to talk for what seemed like ten minutes to Lexi. When I asked her what he did for work she shrugged saying they never spoke about it.

So not only do I take the stand in three days in front of everyone and Davis, but I have to do it without my brother.

Mason said he will be there with me which I'm thankful for. We've been getting along nicely since the scan like nothing bad had ever happened between us. Each day we've become a little bit closer, but there's still that doubt in the back of my mind on whether this is something he truly wants long term.

"Earth to Denny," Harlow laughs, waving her hand in front of my face to grab my attention.

"Sorry, I spaced out. Yeah, he asked me out on a date a few days ago. He said he felt like we never get time together on our own," I tell her, playfully rolling my eyes.

"You're kidding?" she laughs. "He told me the other day I had to wait until today to come see you."

"He didn't?" I gasp laughing.

"He bloody did. Urgh," she moans holding her stomach.

"What's wrong?" I ask concerned.

"Aunt Flow came to visit this morning," she groans making me chuckle.

"That's one thing I've not missed," I laugh, then laugh harder at her expression glaring back at me.

"Oh, by the way, the other day Gram's had the sex talk with me. She was checking to make sure we were using protection. It got really awkward, especially when she told Malik he could take some of Marks condoms whenever he liked because they didn't need them anyway."

"No . . . she didn't?" I laugh, bending over to place my hands on my knees. "Your Nan is completely nuts. What did Malik do?"

"Walked out of the room saying he had homework to do," she giggles and the sound is so sweet. Harlow is so sweet, soft and loveable. She has been that way since the first day I met her. I hadn't had many friends really when I was at school because I felt like they were backstabbers, liars, and out for one thing; but then Harlow came to Grayson High and I knew from how kind and loving she was that we'd get on. We've been besties ever since.

"Did she realise he doesn't go to school anymore?" I ask, laughing at the thought.

"She didn't say anything about it. We laughed about it afterwards, because I asked why he said it. Anyway . . . it got me thinking. When we spoke about . . . you know . . . you and Mason . . . having . . . ," she rambles, her eyes pleading with me to understand what she's trying to say and it makes me grin at her cute face.

"Have sex?" I finally give in chuckling.

"Yes that," she blushes and it's so cute. "Well you told me you used protection, so how did you, you know . . . get pregnant?"

I've wondered the same thing myself. I was never allowed to go on the pill. My mother said it was ludicrous and it was just giving me permission to be a hussy. That night with Mason, every time we had sex we used protection, so I never understood why I got pregnant either. I know they said condoms aren't one hundred percent effective, but still . . .

"I wondered the same thing over and over. Mason must have super spunk or something." We both laugh.

"I'm just happy I'm on my period. I started to worry over it because Malik and I stopped using condoms now that I'm on the pill. I guess if it's going to happen, it's meant to."

"All you can do is keep taking precautions. If it happens, then it happens, but don't worry over it, otherwise you'll put a downer on your sex life."

"Enough about this, Malik will pick me up and wonder why I'm all beet red and flustered," Harlow giggles. "Let's get you ready."

"This is a nightmare," I tell her, flickering through my clothes in my wardrobe. "Most of these are before bump and would never get over my hips or boobs. I swear, I could cry sometimes. The only thing I feel comfortable in is dresses and even then, all my date ones are from pre bump and are skin tight. There is no way I'm squashing my baby into one of them."

"You're such a drama queen," she laughs then grabs something from out of one of the bags she turned up with. "Now, I got you a present because you were always there for me and you always lent me clothes to impress Malik. I have you to thank for catching his eye, so I got you this."

With that, she pulls out a gorgeous green halter neck maxi dress from her bag. It crosses over at the chest with a diamond stud directly in the centre. It's elegant yet stunning. The material at the back of the dress is longer than the material at the front. Thankfully, looking at the length at the front I know it will easily cover my bump and still manage to cover a good amount of leg.

"That is . . . that is beautiful," I tell her feeling my stupid eyes well up. Gah, they're doing it all the time lately.

My parents would never have let me wear anything remotely similar to this. All the clothes I had that were the slightest bit revealing I kept with the excuse to my parents they were for the schools plays and events. I hid most of the clothing easily, but there were occasions when my mother actually bothered with me and checked my room. Even the maids knew to hide the clothing from my mother.

"I know. I saw it and immediately thought of you. I think all your shopping torture rubbed off on me," she giggles.

I laugh remembering the first time I took her shopping for some sexy lingerie she needed to seduce Malik. Not that I thought the girl needed it, but still, it was an excuse to go shopping.

We spent the whole day trying to find something and she vowed never to go shopping with me again after I dragged her into nearly every store we passed by. If only she knew I went easy on her that day.

"I guess it did," I smile, holding the dress up in front of me feeling giddy and excited. "Suppose I best go get ready."

"Yeah, want me to stick around and wait or are you good?"

"Nah, I'm good. You get back, you got court tomorrow. Have they said any more about Hannah?" I question, still worried that she hasn't been seen.

"No. Her mom is adamant that she never ran away, that something has happened to her," she answers, her eyes distant, and sad.

"Everything will be fine I'm sure of it. We have enough evidence to back up our story. He's going to go down," I assure her, gripping her shoulder in a firm squeeze.

"I know. I guess I'm just worried that something did happen and we're all talking badly about her like she has run away. Something doesn't feel right when she's mentioned. I've tried telling Malik I don't believe she ran away. I can feel it in my gut. Now I'm just worried as hell."

"I don't know what to say," I groan, sitting down next to her on the bed. "A part of me feels like she deserves it, that she made her bed, but the other part, the humane side of me believes she doesn't deserve anything bad happening to her. I just feel like I knew how to feel. I hate the girl for everything she put you through, but I still feel bad at the thought of her being hurt."

"I know exactly how you feel," she murmurs, staring off into space. "Right, I'll see you tomorrow morning. What time have you got to be there? Do you need picking up?"

"No I'm good. Mason is going to drive me."

She gives me a sly grin standing up from the bed. "Well I guess I'll leave you to get ready then."

"See ya," I grin, feeling excited about tonight. "Oh and stop worrying. Everything is going to be fine."

"Love you bitch," she shouts making me giggle. The girl never, and I mean *never* swears . . . okay she doesn't swear that much, but when she does, it doesn't sound right coming out of her mouth. She looks too sweet and innocent to be sprouting out curses.

It's just under an hour later when Mason arrives for our first date. I've been pacing the bedroom with so much nervous energy I'm surprised I haven't gone into labour.

The dress Harlow bought me falls beautifully over my bump, making it look slightly bigger with the way it falls. It also gives him a good eyeful of my cleavage thanks to the dress pushing my now large breasts up and together.

I've matched the dress with some plain green flip flops with a diamond stud embedded on the strap. I've put in my silver dangly earrings and my matching silver sparkly necklaces that falls to the top of my cleavage. My hair has been left down in loose waves, my hands too tired to do anything else with it. Same goes for my makeup. By the time I finished getting showered and dressed I grew too tired to do anything else. So my makeup has been kept light with just a tint of foundation, lip gloss and mascara.

"Hold on," I say rushing to the door, my grin stretching across my face. Opening the door I have to grab a hold of it quickly when I open it too enthusiastically and it nearly smashes against the wall inside. My face cringes at the sound and when I look up, Mason is staring at me with such appreciation I can't pull my eyes away from his.

His eyes slowly move from mine, leisurely rolling down my body, to my cleavage which he admires with deep desire, his eyes darkening. They soften once they hit my stomach, a smile tugging at his lips until he drops his eyes to my legs, his eyes darkening once again as he takes me in.

My body hums with awareness, the desire pooling between my legs, and my pulse races with lust.

I want him.

I want him so goddamn much it hurts.

I tighten my legs together needing to ease the ache pulsing between them when his eyes once again reach mine. His eyes are still dark, his breathing heavy and his lips are now curved into his signature smirk; the same smirk that got me to notice him five years ago at fourteen years old. Even then I knew that smirk would be the death of me and that it would only cause me heartache, but not once did I ever care.

I guess I wish I could go back in time and tell my fourteen year old self to open her eyes and tell her she will care.

Because trust me, I do. A lot!

"You look . . . fuck! You look beautiful, Denny," he tells me, his smirk long gone and only honesty written in his expression.

"Thank you. You don't look so bad ya' self," I grin, my eyes now trailing over his body just like he did with mine only moments ago. His large chest is covered by a dark purple buttoned up shirt, his large arms bulging through the material. His sleeves are rolled up to his elbows, but even still you can see how powerful they are with each muscle and vein tensing through his forearms. He's wearing his normal Levi jeans, no rips like most of his other jeans have, and has paired them with a black belt. His legs look as powerful as his arms. They aren't tree trunk built, but they're powerful all the same; I should know, I have admired his body naked. And trust me when I tell you I stored every inch of his delicious body to memory so I'd never forget, including the dimples at the bottom of his large back. And although I'm only getting frontal visual at the moment, I can still picture how tight his ass will look in those jeans. How his muscles tighten when I scraped my nails down his back.

Shaking my thoughts before they go somewhere I'm not comfortable with yet, I make my way down to his shoes. Never have I seen Mason Carter wear a pair of black dinner shoes before. He looks so deliciously handsome I'm finding it hard not to jump him.

Which wouldn't be a good thing at the moment considering this is our first date and I have a baby in my stomach that may get squashed in the process.

"You look real good," I say when I reach his eyes, my tongue slowly licking my bottom lip.

We stare at each other for what seems like eternity, and nowhere near long enough before Mason looks away, his face filled with amusement and lust.

"Come on then before your belly starts demanding food," he chuckles.

"Hey, I'll have you know I'm feeding for two now. I don't have to feel guilty for eating my body's weight in food. It's the only time we can do it without feeling guilty I'm sure," I tease, not knowing what I'm talking about in the slightest.

"Come on then," he laughs, and shuts the door behind me like a gentleman.

———

MASON AND I ARE seated straight away thanks to him booking in advance. The little restaurant he's brought me to is half an hour away from where we live. I've never eaten here before, and from the looks of the decor I'm surprised I haven't. This place is somewhere my mother would have dragged me to if she knew about the place, and I know for a fact she doesn't because, without a doubt, she would have bragged to all her friends she had eaten here.

The place is beautiful with its candlelight settings and old wooden decor. It gives the place a homely, rich aroma. It's inviting.

The place is painted blood red, the colour matching nicely with the dark wood, and beams. The place looks antique with old books littering the shelves, crooked candle holders, and old fashioned lighting. And in spite of all of the accessories decorating the place, it still manages to pull off that rich look to it.

"I promise, the place doesn't look like much from the outside, but I promise the food is great," Mason assures me once we've taken a seat.

He's right. From outside I'd gotten worried he was lost, or he was taking me to a dark, heavy metal bar. It's not in the nicest location and the outside looks worn down from the peeling paint and crappy surroundings. It's nothing like I expected it to be when we were walking up from the car park.

"No, I like it already," I tell him truthfully.

"Good. I'm glad," he smiles widely, making me feel shy. "I used to come here with my Nan. She loved it here. I haven't really been here much though the past year. When I decided to take you out I knew this would be the perfect place to go."

"Their menu is mostly Italian, but I know Nick will make you whatever you like, babe."

Him bringing me here, somewhere he used to come with his Nan has me smiling. I feel privileged that he would want to bring me somewhere so special to him and his Nan.

"What was your Nan like?" I smile. I don't remember much of their Nan; she died not long after they moved here. She used to be good friends with my Nan, my mother's mom who works at Grayson High. They went to the same church, but by the time I was old enough to attend with my Nan, their Nan had died.

"She wasn't our blood Nan, but she was more of a Nan than our real Nan was. She died a few months after we came to live with Granddad. We were lucky that when our biological Nan left our Granddad before our mom was born, that he managed to move on, otherwise we'd never have had her in our lives.

"She never had a good upbringing, but my God, she never let any of it define her. She was so full of life, full of love, that it blew me away whenever she paid attention to me. To any one of us really. We felt the love she had for us. She taught us the sensitive side of being a man, whereas Granddad taught us to be men. If she were here right now, knew what I did to you, she'd kick my ass to Belgium and back. The woman had so much fight in her and she was only four foot nine.

"She also had our Granddad running rings around her. They were best of friends. But if you got on her wrong side you were toast," he laughs and I love it when he laughs. He looks so carefree and his facial features soften. It makes him appear his age and not the rugged, older-than-his-years lad I've come to know.

"She sounds like an amazing woman."

"What about your Nan, the one from Wales?"

"Well, she *will* be kicking your arse when she sees you," I tell him straight faced, raising my brow, then laugh loudly when his face loses its entire colour. "I'm kidding. Kind of. She's cool. She's nothing like my dad. She's opinionated, strong, worldly, funny, youthful, and totally loveable."

"What about your other Nan? I know you have one that lives not far from us," he asks, taking me by surprise knowing that much about me.

"Yeah. We used to get along until the night that I kicked you in the balls," I tell him, my voice trailing off. I really shouldn't have reminded him of that. I wince just thinking about it, remembering the sound of his pain.

When Harlow and I went to a party after one of Malik's races not long ago, Mason had turned up all over some girl. When he started sprouting shit at me I kneed him in the balls.

Not one of my finest moments.

"I remember," he winces, his one hand reaching under the table to no doubt cup his package.

I giggle at his expression and I know that I shouldn't. What I did to him was totally stupid, dangerous, but totally justified.

"Anyway, I was completely drunk and a complete mess and one of my Nan's friends must have reported back to her after seeing me. My Nan told my mom and all hell broke loose. My Nan said I shamed her family and to never speak to her until I got God's forgiveness. I may or may not have answered back and made it worse, but it's not the point," I answer, wincing a little when I remember the horrible words they said to me. "Can I ask you something?"

"Anything," he smiles just as a waitress arrives to take our order. I let Mason pick for me, telling him everything looks fine and that I don't mind. When he gives her our order he sits back in his chair, his eyes locked on me, appraising me. "Go on . . ."

"What was your dad like? I remember you said you were scared about us being together because of him. Can you tell me why? I know some, but it's not something Harlow and I like to gossip about. I heard some stuff from my Nan, but the rest I kind of pieced together and Harlow confirmed."

He groans running his fingers through his hair and I immediately sink back in my chair feeling bad. Why did I go and ask him about his dad when I clearly know he doesn't like talking about him? I'm so freaking stupid.

"Look, you don't have to tell me, forget it. Tell me about your job," I say lightly changing the subject.

"No. It's fine. You need to know. You should know. If we're going to be together we need to be able to talk to one another. I don't know how much I can tell you, or what you know, but my story is a lot different from Malik's."

"I don't want to ruin our date by talking about something that you clearly don't want to," I rush out, my heart beating wildly at the vulnerable look in his eyes, the pain he hides behind his easy going mask.

"The date is so we can get to know each other Denny. For me to prove to you I'm serious as a heart attack about the two of us. Talking about my parents might explain things better."

"Okay, but only tell me what you feel comfortable with." I sadly smile over at him, lifting the glass of Coke to my lips and taking a sip.

"From as far back as I can remember he was violent to us. He publicly beat Maverick and Malik to the point they couldn't go to school on some days, but what they don't know, what they'll never know, is the beatings I received during the night. He'd drag me out of bed to just kick me about, to . . ."

"To do?" I question, reaching over and placing my hand over his.

"He'd make whatever woman he was with at the time to have sex with me. They'd be all for it and would laugh at my inexperience. It's something I've never been able to talk about with the lads. They would never understand. I guess it's the reason I slept around so much, wanting to prove to myself I had a choice . . ." he trails off looking distant and all I can do is cover my mouth to smother a sob, tears streaming down my face. "Please don't cry for me Denny."

His voice is so soft it breaks my heart and I can understand why he slept with so many women. "How old were you when it all started?"

"Eight, nine, I'm not sure, it all blurs together. It was the reason I really pushed you away. You deserved someone better, someone who wasn't tainted and had that evil running through their blood. The way I feel when I'm around you, scares me. Back then it was just as strong and when I woke up, I looked at you and pictured my life. What if I turned out to be just like my dad? What if I hurt you like he hurt us? I didn't want that, not for you, not for anyone."

"So what changed your mind?" I wipe the tears from my eyes, hoping like hell my mascara hasn't run down my face.

"The minute Harlow told me you were pregnant I felt like I'd been kicked in the stomach. Everything around me stopped and I knew in that moment that I'd rather cut off my own arm than ever lay a finger on you. I knew without a doubt we were meant to be together." He shrugs like it's no big deal, but I notice the slight blush to his cheeks that give him away. He's not used to confessing his feelings like this. I've known him for a long time and for him to tell me something so dark, something he hasn't told anyone, just proves how strongly he feels towards us being a couple.

"What about your mom?"

I've always wanted to know about his mom. Harlow said Malik doesn't really remember much about her, only what Maverick told them. I also know she left them as kids and never came back, not even when their dad died.

He laughs, but it sounds off. "My mom was another dad. Maverick painted her out to be a saint, but I know better. He thinks I don't know about the shit she did, but I do. I'd tell you, but it's really Maverick's story to tell."

"That's okay. Has she ever tried to see you?"

"She never wanted us Angel. She wanted us for the benefits so she could feed her drug problem. Granddad said she was really good as a mother when we were first born, and I take his word for it, but the mother I knew was always shitfaced, high off whatever drug she could afford or passed out somewhere. I don't even want to mention the amount of time we walked in on her sleeping with one of dad's friends while he was passed out in the chair next to them.

"I don't even know why they even had kids to begin with. They never raised us, Maverick did. From the age of five years old he was cooking us meals from whatever scraps we had in the cupboard."

"I could never picture doing that to our child. It makes me sick that there are people out there treating their kids that way. There are so many lovable couples out there who deserve to have a child to fill their home, a couple to love and raise them the way a child should." My voice rises and I look sheepishly at Mason, and to my surprise he's grinning at me, his eyes bright. "What?"

"You're going to be a fantastic mother Denny." I can tell he means what he said and it warms my heart.

"And you're going to be a great father."

"I promise you I will be, that I'll never hurt our baby girl."

"I know you won't, Mason, the thought has never even entered my mind. You're nothing like your parents. You never could be. You're kind, funny, loveable, caring, energetic, courageous, playful, and affectionate and . . . protective."

"Really?" he asks lifting his brow.

"Yeah," I smile. "You take care of those closest to you. When you laugh, people laugh with you. If you hurt, people hurt with you, your moods spread like wildfire and for that you give off this aura of safety."

My face flushes when I realise how honest I had just been with him. I'm thankful when the waitress walks over and sets our food down at the table.

The smell is intoxicating, the essence floating around us and sending my senses into overdrive. The smell wafting up through my nostrils and tingling my taste buds has my mouth starting to water.

Mason ordered spaghetti bolognaise for dinner and he picked well, it looks delicious, but the smell is something else.

I lift my fork, twirling the stringy, slithery spaghetti around my fork before dipping it into the rich smelling sauce. My mouth closes over the fork with a moan, my taste buds going into overdrive from the heavenly taste of the rich, succulent, sun ripened tomato sauce. It's practically melting inside my mouth. I don't even finish chewing before I'm scooping up my second mouthful.

"Enjoying that?" Mason teases.

I nod my head, my mouth too full with food to speak. I must look like a right picture, sitting here with hamster cheeks stuffed with food.

"You do realise no one is going to pinch your food don't ya?" he chuckles and I look at him confused.

"Huh?" is all I manage to get out before I'm ramming another forkful into my mouth.

God this is so good.

"You! You're eating like you're worried someone's going to come and take it away," he laughs.

My cheeks flame when I realise I've nearly eaten half the plate already while

Mason has barely put a dent into his larger portion.

"Sorry," I mumble, feeling self-conscious about eating the rest now, but still, not even that is going to stop me from finishing off my plate of food.

"No, don't be sorry. I like it Angel. It's nice to have a woman who likes to actually eat. So don't mind me, have at it," he grins, his hand waving to my plate.

Not needing to be told twice I scoop another fork full and load into my willing, hungry mouth.

This has to be one of the best dates ever.

Despite the conversation we had about Mason's parents, it still feels like things are looking up for us.

I just don't want to get my hopes up only to be let down in the end and have him leave me.

SEVEN

My alarm clock beeps loudly next to me, but I'm too tired to get up to switch it off. Mason didn't drop me off at home until gone half eleven last night and since I never got a nap in yesterday because I'd been too excited about our date, I was exhausted by the time I got to bed.

Yawning I grab my phone off the side of the bed to switch the alarm off. Needing to wake up a bit better, I start to read through my Facebook. I'm excited when I see I've got twenty six notifications, that is until I click on them and they're all for either group invitations or someone posting in a group I didn't even know I was a part of.

Deciding to just check through my newsfeed I'm even more disappointed to find everyone moaning about their parents, about some girl at school, and oh . . . oh, then we have the cryptic messages. These are my favourite ones. They go on about being the bigger person, that 'if you have something to say, then say it to my face' and the best one ever 'next time, if you want to write a status about me, tag me in it.' I really want to comment and say 'can you tag the person you're talking about instead of sounding so cryptic,' but getting involved in Facebook drama isn't me.

Dropping the phone to the bed with a sigh, I get up, wanting a cup of tea to start the day. The second I stand up, a wave of dizziness hits me, and I have to sit myself back down on the bed, waiting for the nauseous, and dizziness feeling to subside.

"Please don't be sick; please don't be sick," I chant to myself, my head resting between my knees. It's something my Nan told me to do from when I first started getting morning sickness.

My phone beeps and ignoring the dizziness and the sickness feeling, I lean back over on the bed to grab my phone.

Who's the daddy: *Do you want me to pick you up to go for some breakfast? Harlow and Malik said they'll come as her lawyer called to tell us it's been postponed for another hour. M x*

I laugh when I read the name he put his number under last night. Only he could have done something so silly. I never even thought to check it last night because I was so tired. Not bothering to change it and quite liking it, I text him back.

Me: *That sounds awesome. I'll jump in the shower now; I'm dying for a cup of tea. D x*

Who's the daddy: *That is not a visual I need right now when I'm having a coffee with Granddad and Joan. That woman can smell a boner a mile off. M x*

Giggling I think of what to text next, loving the fact I get to him in that way. I also wouldn't put it past Joan to have that kind of power. She's like a horny Granny.

Me: *Glad I didn't tell you I'm naked and was just about to get into the shower then. That would have been sooooo awkward. ;) D x*

I can't stop the grin spreading across my face, loving how easily it is to fall into old banter with him. This was how we were when we weren't around people, when we first started to get closer. After last night with him telling me about his past, I can totally understand now why he doesn't let anyone in, why he wears that mask of the playboy, comedian, and hard ass all the time.

Who's the daddy: *Now things just got really awkward. I literally jumped from my chair knocking over Harlow's orange juice into my lap. So, think of me baby, when you're in the shower . . . all hot, wet, soapy . . . naked . . . M x*

Who's the daddy: *I'll be there in twenty minutes so get your cute ass in the shower. M x*

Me: *Now you've got me all excited. I'll think of you while I'm in the shower. When I stand under the hot steam, rubbing soap all over myself, naked, wet and slick . . . see ya soon D x*

Who's the daddy: *Now I need a shower. . . .* M x

I leave the phone on the bed, not wanting to text him back; otherwise I'll never get up to get ready. I grab my court outfit, an outfit I'm not too sure about. It's a black sleek maternity dress, the material clings to me in all the right places, but when Nan and I bought it, sole purpose being for court, I was a lot smaller. Now I'm worried it's not going to fit me the same way.

My Nan complimented me when I tried it on. She said from behind I didn't look pregnant, but when I turn around you can totally see my bump.

I manage to finish getting ready when there's a knock at the front door. Grabbing my bag off the bed, I walk to the front room, throwing the bag over my shoulder.

"Hey," I smile, and blush when Mason's eyes rake over my body, his eyes yet again lingering on my obscene cleavage. The dress is tight around the bust making my breasts push together in an uncomfortable way. "You finished?"

His smile knocks me for ten and has my knees knocking together. How can he effect me so badly? The hold he has over my body is scary. It's like when he's around I have no say or will power.

"Not yet," he smirks, his eyes again doing a once over.

"Oi! Once you've finished ogling the hot MILF can we get going?" I grin hearing Max yell from out of the car window, a massive grin upon his face.

"Bro," Mason growls, his eyes glaring towards Max who is still grinning and just to annoy Mason more, Max gives me a slow scan, admiration clouding his eyes. "He's freaking dead," is all I hear muttered when I step out, loving it when Mason yet again closes the door behind me. We walk down the path with his one hand at the small of my back, sending delicious shivers up my spine.

"You look seriously fucking hot by the way," he whispers once we round the car. Looks like I got shotgun I think when Mason leads me to the passenger side.

"Thank you," I blush, secretly liking the fact he finds me attractive even with a huge bump.

"No, *thank you*, I've had fantasies about you like this for so long. You look like a hot, naughty, school teacher or a secretary. I think I'm still dreaming the way today is going," he says, shaking his head as he opens the door. I'm too stunned about the comment he made about having fantasies about me to even try and get my head around him thinking I look hot.

He helps me get into the front of the car before shutting the door behind me.

"Denny," Max groans, "You're gonna kill me love."

"Huh?" I ask when I finish buckling my seatbelt. Max has to have the worst timing with his idiocy. He chooses when Mason gets into the car to answer my question.

"I had a semi hard on over your outfit, and now I've got a raging boner from looking at your tits, especially now you've got your belt on."

He says it so bluntly and so loudly, I don't just blush, I just burst out laughing. "Stop looking at m . . ."

I don't get to finish the sentence because Mason is out of the car and rounding the back to drag Max out. Luckily the little shit never had his seatbelt on or things would have gone awkward quickly.

Mason slams the door shut making me jump, and although I can hear them, it only sounds like mumbles. I manage to make out the threat of a pole shoved up his ass and something about telling everyone he had an STD if he addressed his girl like that again.

His girl!

He called me his girl. My belly does a flip and I'm grinning like a fool when they both get back in the car.

"Sorry Denny," Max frowns, but soon sneaks a wink when Mason isn't looking, making me giggle.

"What are you happy about?" Mason asks, looking at me warily, and quickly looks up in the rear-view mirror to check on Max.

"I'm just excited about eating. I didn't feel too good when I got up."

"Why didn't you tell me? You should have called me," he frowns pulling out, his eyes flicking to me with concern.

"You texted me and made me forget I had it, so the point's moot, don'tcha think?"

He's grinning like a mad fool when I chance a look at him, "Good," is all he says and he looks so darn proud of himself it's cute.

We arrive at the cafe at the same time Harlow, Myles and Malik do. We had to park nearer to the court as that's where we'll end up.

"How are you doing?" I ask Harlow, knowing she's terrified of seeing Davis again.

"Okay. Just nervous I guess. He's going to be so close. What if he attacks me?" her bottom lip trembles and I wrap her up in my arms just as Malik walks over to us.

"What's up?"

"Nothing," Harlow replies the same time I reply, "She's worried about Davis being in the court room."

"I knew there was something you weren't telling me," Malik growls, frowning at her.

"I didn't want you to worry."

"I'm not worried, babe. He won't get near you, I promise. If it's just seeing him in general then I'll make sure your attention is focused elsewhere," he grins, but I can still read the concern in his eyes. He doesn't like seeing her worried.

"You can't do that in a court room," she whisper yells making Malik and I chuckle.

"I can and I will if you worry babe. Go grab the table over there and we'll bring the food over."

Shit!

I didn't go to the cash point machine before coming. I can't see a place like this taking cards either. Not that the place is horrible, it just doesn't seem to be updated into the twenty first century. I mean come on; they have what has to be the oldest till in history.

"Any chance the cafe isn't as old as it looks and it takes cards?"

"I don't think so," Malik answers confused, his eyes watching Harlow's ass walking over to the table.

"I'm just going to pop down to the cash point. There's one outside Tesco," I tell him, ready to turn around until a demanding voice stops me.

"I don't bloody think so woman. Go sit your ass down. I've already ordered for you," Mason warns. I turn to find him looking at me like I've grown two heads and it kind of pisses me off.

"Excuse me?"

"Yeah, excuse you. Did you really think I'd let you pay for your own breakfast?"

"Mason, you didn't exactly mention anything to me or even ask me what I even wanted to eat. I'm not a fucking mind reader."

"And that's my queue to leave," Malik mumbles walking off.

"I shouldn't have to," he says completely ignoring Malik. "You're my woman and I asked you to come. Now let's go sit down. I've ordered you a large tea and a full English breakfast. I made sure there wasn't anything you couldn't eat on there."

I stand still for a moment, not following him, I'm too shocked. Was that an argument? If so, who won? Because to me it sounded like I just got bossed about and treated like a dog.

"I'm not a fucking dog. I'm not going to heel because you said sit," I snap, feeling my blood pressure rising.

"I didn't treat you like a fucking dog, Denny," he groans running his fingers through his dark hair. His muscles bulge as he does it and my mouth waters and I can't help but ogle the way he flexes, or notice the way the tension has risen in the past few minutes. "You finished?" He says throwing my earlier question back at me.

I slyly grin up at him, moving forward just an inch before leaning up to whisper in his ear. I nearly forget what I was going to do when I feel his large, warm hands going to my hips. The sensation sends tingles through the material of the dress and has me sway unsteadily on my feet.

Remembering what I was doing I move my lips closer to his ear, so they lightly touch before talking. "No, because your clothes are in the way." My voice is husky and not at all how I usually sound, it's shocking even to me. To be honest I hadn't expected that to come out of my mouth, I was going to say something sexy, but nothing came to mind.

My face is flushed when I pull back, my lips lightly skimming his jaw. His eyes are hooded as we stare at each other, both of us breathing like we've just been running a marathon.

"I wouldn't bother Denny, he always wins staring competitions," Max hoots from the table making me jump. He obviously didn't catch the tension burning between us, or if he did, he interrupted to piss his brother off for the second time today.

I quickly rush over to the table, pissed when I have to squeeze in behind one of the chairs because of the man on it wouldn't push his seat forward for me. My stomach nearly touches him when Mason walks up beside me and pushes the man's chair in for him.

"Thanks," I smile, ignoring the man when he protests since he clearly just ignored me. When I look down at him he's glaring up at me, his face bright red, and his moustache covered in either beans or tomato sauce. My guess . . . could be both. The jury is still out.

"Oh and you're going to pay for that little tease back there," he whispers down to my ear making me blush. I quickly move to our table to get away, gutted when I find the only other empty seats are the ones next to each other. Myles grins at me when he notices my displeasure and I know he has something to do with it. I give him the glare that says 'shut it' which only makes him laugh harder.

I'm not halfway through my food when my belly starts to tighten. Brushing it off as nerves I take a sip of the orange juice that I got Mason to buy for me.

Seconds later I'm on my feet with my hands covering my mouth rushing to the toilets at the far end corner.

Trust us to be sitting the farthest away!

I'm not even in the loo before I'm throwing up my breakfast. I whimper feeling uncomfortable from not only being sick in a public place, but kneeling down on my freaking bare knees in a public toilet.

Gross!

"Denny . . . Are you okay?" Harlow calls and I ignore her, not being able to stop the horrid retching.

What sounds like a scuffle soon turns into arguing on the other side of the door and I hope to God that they aren't complaining about me. I'm pretty sure the shop next door could hear me throwing up, so I hate to think I'm putting people off their food. Especially after seeing the price for a small breakfast when we walked in.

"Fuck off!" is all I hear before another door is slammed shut. "Denny . . . Babe, is everything okay?" Mason's worried voice comes from the other side of the door. I inwardly cringe at him hearing me like this. Not really attractive.

I groan not able to speak as the heaving stops. I rest my head in my hands, my elbows resting on the dingy toilet seat.

"Can you let me in please? I need to see you. Do we need to go to the hospital?"

I wipe my mouth with the tissue, well tissue paper, wincing at how painful it is against my skin before flushing the toilet. I reluctantly open the cubicle door and wince when I see his worried, concerned expression.

He braces me in his arms, hugging the life out of me, and I have to catch my breath. "Oxygen is becoming an issue here, Mason," I growl, hoping to Christ I don't smell like vomit.

"Are you okay?" he asks looking me up and down like I had just fallen over and not thrown up everything my stomach was storing.

"Yeah. It's normal to get sickness during pregnancy. I had it a lot when I moved in with my Nan and a little before, but I haven't had it since," I shrug moving out of his embrace so I can swill my mouth out in the sink. I look at the dirty, rusty sink and nearly pass swilling my mouth out, but then Mason produces a bottle of water and I sigh with relief.

"Use this, not the tap water. I asked Myles to get it for you," he smiles sheepishly, and my eyes soften towards him. He's so incredibly sweet, it's like he's a brand new person.

"Thank you," I croak out, feeling embarrassed as I swirl my mouth out before taking a large swig of the refreshing cool water.

"You really should have sipped that," he winces.

"It's okay," I giggle, feeling like I could easily go back to sleep.

"Look, I'm going to go talk to the lawyer. Why don't you go sit in the car until I get back."

"What? Why? I've got to be in there in . . . Shit! I need to be there in ten minutes," I squeak, rushing towards the door, but a large arm goes around my waist, under my belly, pulling me back.

"You can't stand up in court when you look like you're about to pass out, Denny. You need to go home and rest."

"I'm bloody doing no such thing you idiot. I'm going. I'm fine. I was just sick, which is normal during pregnancy, Mason. I'll go home to sleep after. Don't make me use your brothers against you," I warn him and see his lips twitch.

"I don't think it's a good idea though. You've just been sick," he points out.

"I know, I was there," I tell him, giving him a 'duh' look.

"Christ!" is all he says before opening the door to four worried looking faces. "Oh and before anyone says anything, not my idea."

"What happened to your eye?" I gasp when I see Max's black eye.

"Walked into a door," he whispers looking like a lost puppy. Malik, Myles and Mason all look over to him with shocked faces. My arms reach out to touch him, but he flinches like I'm about to hit him. Harlow giggles from the left of me and I give her a glare.

"It's not funny. Who hurt you Max?" I urge, wondering why his brothers haven't kicked their asses.

"Mason," he squeaks out, his eyes wide and full of fear.

I turn so quickly, pointing my finger hard into Mason's chest. "You say you're sorry to your brother right now, Mason. You can't go around hitting people for no good reason," I snap, shoving my finger at him again.

"Trust me; there was a reason," Malik mumbles amused.

Ignoring him my head turns back to Mason, giving him a warning glare. "Now!" I shout loudly causing a few customers to turn our way.

"I'm not fucking saying sorry to him," He growls, sending Max glares over my head. He steps forward as if to attack Max again and I hold my hand out to stop him. I turn around to take Max to get some ice when I catch him grinning smugly at Mason. He soon loses it when he sees me looking.

"It really does hurt Mase, you should say you're sorry," he whimpers.

Knowing I'm being played for a fool, I play along walking over to Max. "Oh dear Max, we should get this looked at," I tell him sympathetically. He gives me a sad pout which would have been so believable had he not been grinning smugly two minutes ago. "Let's take a look," I say and he leans his head down for me to look at his eye, that's when I notice his eyes roam to my chest. I poke hard over the forming bruise and grin smugly when he howls in pain.

"What was that for?" he cries.

"One, for trying to make me look like a fucking idiot, second, for doing something to piss Mason off and three, for looking down my dress at my tits," I growl.

"You looked at her tits," Mason snaps, the front of his body pressing against my back.

"Oh no you don't, Rambo, let's get to court. We're going to be late."

"Holy shit! Malik we're going to be late. That's not going to look good if we're late," Harlow cries, rushing over to grab our bags.

We all head out of the cafe and make our way to the court house. When we reach the courts, all of a sudden the sickness feeling swarms my belly again and I know for a fact I'm not going to get through this day without emptying my stomach again.

Great!

IT DIDN'T TAKE ME long to go talk through what I'm supposed to say in the court room with Harlow's lawyer. Not that he needed to remind me, or prep me. I'd never be able to forget what a jerk Davis was to her.

"Denny Smith, please make your way to court room one," a woman's voice calls over the intercom. All witnesses have been put in a separate room, so I won't be able to see Harlow or anyone until after I give my statement.

Mason argued with the lawyer to make an exception, telling him about me being sick and really shouldn't be alone, but the lawyer was having none of it.

Standing up on shaky legs I make my way to the door where the security personnel bloke is waiting for me.

"Follow me Miss," he says and I follow him to court room one, my face heating because of the nerves pumping through my body. My heart is beating so fast I'm afraid it's going to burst. It only escalates when I see Davis sitting in the defendant box making my skin crawl.

After finding out why the court has been adjourned so many times, all I want to do is scream at him.

He's telling the courts he's not guilty, that the bodily assault on Harlow was caused by Malik when he found them about to sleep together. And that Harlow is trying to say it was him to protect Malik or some bullshit. He's also got an answer to why I got hit over the head. Apparently I must have fainted and hit my head. I think I'd have known if I had fainted.

"Will the accused please rise," the judge calls and I watch from the witness stand as Davis stands up, his eyes narrowing in on me. Ignoring him, I turn my head making sure to look directly at the judge when addressed, just like Harlow's lawyer told me to.

They go through the motions where I have to take an oath, swearing to the almighty God to tell the truth, the whole truth, and nothing but the truth.

As soon as the oath has left my mouth they begin. Davis's team wastes no time asking any questions, not that I thought we were going to have biscuits and tea beforehand. I just presumed they wouldn't be so aggressive; he's the guilty after all.

"What would you say Mr. Davis and Miss Evans relationship was like Miss Smith?"

Huh? He's been asking me the stupidest questions for the past fifteen minutes, but this one just takes the biscuit.

"I'm not sure I understand the question. They've never had a relationship of any sort. Not unless you count him bullying her as one," I shrug, finding it hard to look at the judge when I speak. I've had it drummed into me since I was a kid to always address the person you're talking to, but instead, today, I have to listen to the lawyer question me, but give my answer to the judge and jury.

"So they weren't intimate on any level? Miss Evans didn't move seats on the first day of school because Mr. Davis told her to after she tried to 'feel him up,'" he exclaims, reading from off the piece of paper in front of him.

"No, that is not what happened. Harlow was new, she had just started and when she sat by him he made her feel uncomfortable."

"Uncomfortable how?"

"He smelled badly; he hadn't showered and had been doing drugs the night before. When he tried it on with her, she moved seats, from there on out he continued . . . "

"That's all we need," he says holding his hand up interrupting me, and it's not the first time he's done that either.

Rude!

"Last question on the matter before I move on, how did he 'try it on with her,' as you put it?"

"I'm not sure, I wasn't sitting next to them." I'm beginning to feel frustrated, especially when the smug fucker looks pleased with my answer, and looking over to Davis, he does too.

"So you weren't close enough to hear what was going on?"

"No, I sit on the other end of the classroom," wondering what this has to do with anything.

"So Miss Evans could easily have tried it on with Mr. Davis and then felt embarrassed when he kindly rejected her, so she ended up twisting the story."

"From my point of view of the room, I guess you could make that up, but there are plenty of other students in there that day who heard clear as day what was said and what happened, so my opinion is irrelevant."

"I see," he says, looking none too happy about my answer. "The night you were found unconscious, Miss Smith, can you tell us what happened?"

"Harlow and I went to the bathroom. I became sick," I tell them, rubbing my rounded stomach in a soothing gesture. "So we went outside to get some fresh air. When we did Harlow started to complain about feeling funny. When I turned to help, something hard hit me on the head."

"So you didn't see anyone approach?"

I shake my head 'no' really wanting to get out of here, my eyes are becoming tired, my feet are killing, and I can feel myself being sick again with the way this lawyer is digging at me.

"So you could have fallen and hit your head when you fainted?"

"I never fainted. I felt fine other than I had just been sick. I felt whatever it was they used to hit me with to knock me out. I assure you I never passed out."

"I have no further questions your honour," he says, sitting back down in the seat. Harlow's lawyer smiles at me encouragingly.

He continues to ask me similar questions as the other lawyer and by the end of it all I'm exhausted and hungry, which doesn't surprise me after throwing up all of my breakfast this morning.

Hoping to get it all dealt with today I'm angry when the judge adjourns the hearing, asking us to come back in two days.

Walking outside to the others they all rush over to me, bombarding me with a million and one questions.

"They were ruthless. I honestly have never wanted to punch someone so much in my life. Your lawyer said not to take it to heart, but I couldn't help not to when they were making me feel like the accused," I growl.

"Oh God," Harlow frowns, looking worried as hell. "I don't think I can do this. Richard told me about the statement Davis had given to the police and I can't believe he even thought up something like that."

"I know right, he has answers for everything, even for the first day in class when you moved away," I tell her, hoping I'm allowed to talk about this with her.

"Come on; let's go get a drink and some food. It's been a long day," Mason butts in the same time Malik walks up to Harlow and places his arms around her front.

"I've spoken to Richard; he said you can do a video link to give your testimony if you're that worried. You won't have to see Davis. They'll see you, but you won't see them, you'll only hear the questions."

"That sounds like a good idea," I tell her, wishing they offered that to me.

"I dunno. I'll think about it. The thought of him watching me, and not seeing his reaction or what he does creeps me out. I don't know why. Why can't they just take him out of the room?" she whines as we make our way outside the door, nearly bumping into a group of people.

Mason stiffens and I look over his shoulder to see Davis's older brother, the one in a gang, Carl, staring holes into us. Harlow doesn't know who they are, which I'm grateful for and I'm about to do a victory dance that he or his family didn't make a scene when he speaks up.

"Put your lying fucking slut on a lead Malik," he shouts. Malik turns, his glare deadly as he stares down Carl.

"What the fuck did you just call her?" Malik thunders, stepping forward, but Max, Myles and Mason step closer to him.

"You heard me. My brothers in there looking to do some serious fucking time, all for a bitch who can't keep her legs closed."

"Keep telling yourself that Cam," Max sneers before Malik can open his mouth.

"It's Carl," Carl snaps, shooting daggers at Max.

"Like I care. You could be named Carlie and I wouldn't give a fuck. What you need to worry about is buying soap-on-a-rope for your brother. A bar of soap won't be good for a rapist in prison," he snarls and Carl takes a step toward him when two security guards walk out, telling us to move on.

We listen, but the tension is still thick in the air and I'm glad when Myles suggests we go back to Wellingborough where my brother lives to find somewhere to eat.

Today has been long, and I can't wait to get back home, showered and into bed. I'm so freaking tired I reckon I'll fall asleep eating my food.

EIGHT

A BANGING NOISE IN the distance wakes me up from my deep slumber. Still feeling tired I lay there listening, my head going over the previous day's events.

After dinner Mason picked up on my tiredness and offered to bring me home. He also gave me a kiss on the cheek before leaving which had me feeling giddy and more awake than I was actually feeling.

Once I had showered I went straight to sleep, only to be woken up by something I obviously dreamt about.

Sitting up I rub at my tired eyes yawning. Needing a glass of water I throw my legs out of the bed and get up, but stop suddenly when I get closer to the door and hear glass shattering. Shaking, and stupidly, I open the door a crack, enough so I can peek my head out and look down the hall. The moonlight shines through the kitchen blinds casting a dim glow on the front room, and that's when I see a darkened shadow moving in through the window.

Frozen, it takes me until I see the light reflect from a knife to shift myself into gear, shutting the door as quietly as I can and locking it, even though I know it won't hold off an intruder. My heart is racing and it feels so loud against my temples I'm wondering if he can hear it too.

Shit! I cry inwardly when I look around the room. There's nowhere to hide and there is no way I'll be able to fit myself through the bedroom window. Hearing another loud smash I clamp my hand over my mouth to smother the scream and I'm startled to hear a voice I vaguely recognise.

Moving as fast as I can, I grab the magazine I had been reading and start ripping pages out to start using them as wedges for under the door, knowing it will be harder to push open if he does manage to get past the lock. Once I've done that, I shakily get to my feet, jumping when a knock bangs on my door.

"Open up now!" the voice snarls, and for some reason I can tell he is putting on an accent, his voice sounding off.

Quickly grabbing the chest of drawers in a dazed panic, I drag them as close as I can to the door before pushing them over. Now they're leaning against the door and I pray with that and the wedges of paper under the door it will be enough to hold him off.

Police!

Grabbing my phone I quickly dial 999, screaming when a knife slices through the door. I don't watch, but listen as he struggles to pull it back out. I'm too busy crouching down in the wardrobe, hoping the police can get here soon.

"999 what's your emergency?"

"Police please. I have an intruder in my home," I cry out on a whisper, my whole body shaking to the point of pain.

"Okay Miss. Can you tell us where you are?"

I rattle off the address before addressing the real issue, "I'm twenty seven weeks pregnant, he has a knife," I cry, my whole body racking with sobs.

"Calm down, we have dispatched a team right out to you. They are two minutes out," she says as another bang that sounds like the knife cutting through the wood happens making me squeal and this time I don't bother covering the sound. He already knows that I'm in here.

I'm sobbing and trying to concentrate on the ladies voice on the phone who is still trying to calm me down, but my attention is on the door, praying like hell he doesn't get through. The next thing I hear is a commotion at the front door and more glass shattering. Putting the phone down when I hear the police, I rush out of the wardrobe, finally able to catch my breath. Walking closer to the door to see if I can hear what's happening, I step on a piece of paper, at least I thought it was until I look down noticing writing on the back. Picking it up I read the words out loud, my mind too far gone to stop myself from reading them. "This is what will happen if you continue to be a grass." With shaky hands, I turn the picture around to see the most horrific image I'll ever lay eyes upon. I let out a blood curdling scream, falling backwards onto the floor with another scream, a painful one this time.

NO! NO!

"No, no, no, no. I want to go. I want to go," I chant to myself, clutching the phone in my hands and through my tears I call the last number, which happens to be Harlow.

"Hello," she answers groggily.

"I need to go. I need to go. Please," I whimper, a sob tearing through my throat.

"Denny. Denny, are you okay? What happened?"

I don't answer her, instead I drop my phone when a loud banging starts on the bedroom door and I scream moving backwards, hitting my head on the wardrobe door.

My eyes stay glued to the photo, not able to take my eyes off it as I rock backwards and forwards, tears streaming down my face and pain skirting all over my body.

Please no! Please don't let it be true.

The picture is a good distance away, the image blurry from my teary eyes. Hannah lays motionless, her bruised body covered in dirt, her face cut and bloody. It's the missing bottom half of her clothes and the blood pooling between her legs with the scared look in her wide, open eyes that has me puking on the floor next to me.

Who could do that to someone? Is this what they are going to do to me? Feeling sicker by the second, I block out all the loud voices around me and the banging on the bedroom door, too afraid to move.

Finishing emptying my stomach I crawl back into the wardrobe, curling into a ball, my whole body shaking with fear. My stomach hurts painfully, and I try to rub the pain away, but it doesn't leave.

I don't know how long I lay there in pain, or when they smashed through the bedroom door, but the next thing I know paramedics are in front of me and I can hear shouting close by.

The next thing I know a form comes skidding across the floor near to me. It startles me at first causing me to break out of my trance and I notice it's Mason.

Another sharp pain causes me to whimper.

"Mason?" I croak out, my voice hoarse from screaming and crying.

"Yeah baby, it's me. Can you come out so the paramedics can take a look at you?" he asks me softly and I look at him confused, then notice two paramedics close by waiting.

It takes me a second to remember why I'm here before it all comes flooding back, and I cry out. Rushing out of the wardrobe quickly, I throw myself in Mason's waiting arms. He barely has time to steady himself to stop us from falling backwards. The pain in my stomach tightens and I whimper again before burying my head deep into his neck, breathing in his intoxicating scent.

"Hannah, someone killed her. They said . . . they said 'that's what happens to grassers.' Mason, she looked so scared," I sob, but it turns into a cry of pain when a fresh wave of cramps hits me low in the stomach. "He was going to kill me wasn't he?"

"Shush babe, everything's fine. I promise," he says shifting me so I'm looking directly into his gorgeous, chocolate coloured eyes. I know he's trying to mask that he's worried, but I still see it in his eyes.

"It hurts," I breathe out, finally admitting for the first time out loud about the cramps in my stomach.

He gives a nod to the paramedics who rush over and start checking me out. Another cramp hits me and I cry out louder with a scream.

"What's wrong?" I cry.

"We need to get you to the hospital," the woman paramedic tells me calmly.

"What's wrong? Is it the baby? Did I do something?" I cry at them, and then look to Mason for answers, but he looks as lost and pained as me. He reaches for my hand when they strap me to a stretcher, telling me everything is going to be okay.

"What's wrong?" he asks them, his voice firm and demanding.

"We can't be too sure because of the night's events. It's put a lot of stress on mum and the baby, so she could be going into labour," she tells us, rushing us out to the ambulance.

"It's too early," we both cry at the same time.

"Oh my God is she okay?" I hear Harlow cry when we reach the ambulance.

"They're taking her to St. George's Hospital, meet us there. I'm going with Denny," Mason tells them just as another pain hits my stomach. Everyone around us must have caught on to what was wrong and Harlow gasps in worry, crying to Malik.

"She can't have the baby yet, it's too early. We read a book about birth, it's too early," she kept repeating, but her voice drains out as soon as the back of the ambulance door closes.

"Please make it stop," I beg them, the pain feeling excruciating. I'm frightened I'm losing the baby, or that I've hurt her from everything that happened tonight. My mind is too preoccupied to even think about the break-in. It seems so insignificant compared to the horror I'm going through right now.

An oxygen mask is placed over my face, and I start sucking in deep breaths, my head becomes woozy, my body relaxing as the pain in my stomach starts to ease a little. The hold on my hand tightens and I give it a light squeeze back, tears running from my eyes.

We arrive at the hospital twenty minutes later. We're rushed through the side doors and into a waiting side room where a scan machine and another machine are waiting for us.

"I'm Doctor Harold; I'll be treating you this evening. Can you tell me where the pain is?"

I show him, pointing to the lower end of my stomach close to my bladder.

"Is it there now?" He asks touching my lower abdomen.

"No," I tell him shaking my head, feeling tired and exhausted. A fresh pain hits me low in the stomach and I breathe through it, just like the paramedic showed me.

As soon as it eases off, the doctor resumes his examination on my lower stomach.

"I just want to do a quick scan, and then I'm going to put sensors across your belly. They'll track your baby's heartbeat and it will show us the strength of the contractions. Are you happy with that so far?"

I nod my head yes, the panic not easing any since the pains started. He nods his head to the nurse to come closer.

"The nurse is going to put an IV in your arm to get some fluids inside you. I'll also be doing an internal examination to make sure your cervix hasn't dilated. Am I okay to do it or would you prefer a female doctor?"

At this point a monk could do it and I wouldn't care, just as long as they knew how to help my baby.

"I don't mind," I assure him, then spend the next twenty minutes or so being poked and prodded in the most intimate places.

After leaving us for half an hour the nurse and doctor walk back in. The doctor walks straight up to the heart machine monitoring the baby's heartbeat, and pulls out the sheet of paper that's been printing the progress since they attached me up to it. The contractions have gone and I haven't had a pain in almost fifteen minutes.

"After an internal examination and from what I can see here, the stress you endured tonight has caused you to experience Braxton Hicks; which is your body's way of preparing itself for birth. However, Braxton Hicks contractions aren't usually that painful, the contractions can be closer together, but usually they are just mild pains. After monitoring you it's safe to say you aren't going into labour. I'd advise you to go home and get lots of rest for a few days. Do you have any questions?" he finishes.

"So, Denny is going to be okay? And so is the baby?" Mason breathes, relieved.

"Yes. It happens in most pregnancy's, especially at this stage in the pregnancy. It just so happened that the stress from tonight brought them on."

Mason slumps back in his seat, his hands running over his face. When he looks back up his eyes are glassed over when he looks at me.

"Can I go home?" I ask, not turning my eyes away from Mason. Something in the look he's giving me is so powerful it's choking me. I've never needed anyone in the way I've needed him tonight. I hate depending on people.

"Yes. I'll get you your discharge papers ready and then you are free to go," he tells me before leaving the room.

I wait for the door to close behind him before turning my attention back to the nurse.

"I need to remove the IV from your arm," she says softly, setting up the stuff she needs beside me.

"Are you okay?" I ask turning my attention back to Mason, keeping my mind off the nurse removing the IV.

He laughs, but there's no emotion in it. "Am I okay? Denny, I'm far from okay, but the bigger question is, are *you* okay?"

"Still shaken up, and glad everything with the baby is okay. Have the police said anything?" I ask, mentioning the break-in for the first time. I can't remember if Mason has left the room or not since we arrived, my attention has been emotionally and physically on the safety of my little girl.

"I'm not sure. I haven't spoken to anyone. I know my brothers, Harlow, Granddad and Joan are outside waiting."

"Go see them. Tell them to get home," I gasp, horrified that they've been waiting out there this whole time. We've been here for three hours. It's four in the morning now, so they must be tired as hell just like me.

"I'll go out and let them know what's going on. I don't think they're going to leave until they've seen you're okay for themselves. I'm so sorry I wasn't there for you," he tells me on a whisper, his voice hoarse.

"None of this was your fault Mason."

"I should have been there to protect you. I hope you know you're not getting out of moving in with me now," he warns.

"Don't start Mason, I'm not moving in with you."

"Yes, you are."

"No, I'm not," I snap, ignoring his 'we'll see' look as he leaves to tell the others that I'm okay.

NINE

MY LEGS ARE REALLY sore when I wake up from the long day I had yesterday gathering the rest of my belongings from my parent's house. It took a toll on me, not only physically, but emotionally too.

I honestly didn't believe Mason when he told me they'd have my stuff still. But when we got there and my mother wasn't there, only my dad, he told us he shifted the boxes into the cellar so my mother wouldn't find them. Turned out she wanted them binned.

Totally not surprised that she wanted that, but what did surprise me was her not burning them the second I left the house. It's something I could totally see my mother doing, or well, getting someone else to do the dirty work for her.

We managed to get most of it in the trunk of Mason's car when she pulled up in her flashy car, wearing her over-the-top fancy clothes. She immediately went crazy at us all as soon as she got out of the car. She even threatened to phone the police on us. Dad had talked her down and pleaded with me to leave before things got out of hand. He didn't even need to give me *the look*; I had already decided to hightail it out of there. I didn't want to argue with her after everything that has been going on.

The rest of my stuff is at my Nan's, who surprised me when she informed me it was already boxed and ready to go. Best part is that she is moving to town to be closer to me. She told me she doesn't want to spend the rest of her life miles away from her granddaughter.

That was two weeks after the break-in, just when I finally agreed to move in with Mason in the new house on his granddads property. He pleaded, begged, guilt tripped me until I relented. It's now been three weeks since the break-in and today I move into the new house, with Mason.

I've been sleeping in Malik's old bedroom until they had the new one sorted, and I don't know whether it's because he was being a gentleman or because he knew I wasn't ready to share that personal space just yet, but not once since I moved in here has he tried to sleep in the same bed as me. As from tonight though, that is going to be another matter. Tonight we will be sharing a bed and I'm afraid I won't be able to control myself when I'm around him. Every minute I spend with him is another minute of torture. My body is burning for him, craving for him so deeply that it's gone beyond what people would, call healthy.

"Oh, hey, you're awake," Mason says startling me as he moves into the room.

I cover myself up; conscious of the fact I'm only wearing knickers and one of his t-shirts that I robbed off him the night he brought me home from the hospital three weeks ago. Don't worry. I washed it. Then I made him wear it again so it smelled like him.

"Um, yeah, why wouldn't I be?"

"I thought you'd sleep longer. Want to come over to the new house when you get dressed? Max has just gone to the chippy, so if you want some I'd hurry up," he grins.

"I could eat. What time is it?" I ask trying to look around for my phone. It seems too early to eat fish and chips.

"Half twelve."

"Half twelve? Are you kidding me? I've been asleep for fourteen hours?" I grumble getting out of bed.

"It's fine. Joan told us to leave you to get some rest when Max started moaning about you getting to sleep in and not him. She had to remind him that in a few months it will be you not able to have a lie in."

"She could be a good baby," I defend rubbing my stomach.

Grabbing my clothes I turn to look for my boots. When I see them over on the chair, I lean over to grab them when Mason starts choking, startling me. Turning around I find his eyes glued to my ass and I blush knowing he's staring at my red lace maternity knickers.

"I'll um . . . I'll go wait at ours and I'll see you over there," he stutters, his eyes giving my ass one more glance before he stumbles out of the door. I want to laugh at his quick retreat, but then it has me wondering if it turns him off. I've been putting on a lot of weight over the past week and maybe he's not into big girls. The weight doesn't even bother me. After being skinny with no figure for all of my life, it's nice to have some shape to me.

Not wanting to get upset I cross the hall to the bathroom to get washed and changed, ready to get this day over with. Oh, and to get some food before Max purposely tries to eat it all. Although, after this past week, since I agreed to move in officially, Mason has been the one pinching my food. Just the other day I was eating some tikka wraps that I made when he walked in, took a huge bite out of one, leaving me with just a mouthful. I shrugged it off trying to not let it bother me, but then he did it again when I made more. He has also tried doing it over the week when we've had dinner, pinching little things or wanting a taste. I swear he's so lucky he has balls at the moment, because I was determined to ruin them a few days ago when he pinched the last slice of pizza. Before him, it was Max. I was eating a lot of sweets the first week I was here and he had a tendency to help himself, telling me sharing was caring.

Walking over to the house, boxes are stacked up outside the front door on our little makeshift patio. It's kind of cute.

I walk in without knocking (I mean, it is my house now. Kind of) I turn right into the living area where I'm thankful to find the sofa already there. Mason, with help from Harlow when I was living at my Nan's and my brother's helped decorate the house the way I would like it. It still amazes me that he was that sure of me moving in. But he did.

The front room is painted a warm brown and green, the sofa the same colour brown with green shaded cushions. The rest of the place is decorated with similar matching green ornaments and the TV . . . huge. Not that I expected any different in a blokes house. I'll never understand why they have to have them so big. It's not like they're going to see anything that the portable TV can't.

"Wow. It looks amazing in here," I voice out loud.

"Thank God. Mason has been on my back worrying," Harlow giggles standing up to give me a hug. "You okay? You've been sleeping a lot more lately."

"Yeah I'm doing okay. I think it's just the heat, but it's starting to cool down now so the sleeping should ease up. Hey, what are you doing?" I shout when I see Mason mooching through a box with my name on it.

"Um . . . what's it look like?"

"It looks like you're going through my personal belongings that I'm pretty sure on the other side says do NOT open unless you're Denny," I tell him, raising my brow. The box is filled with diaries and other personal items. So you can understand my panic if he ever read any of them or saw what I have stashed at the bottom. I'm pretty sure the last three diaries which are from over the past three years would give him a heart attack if he ever read them. They are all about him, my fantasies about him and my overactive imagination on what our life would be like together. Yep, totally creepy, especially when you add what I have hidden at the bottom. I don't even want to imagine the things he would think.

"Well I didn't see your name," he snaps, having the audacity to blush.

"Now you do need to get your paws out of there," I warn, and then jump when a voice startles me.

"I hope you didn't wake fucking Denny up brother. I'm not having her eat my. . . . oh, hey Denny. Shit . . . I was just telling Mason that I hope he didn't wake you up because I was going to bring you a plate in bed," he says stuttering, his eyes pleading with his brothers behind me to help.

I shake my head feeling deflated. Am I that big of an eater that they're all scared I'm gonna pinch their food and eat it?

Whatever!

"I'm not hungry anyway," I lie and move to sit down on the sofa feeling ready to burst into tears.

"What the fuck, Max?" Mason snaps, walking up to his brother and smacking him across the head.

"Sorry man," he groans. "It's okay Denny. There's plenty of food to go around for all of us."

"It's fine Max," I grit out, feeling ready to explode. First Mason this morning and now this. I can't take it anymore. They think I'm disgusting.

"Ahh shit, you're going to cry," Max says rubbing the back of his neck.

"No I'm not," I grit out defensively, the top of my nose stinging. My throat starts to ache and to make it worse, I'm pretty sure my eyes just started to water.

"Yes you are," he tells me just as Mason takes a seat next to me.

"Are you okay, Angel?"

"Jesus, it's not the end of the world, Mason. I can reject food if I want to. It's not like I'm going to waste away is it. I mean, I wouldn't want to starve the rest of you," I say, but the more I speak, the higher my voice gets.

"He didn't mean it like that, Hun," Harlow softly tells me, coming to sit down on the other side of me.

"It's what everyone's thinking. Max can't stand to eat in the same room with me because he thinks I'm going to eat all his food," I say hysterically. Max takes a step back, his eyes wide while Harlow rubs up and down my back. "And to top it off, Mason thinks I'm fat," I cry out, a sob tearing through my throat. Harlow pulls my head to her shoulder soothing me.

"Mason, I can't believe you would think that," Harlow snaps; anger evident in her voice.

"I never said she was fat," he says defensively with his voice filled with confusion and I can feel his eyes on me.

"But you thought it. You're repulsed by me. Running off as soon as you see me half naked," I cry harder into Harlow's shoulder.

"When did I see you half naked?" he asks.

"Dude . . . burn!" Max laughs, and I send him a glare that has him retreating. He steps back bumping into Maverick and Myles who have just walked in.

"What the fuck? Who upset Denny?" Maverick snaps, his eyes glaring at everyone.

"Bro, you don't want to get involved," Max warns him, taking another step back.

"You all think I'm fat," I wail, feeling like I've just stepped on to the crazy train. I don't even know why I'm acting like this and a deep part of me knows I'm being irrational, but I don't care. All I care about is Mason thinking I'm fat.

"Who said she was fat?" Myles says outraged walking farther into the room.

"Can everyone clear out a minute and let me talk to Denny alone?"

"I don't think that's a good idea," Max warns with a mouth full of sausage.

"That sausage is going to be shoved somewhere other than your mouth if you don't fuck off," Mason growls and everyone starts to clear out of the room.

"Will you be okay?" Harlow asks sweetly.

I nod my head, wiping my runny nose with the back of my hand before wiping it on the back of Mason's jeans.

"Please tell me you didn't just do that, Denny," he pleads sounding disgusted, which just sets me off again. Harlow takes a step towards me, but something Mason does has her retreating and following the rest of the brothers to wherever they are heading, probably in to the kitchen to eat all my food. Just smelling the salt and vinegar in the air has my stomach growling. "Now tell me what this is all about?"

"Nothing, it's just the pregnancy hormones," I lie feeling foolish now for wiping snot unladylike on his jeans.

They're good jeans too.

"Bullshit, I can piss a better excuse than that," he remarks crudely.

"It's not an excuse," I sniffle not looking at him.

"Tell. Me. What's. Wrong, before I go Jessica Fletcher on your ass and find out for myself."

"Jessica Fletcher?" I question, scrunching up my features.

"Um . . . yeah . . . My Nan used to make me watch it as a kid okay," he says holding his hands up in surrender.

"And you liked it?"

"You're kidding right, I loved it, she was a bad ass detective," he gushes before straightening his own features. "It was okay I suppose."

"You suppose?" I tease, amused.

"Stop changing the subject," he snaps and I raise my brow at him. "Tell me why you're so upset."

"Because you're disgusted by me," I yell throwing my hands up heavily.

"You're seriously having me on right now. Please tell me you are Denny because this isn't a joke," he warns taking a step closer, his hard chest resting against my bump.

"No," I whisper looking away again, but his hand shoots out grabbing my chin to face him.

"Look at me. When have I ever gave you that impression, Angel?" he asks softer this time.

"Earlier when I was bending over," I cry out embarrassed. "You got one look at me and hightailed it out of there, Mason. What do you expect me to feel like when you do something like that? It hurt Mason, really fucking hurt, especially knowing you can go to work each night and bang some skinny ass bitch who doesn't have stretch marks, cellulite or a rounded stomach."

The sound of my heavy breathing is the only noise you can hear in the room after my rant. When Mason still hasn't spoken, my fears were confirmed. He knows I saw what was running through his mind and he's just too scared to admit it.

Coward!

When his loud booming laugh echo's around the room I snap my head in his direction and scowl.

"Why are you laughing?" I growl feeling more pissed.

"You! Babe, there is nothing that could ever get me to stray from you."

"We're not exactly an item and you did before," I remind him which makes him give me a death glare.

"No Denny, I didn't. If I never acted like such a dickhead the morning after we fucked then we would be together. That night, it meant something to me whether you want to believe it or not. I've had enough of pussy footing around you wondering if you're going to wake up one morning and realise what a mistake you've made being with me. We are together now. The minute I realised what a fucked up mistake I made, we were together. As for not finding you attractive, would this happen if I didn't?" he asks which confuses me, but then he quickly grabs onto my hips and presses his erection against me. I'm actually surprised he managed to reach with my bump in the way, and more than that I'm surprised by the simple fact he got a boner over me.

"I'm always hard for you, Denny. It's killed me not being inside you, but I need you to know you mean more to me than just sex. I want to do this right, I want us to work and I don't need me and my dick ruining that."

"You'll get bored Mason, you'll see some much prettier, skinnier girl, you'll flirt, and before you know it you're in the back alley of some club fucking her up a wall."

"As much as I love your dirty imagination right now I'm not a cheat Denny. There is no one on this earth that could get me to cheat on you or even contemplate doing it. That is one thing, without a doubt, I can promise you without the worry of knowing that maybe someday I'll break it. I keep my promises. I've had a whole childhood full of broken ones to know never to make one I can't keep. You're going to need to know you're enough for me and trust me," he whispers, leaning in, his lips a breath away from mine and my pulse races miles a minute in anticipation.

I lean my head back to give him easier access. His lips press softly against mine, kissing me gently as my hands run up his strong, hard biceps slowly. His tongue licks at the opening of my mouth and I moan holding him tighter. Just as the kiss starts to deepen, the door opens and Maverick walks in, coughing loud to show his presence.

"Bro, the lawyer is here and wants to see you both in the kitchen," he says and I can hear amusement in his voice as I hide my head in Mason's chest in embarrassment.

"Coming bro," Mason replies before I hear the door shut again.

"Well that was awkward," I groan.

"Not as much as you crying over food," he grins rolling his eyes. "Max is just territorial over his food. He's worried he's met his match, that's all. None of us can out eat him. My Nan used to moan at him all the time for all the food he went through, asking where he puts it all. She'd say, 'If I even looked at the food you ate I'd gain three stone' and she'd shake her head at him."

"I wish I could have met your Nan, she sounds great."

"She's just like yours," he grins and I look at him confused.

"I've met her. We talked on the phone the other day arranging some things. She'll be here soon so let's go see what the lawyer wants with all of us. Make sure you have something to eat, if Max says anything tell him you'll tell his niece he made you starve when you were pregnant," he grins wickedly and I laugh.

In the kitchen Harlow's lawyer Richard Cole is sitting down on a stool at the small breakfast bar. In the room Harlow's Gram's, Mark, Harlow and the all of the Carter brothers stand waiting for Mason and I to enter the room.

Maverick sends me a cheeky wink smirking, and I blush at him like a school girl. Mason tenses beside me and pulls me into him as we stand waiting for the lawyer to tell us whatever he interrupted our day for.

"I'm sure you're all guessing why I called you here today," Richard says, looking at me, to Harlow, and then over to Malik.

We nod our heads wondering what is so important that he would turn up out of the blue and not wait until our next meeting in a few days.

"Well, a new witness has come forward with what could be vital evidence."

"Who?" Harlow and I interrupt gasping. We both take a step forward wondering the same thing. Who else did he rape?

"I'm not at liberty to say. The witness has been held in protective custody until the trial. From what the police have informed us Hannah Gittens case has now been moved up to a murder investigation. From the picture Denny had posted in her house the police are almost certain she is dead and that whoever killed her is targeting the witnesses. After the break-in at Denny's brother's house it seems that way too."

My stomach turns and I feel like I'm going to be sick. I've tried so hard over the past few weeks to forget about that picture, most of the time it works, but then there are times when it's all I can think about. I wish it could be unseen, but I know it's never going to happen which kills me more inside.

The break-in itself is something that hasn't gotten to me as much as I originally thought it would. Yes I have nightmares over it occasionally, but that's mostly because of the baby. In my nightmares I wasn't able to keep him out and he hurt my baby girl. Something about the nightmare feels so real it scares me to death. It's why I've been sleeping a lot during the day. During the night when I need to sleep is the worst. The darkness consumes everything around me, and the deafening silence pierces my ears and that's when the nightmares creep in and takeover.

"So why can't we know? What is the evidence she has on him? When did this happen?" Harlow asks panicked.

"Babe, calm down," Malik soothes her. His arms go around her waist, pulling her back to his front.

"No, I can't. If he raped someone else then I need to know. It's my fault, don't you see that? If I had gone to the police sooner about him instead of worrying about making the situation worse, then we wouldn't be standing here right now."

"I disagree," the lawyer speaks up. "They wouldn't have charged him by hearsay; they would need solid proof to arrest him, Harlow. I'm not saying you getting attacked is a good thing, but you're taking a stand now, and that will put him in prison for a long time."

"What if it doesn't though?" I speak up. "He's claiming a pretty good alibi, everything he's saying adds up, even if we know none of it is true. You can see by how protective Malik is he'd never touch Harlow and you know from meeting her for a few minutes she isn't one to cheat or lie. Someone needs to be able to put our minds at rest, so we can sleep at night. So please tell us something," I plead.

"Alright," he sighs running his hands through his hair. "I'm not allowed to mention names, but the witness stepped forward a few days ago by going to the police station and handing in the clothes she had been wearing the night of the rape. We also have a hospital report claiming her story to be true. It happened years ago, but she's finally stepped forward claiming she was too scared to press charges at the time. I guess she found out he did it again and heard of his alibi and decided to step forward."

"So will this help our case?" Harlow asks, tears in her eyes.

"They might overrule it, but we're digging up the results of the rape kit at the hospital. She hadn't gone straight there, so DNA might not be conclusive, but something might be able to pin him at the crime. We've also taken the clothes to forensics. I'll be going over a few things from her statement and I'll find out as much as I can with the leads I've got."

"What about the clothes she kept?" I ask wondering why she would do that. My mind wonders back to Kayla, and wondering how she is doing. I know the girl who has stepped forward isn't her because her mother would never allow it, but half of me wants it to be her. I want her to get the justice she deserved all those years ago when it happened. The other half is being realistic, and doesn't think her mother would ever let her stand up in court and testify.

I miss her, and I hope she's okay.

"She bagged them as soon as she got changed into a sealed plastic bag. If there is any DNA, it will be on them, but it can take up to a week to find out."

"Which will still be in time for court?" Malik speaks up.

Mason starts running his hands up the side of my body and I relax my back against him. When he moved to stand behind me is anyone's guess.

"That's the other news I'll be giving you. The witness is testifying the day you were meant to and you will be testifying the day after. If the court hearings go well, then the sentencing should be held not long after."

"Why can't they just hurry the process up? It's been months and months since it happened and the case is still on-going."

"I know that must be hard for you, Harlow, but we have to follow procedure. I'm sorry. If a closer date clears up then I'll bring the date forward. Until then we sit and wait and hope with the new witness things start to speed up."

"Okay," she whispers nodding her head. I know she's worried something will happen between here and the court date. Especially with whoever is targeting witnesses. Harlow is the main witness in this case, so I understand her anxiety.

"I'll leave you to it. If you have any further questions please don't hesitate to call me. If anyone confronts you over the case other than me and your family then please call me immediately or the police. I'll call with any updates," he tells us standing up.

"I'll see you out," Gram's tells him. I forgot she was there. She's usually mouthing off and telling the lawyer where he can stick his degree. I guess the talk Mark promised Malik he would have with her worked.

"You okay?" I ask Harlow.

"I feel bad for feeling relieved that someone else will be standing up in court, but then I remember why they're standing there and I feel sick. I'm sick of it all. I just want him to get sent down. How can the judges not see that he's a criminal, that he shouldn't be able to walk the streets for the rest of his miserable life? I just want this to be over," she slumps back, using Malik for support.

"He will never hurt you again, baby. There's no way they'll find him innocent. As for feeling guilty, don't. You have nothing to feel guilty for. We'll get through this, Harlow, together."

I look at the two as Harlow turns in his arms and hugs him, her head thrown into the crease of his neck and shoulder. Her cries echo around the barely there kitchen and cause my own tears to fall.

"Fuck," Max and Maverick say before clearing out the room, taking the damn chips with them.

"Don't you dare," I snap, shoving away from Mason and over to Max. "I'm hungry, if you want to starve your niece then I'll happily remind her all the time when she's older."

"Jesus, that's blackmail."

"That's life; now give me that," I smile in triumph, grabbing the bag.

Everyone else reluctantly follows, grabbing plates out the boxes before sitting down to eat.

It's getting late when Max walks downstairs into the front room where I've been lying down on the sofa catching up on some soaps. *Coronation street* just finished when he comes barrelling in looking sweaty in his ripped jeans and black tee.

"Having fun *just* sitting there, you look far too comfy?" he sarcastically asks to which I return with a twisted smile when he wipes the sweat off his forehead.

"Oh I most certainly am," I grin, stretching out on the sofa.

He grunts again before shaking his head in disgust at me. "You're lucky I didn't want to be a part time uncle, Denny, because otherwise I'd be making you carry those goddamn clothes up yourself," he whines.

"I'm pregnant you dipshit. We aren't supposed to lift anything heavy," I tell him laughing. "What crawled up your ass?"

He grunts again which he seems to be doing a lot around me today. I know his behaviour isn't malicious towards me, that he's treating me like he'd treat Harlow or one of his brothers.

"If you didn't have so many fucking clothes I wouldn't be in this mood. Do you seriously need that many? There is seven days in a week Denny, you only need seven outfits, but with that many clothes I'm sure you could wear a new outfit every day for the next three years," he growls sounding pissed.

I just burst out laughing not able to hold it in. My laugh gets louder and harder when I hear Malik calling Max to come help with the boxes of shoes. Max's face is priceless and just so I never forget his face like that again I snap a picture on my phone. I had just been playing Candy Crush when the commercials started when he walked in, so the phone was already in my hand.

"I'll make you pay for this one day, Denny. I really will," he grunts before stomping his way out of the room.

I'm doubled over laughing when Mason and Harlow walk in looking exhausted and half confused and concerned for me.

"What's got you so happy?" Mason questions.

"Yeah, I'd be careful of that bladder of yours," Harlow giggles which calms my giggling down somewhat.

"Max. He came in moaning and when Malik shouted to help out with the boxes of shoes, his face was hilarious, look," I tell them, showing them the photo on my phone.

"Oh my God, send me that," Harlow laughs. "Max's and Myles's birthdays are coming up soon so we can use this to our advantage. It's so going in the paper."

Mason and I chuckle and I'm glad I've managed to put a smile on Harlow's face. She has been down since the lawyer came over this afternoon.

"I'm hungry," I murmur once we calm down.

"Me too," Harlow replies sitting down near my legs. I manage to lift them in time before she sat down, and I plop them back down on her lap once she's seated.

"Me three," Mason grunts sitting down near the fireplace.

"Me four, for whatever it is," Max snaps when he storms back in the room, his face red and sweaty.

"It's to clean up the garden so that Denny doesn't trip. We needed another helping hand," Harlow teases.

"Fuck! I just remembered I can't. It messes with my allergies. Sorry peeps."

Max sits back down in the armchair, not looking sorry at all and I want to laugh.

"Well, thanks for your support, asshole," Mason grunts at him, shaking his head.

"You didn't carry all those clothes, Mase, they were fucking heavy as shit and did you see how many runs I did to get them all up the stairs? How the hell are you supposed to get them in that wardrobe? I know it's big, but bro . . . bloody hell man, those clothes need their own house."

"That's an over-exaggeration and you know it," I snap outraged.

"Babe . . . I'm the one that packed them into the van," Mason laughs. "There's tons."

"Sorry for dressing nicely. You'll probably have to get rid of most of them anyways. I probably won't fit in them after the baby is born."

"Don't call me," Max warns looking sternly at Mason.

"What we having for dinner then? I'll buy it this time," I tell them.

"I'm fucking starving," Max groans.

"When aren't you?" Harlow teases.

"When I watch those programs, 'How clean is your house?' they put me off food. Oh and at school. Whenever I think of the cafeteria, I lose my appetite."

I playfully roll my eyes and open my mouth to ask where the rest are when Maverick and Myles walk in with bags of Chinese takeout.

"We brought gifts," Maverick grins. "Malik's just gone to get some plates."

"We were just about to order something too," Mason grins.

"We knew Denny and Max wouldn't last another twenty minutes so we called them half an hour ago and went to pick it up on our way back. You finished with the boxes?"

"Yeah. Everything is mostly unpacked apart from Denny's clothes and shoes," he shrugs.

"The place does look homey now that everything is moved in," Maverick comments.

"Just needs some pictures up and it will be a home," I suggest, speaking out loud.

"And a baby girl," Mason says softly and my heart melts. I look over to him to see his warm eyes focused on mine and I smile.

"Any chance you could scoot up, babe?"

"Oh yeah, sorry," I grin sheepishly. I scoot up the sofa as Malik walks into the room. Mason takes a seat in between Harlow and I and Malik takes one in front of Harlow on the floor. We only bought a three seat sofa and an armchair, so Maverick, Myles and Malik will have to make do with the floor, but looking at them piling mountains of food on their plates, they don't seem to care. I will have to buy some beanbags from a store that I saw in town, they would go perfect in this room.

Myles helps himself going through the box of DVD's we got from my parent's house and picks one out with a grin.

"Love this film, *Nightmare on Elm Street*," He grins excitedly.

"Can't we watch something else?" Max whines like a two year old.

"Nah, I want to see this. I didn't pick you as a horror film chick," Mason grins, his eyes sparkling.

"They aren't horror movies, Mason," I tell him dryly.

"Yeah it is. I fucking shit my pants and couldn't sleep for a week because of Freddy. I was scared he'd come for me," Mason tells me wide eyed.

"Don't even get me started on the freaky show. I watched *Scream* once with a girl at the cinema. I wasn't paying attention to the movie at first, I was staring at the girl's tits, but then everyone started gasping, so I started watching it. It was fucking horrible. Let's just say the girl got freaked, practically jumped in my lap, but all I could do was shove her off screaming 'I can't watch this, I can't' like a little girl. Worst date ever. I didn't even get to touch her up."

We all look to Max who is also piling food onto his plate at the same time as talking and we all burst into laughter. He looks at us all offended before grabbing a tray of curry and sitting back in the chair.

"Remember that time as a kid when we made him watch *Hocus Pocus?*" Maverick asks Mason chuckling.

"Shut the fuck up," Max warns making me grin, even though I don't know what they're going on about.

"This I have to hear. I love that movie and I'm still shocked over you crying over *Scream*, because that has to be one of the funniest horror movies made," I grin.

"Well, our dad had left us for the night this one time and told us we could watch the tele. The choices of films that night were *Hocus Pocus*, and a few other boring films, so we made him sit and watch *Hocus Pocus*. We weren't even halfway through the movie before he started screaming and crying. You know the zombie,

Billy? Well when he rose out of the grave Max nearly wet himself," Maverick laughs and we all laugh with him apart from a scolding Max.

"Hey, Mason, I don't know why you're laughing, I can remember you nearly pissing yourself crying over the *Wrong turn*," Max taunts looking smug.

"I was laughing that hard my eyes started to water," he replies dryly and I grin looking at him. He must sense my stare because he turns to look at me and the look he gives me sends shivers up my spine.

"You okay?"

"I laughed at that movie too. You'd run the way you came wouldn't you? You wouldn't run *in* the forest?"

"Oh God," Mason groans. "And when they run into the abandoned shed looking for a phone," he says rolling his eyes. "Why would they even think there would be a phone in there, the place had campfires outside for heaven sakes."

"Don't get me started, it's just as bad when they hide under the bed or they walk to find out what the noise is. Me . . . I'd lock myself up in my room until I heard something else then call the police." Which I did, I want to add, but I don't, I don't want to put a downer on the day. I've managed, even between them all moving boxes to get to know the rest of the Carter brothers more and I'm so thankful to be a part of this family. I just hope they will still have me once Mason realises he's making a mistake being with me. And a huge part of me has a sinking feeling he will. No matter how many times he's tried to reassure me he's here to stay, or how strong my feelings are growing towards him again, I know in the end he will break my heart when he realises he wants to be single and ready to mingle.

"Okay you two love birds, break it up. It's like watching some kind of freaky foreplay with the way you two are getting excited over a horror movie," Max frowns disgusted.

We both laugh, but I can't help the faint blush to my cheeks at the word foreplay, knowing for a fact what I'd rather our foreplay to be like. After all, I know what his fingers can do and how they feel.

"Fuck off," Mason grins putting his arm around me as Maverick takes our plates to the kitchen and Harlow packs the leftovers up. Not that there's much left over.

After everyone leaves, Mason and I straighten out the sofa, clean the drinks up and lock up. By the time we've entered the bedroom there's an awkward silence that is starting to make me more nervous. I know we're sharing a bed. I'm going to have to be close to him, close enough to smell his spicy aftershave, his body scent and everything. It's going to kill me.

"So . . . how do you want to do this?"

I want to say 'on my back' and he must see it written on my face because the devil smirks.

"What do you mean?"

"The bed, which side do you sleep on?" he asks as we both stare from opposite sides of the bed.

"Oh, on this side." I point to the side I'm standing by, not really wanting to tell him I sleep in the middle, that this girl doesn't do sides.

"I'll go wash up," he says walking back out of the room to the bathroom. I pull back the blankets, then walk over to the curtains and shut them while I wait for him to finish.

Out of all the rooms in the house the bedroom is my favourite. It's a deep purple, with black empty frames, and a few 3D butterflies lining the walls with a black fan centred in the middle of the ceiling. Even the doors to the walk-in wardrobe are black along with the bedroom furniture.

The best feature in the room is the window. It's lower to the floor than the other windows in the house and Mason has installed a mini cushioned sofa for a reading area. I know for a fact Harlow had something to do with this room because it's nearly the exact replica of my dream bedroom. The only thing missing is the four poster bed with the white canopy that falls above and down the sides of the bed.

"Bathroom's free," Mason calls walking into the room making me jump.

I make quick work of grabbing my night shirt and running quickly through my night time ritual before slowly making my way back into the bedroom.

The room is dimly lit, the soft glow surrounding the room making it look warm and inviting. I smile shyly at Mason and walk around to what now is my side of the bed and get in. Mason doesn't move until I'm lying down, he switches the lamp off and I feel him get back under the covers, and I swear he's facing me.

My body is rigid and I lay there straight as a plank looking up at the ceiling until Mason's voice startles me.

"Relax, I can feel how rigid you are from here."

"I can't help it," I whisper, following his lead by turning to face him.

"Everything will be okay, I promise."

"That's not why I'm nervous," I tell him honestly. "I'm scared that you're going to hurt me again." I leave out the part where I want to jump his bones, that with him just lying this close to me is pure torture for me.

"I didn't want to hurt you the first time, Angel, I just wanted to protect you. I promised you I would show you how much you mean to me and I will. I don't know where we'll be in five years or if we'll last, but I do know I like who I am when I'm with you. I can finally be myself without having to put on this easy, uncaring, joker persona in front of everyone. I'm just the real me when I'm around you and I like it," he whispers before his hands touch my hip and sparks light between us. "Now get some sleep."

I nod my head then let out a startled whimper when he brings me flush against him, and instead of pulling away I lay my head down on his chest loving how warm he is under my touch. My eyes close instantly and for the first time since the break-in I fall asleep peacefully lying in his arms.

TEN

A WEEK OF LIVING alone with Mason, sleeping in the same bed and walking around in confined spaces with him has been total and utter chaos on my mind. Everything he does drives me wild, the way his lips close around a spoon, or the way he looks when he walks out of the shower wearing only a towel around his hips, showing his well-defined body. Oh my God, that 'V.' I'm literally losing my mind. I've even resorted to being a bubbling mess when I'm around him, always stuttering on my words. The once sassy, take no prisoners woman is long forgotten. It's like he's put me under some sort of spell, one where I can't make one lucid thought for myself.

He doesn't seem to be affected like I am; but then again, he has changed since I got back from Wales. The playboy I once knew has long gone, and in his place is a grown man, making a living, and acting sensible. The old Mason would have had me stripped down, naked, and thoroughly fucked me by now. Don't get me wrong, he can still flirt outrageously and leave me feeling dizzy. He even still acts like a two year old. He even leaves the toilet seat up, even after I stuck a post-it note above the flusher to warn him to put the seat back down after he's used it, but he's still grown up a hell of a lot since the day we became more than just friends.

Just the other day Harlow was saying how the brothers have noticed the change in him, and I began to worry they thought it was my doing. She must have read my thoughts because she assured me they are thankful for whatever had gotten him to grow up, to see that there is a future for him. They said they were afraid the road he was travelling down was on he'd never come back from. His life before me and the baby consisted of girls, sex and beer. In whatever order you wish to categorise them in.

I'm just glad I have him. The other day I had another bad case of Braxton Hicks and bless his soul, Mason stayed with me, rubbing my back until early hours of the morning.

He also makes me breakfast every morning, and if I'm not awake he will bring it up to me, depending on whether he has to go into work to let in the cleaners or not.

"Are you sure you have to go?" He asks pouting, a gleam shining in his eyes.

I do need to go. As much as he has been attentive all week, I need my space. I still don't know what we are, but a few times this week I swear I felt him lying to me, like he was deliberately hiding something from me. It ended up consuming my every thought, so the other day when he came back soaking wet from the rain, I asked him where he'd been and what he was hiding. He said at work, but no way would he have gotten that wet walking to and from his car. He had to have been out in the weather longer to get that soaked. Then I heard him on the phone, and when I walked into the kitchen to try eavesdropping on his conversation, he finished the call so quickly it made me even more suspicious.

Honestly though, I just want him to want me the way I want him. I've always wanted him. I've always felt that deep rooted connection between us and the chemistry between us has always been off the charts explosive. But since I got back from my Nan's I feel like he's not being himself and that it's stopping us from finding out where we are heading. We don't act like a couple, we don't seem like a couple, and we're certainly not intimate like a couple.

Now can you see why I'm so freaking stressed? I'm a horny pregnant woman about to combust because the only man she's attracted to seems to want to 'talk' all the time. He doesn't even kiss me. He's driving me completely insane and I'm going to be getting a one way ticket to D Block if it carries on.

"I need to get out for a bit," I tell him, not facing him and instead shoving shit in my bag to get ready for when Nan and Harlow arrive.

We've decided to go into town to look for some maternity clothes and underwear. With my hips growing some actual meat on them, my usual jeans don't fit as snug and neither do my leggings.

"Is everything okay?" he asks walking up behind me, and I feel his presence there surrounding me.

"Why don't you tell me."

"Huh . . . what does *that* mean?"

I can hear the confusion in his voice which only makes me feel more upset and angry. He must know what this is doing to me. Living under the same roof, sleeping in the same bed and not feeling like a family. It's times like this that I wonder if he truly is only with me because I'm pregnant with our daughter.

"It means I'm fed up of not knowing what the hell is going on with us. We're living together, but we're not really together, *together*. You kissed me the other week to prove you were attracted to me, but since then all you've done is be secretive, stealing quick glances at me here and there to see if I'm looking at what you're doing. What gives?"

"Look, I'm going to come right out and say this before it goes too far." He talks calmly, too calmly, and I know he's going to ask me to leave, that all of this was a mistake and I can feel my heart crumbling once again.

"What goes too far?" I grit out, not able to help the quiver in my voice.

"I haven't touched you because you left. You left with our baby without even talking to me face to face," he says and when I go to interrupt he holds his hand out stopping me. "It killed me just as much as it killed you, and you'll never know just how sorry I am because now there isn't just doubt in your mind, there's doubt in mine too. What if you don't really want to be with me? What if you're only here because you don't want our girl to grow up without her father?"

"Are you being serious?" I ask, but I already know the answer.

"Deadly."

"Mason, you must realise that it's me you don't want to be with, that you feel obligated. I have no obligation to you. Do I want what's best for my child? Yes. Would I do whatever it takes to achieve that? Yes. What I won't do is ruin her life by being in a loveless relationship. My parents are in that and look how that turned out. If I truly didn't want to be here, with you, with our baby, I would never have come back and stayed."

"So you're not with me because of the baby?" he asks, hope filling his voice.

"God, no, Mason! I'm here with you because I want to be. I just feel like you don't feel the same way that I do."

"Knew you couldn't resist me, babe," he grins playfully grabbing me in his arms and swinging me around.

"I'll be sick," I warn, giggling.

"I don't care babe. I've been stewing over this for far too long, but didn't want to say anything because I'm selfish and didn't want you to leave me again."

I playfully role my eyes as he positions me between his legs while he rests against the side of the kitchen counter.

"Cooeyyyy!" my Nan's voice screeches outside of the house. "Oh my, aren't you a sight."

Hearing her flirtatious voice I quickly move out of Mason's arms and rush over to the door in time to see the interaction between my Nan and Myles.

"I'm really sorry Miss, but this is private property."

"Back in my day they never made men like you. Such a shame too, you have such a fantastic body young man," she flirts and I know she's only playing.

I think.

Myles blushes and I feel sorry for him so I step outside interrupting before she says something I can never erase from my mind.

"Nan, leave Myles alone," I giggle.

My Nan turns around wearing a huge grin on her face. Her eyes are sharp on mine but soon fly to the side when Mason steps up next to me and she grins bigger.

"You do pick well my girl. I could have you for dessert," she says looking Mason up and down, and for once, I'm glad he has clothes on.

"Seriously, Nan?" I ask, playfully rolling my eyes.

"Alright, alright, but come here, I miss my favourite granddaughter."

"I'm your only granddaughter," I tell her giggling.

"Yeah . . . well, it's the title that matters. Have you spoken to your father?" she asks attentively and something from the look in her eyes tells me she's hiding something.

"Um . . . no."

I leave emotion out of my voice. Since we picked the rest of my belongings up at my parent's home, my father hasn't bothered to come see me or bothered to contact me. He's so far up my mother's ass that I'm surprised he doesn't take a piss without her permission.

"Well, he's meeting us at a cafe in town. He needs to talk to you about something before we go shopping."

"Nan, I'm not talking to him. Please don't ruin this day for me," I plead and feel Mason walk up behind me and pull my back to his front. The position is oddly comforting and feels right, so I lean back into him, relishing in his embrace.

"Shush babe, hear her out," he whispers in my ear and I sigh. Myles moves over to the other side of the garden and starts messing with the flower bed, but I can still tell that he's listening. He's a Carter after all.

"He only wants five minutes of your time, honey, at least give him that," she pleads and if this was anyone other than my Nan then I would just ignore them and tell them to fuck off. "Plus I'll disown you if you don't."

"Are you freaking kidding me?" I squeal outraged and notice Harlow walking into the garden, but stops short when she hears my outburst.

"Jesus . . . It's a joke, not a dick, don't take it so hard," Nan mutters and I look at her confused. Mason doesn't help when I feel his body shaking with laughter or when I hear laughter coming from Myles, confirming my earlier suspicions that he was still listening.

"Huh?"

"I'd never disown you sweetie, but I know what your father wants to talk about and it's something I think you'll want to hear."

"Well if you know then why don't you just tell me?"

"Where would the fun in that be? Come on, he's waiting."

I groan, really not wanting to go now she's spoiled the day by bringing my father into it. I'd been really looking forward to some girl time, and of course getting some clothes that actually fit me. I turn around in Mason's arms and give him my puppy dog eyes which only makes him grin.

"Babe, he's your dad. If you don't feel comfortable and you want to leave, then just call me, I'll come and get you."

"You promise?" I pout, liking the feel of him pressed up against me.

"Always," he grins, kissing the tip of my nose, the notion has me melting towards him. "Now go on before your Nan strips the rest of Myles's clothes off," he chuckles.

I turn to find Mason isn't far off on the matter and have to snap my hands in front of her face to bring her attention away from the poor boy.

"Can Harlow still come?" I ask, gesturing to Harlow behind her.

"Of course," she says then sends a look to Mason behind me and I turn to catch a quick glimpse of him nodding his head.

"Is something going on?"

"No," they both say suddenly and I shake my head.

Weirdoes!

"Well come on then, we haven't got all day," I snap going back inside quickly to grab my bag.

It doesn't take us long to arrive at the cafe where my dad is waiting for us. Harlow trails in behind my Nan as she walks in front of us, weaving in and out of tables, directing her way over to the table my dad is sitting at.

"Is he like your mom?" Harlow whispers sounding genuinely scared.

"No, but he's just as bad with his silence," I whisper back feeling deflated. When my dad comes into view I nearly gasp. His face is sunken and he looks like he hasn't slept or eaten in a few days. The dark circles under his eyes are proof of that.

"Hey Denny," he chokes out, standing up to greet me and bring me into a hug. I'm uncomfortable at first with the affection. It's the first time he's ever shown me any affection since I was five years old. It feels foreign to have his arms wrapped around me in such an affectionate embrace, like he feels like I'll disappear if he lets me go. It has me choking up, and my eyes begin to water, but then I remember all the years he's abandoned me and I harden my stance.

"Dad . . . I need to breathe," I choke out.

"Sorry. Yeah . . . you need air. I'm sorry," he stammers and I look at him with an eyebrow raised wondering where the hell my dad has gone. The man in front of me just seems like a complete stranger.

"Why am I here dad?" I sigh.

"Hear him out Denny," Nan warns gesturing to the chair I'm standing in front of, not making any moves to take a seat. When she gives me that 'I'm warning you right now' look, I quickly pull out the chair and take a seat.

"I'm going to . . . um . . . order a milkshake. Yeah, a milkshake. Does anyone else want anything while I go up there?" Harlow asks nervously.

I know she's doing it to give us some privacy, but I really don't want her to leave me alone with them right now. I grab her hand, looking at her with pleading eyes not to leave me. Thankfully my dad speaks up making me relax.

"They come over to take your orders," he smiles. "And it's on me."

"Thank you, Mr. Smith."

"Call me Charles."

"Dad?" I call again, wanting him to say whatever it is he has to say so I can go and get me some trousers that stretch over my large frame.

"Yes, sorry Denny."

He opens his mouth to reply when the waitress walks over taking our orders. If I'm honest I just want to strangle her and tell her to fuck off while my dad talks to me, but I'm not that sort of person. One thing my parents *did* teach me, was manners.

As soon as she brings back our drinks we all settle in to listen to my dad.

"How are you? And the baby?" he says looking down at my stomach and I swear I see his eyes soften, but that can't be right. He didn't want me to keep the baby as much as my mother didn't.

"Why do you care? You made yourself perfectly clear where I stand, dad."

"Denny, please listen," Nan snaps and I whip my head to hers wondering why she's pushing me to listen to him when she told me she was on my side, that she didn't agree with what they had done to me.

"Denny, for me to explain the choices that I made in my life I need to explain a few other things to you. Before you were born I was in love with a woman named Katie. We had been together for several years. She had broken up with me and it devastated me to the point I went out every night to drown my sorrows. She left town shortly after, never telling me goodbye or where she was going.

"When I met your mother I was on the rebound and just needed to feel loved. We kind of dated for a few years, and I did start to care for her in my own way, even though everyone warned me she had just pulled the wool over my eyes. When I found out about you, I wanted you straight away. I needed you in my life, but then I found out a few things about your mother, who she really was and that's when everything turned to shit.

"She deliberately got pregnant for my family's wealth. She knew I never loved her, or wanted anything more than what we were. So she got pregnant with you because she knew I'd marry her because of you. Mom and dad warned me not to. Said that she was bad blood, but I didn't believe them. Not until you turned two and Katie came back into my life.

"I found out the reason Katie left me was because of your mother. Katie and I made plans, she had some big news she wanted to share, but she needed to show me, so we planned to take you away, to get you out from under her control. We were on our way to our new home when the car brakes stopped working," he says on a whisper, his eyes full of tears.

"Oh my goodness," I gasp, tears filling my own eyes. He tried to take me away from her. I think it over, and I know for a fact my life would have been better if she hadn't been in it.

"I don't have proof, but I swear your mom cut those brakes. The front of the car took most of the hit and Katie died. I barely made it out of there alive myself.

"When we came home from the hospital I couldn't walk, so your mother had to take care of me," he whispers looking ashamed. "She didn't treat me well when I was in her care and because of the depression of losing Katie and nearly you, I just let her do what she wanted. I felt like I deserved it when Katie had just lost her life.

"I questioned your mother about the car. I told her that I'd leave her as soon as I was better when she said to me, 'Charles, look what happened the first time you left me, you wouldn't want Denny to die next would you?' It was then I realised I needed to stay, too scared to get on her bad side."

"Why did you let her treat me the way she did then? No . . . Why did you treat me the way you did?" I snap, starting to feel angry with him. All those years he was in a loveless marriage, one where he could have gotten away. He could have just taken me away as soon as I was old enough, but he stayed, letting her torment me that much more.

"I was scared of what she would do to you."

"I'm eighteen, dad. It's taken you eighteen years to tell me all of this? Why tell me all of this now? Why couldn't you have taken me away from her? And why did you ignore me for all these years?" I cry, tears running down my face.

"I didn't want her to have more ammunition to hurt you. Whenever I paid you attention as a kid it caused her to be cruel to you. The further I pushed you away, the more she left you alone."

In a way he's right, she ignored me for the most part, but then there were days when she would be so cruel I questioned her reasons for having me. Now I know why.

My father's money.

"You're a coward," I snap on a sob.

"I've left her," he cries on a whisper. "I won't live without you in my life Denny. I can't. All I've lived through, all I've had to stand back and listen to has been to keep you safe, to keep you in my sight. I was so scared that one day she would take you away and disappear. She threatened me on so many occasions to do it, and I knew she wasn't lying."

"Why leave her now?" I question, wiping the tears from my face, ignoring the stares aimed at our table. If I look I know I'll run and I need answers.

"Because I have nothing to stay for now you're gone. I need you in my life Denny."

"So why has it taken you until now to leave her?"

"I needed to know you were safe. I needed to make sure that you had people to protect you when I couldn't."

It all feels so surreal. I know my mother is a bitch, but to hurt her own child . . . okay, I do believe she would. I don't know why I questioned it really; she's never cared about anything other than herself and my dad.

"And am I?" I ask, rubbing my stomach where my baby girl wiggles, kicking out inside of me.

"Yes. She'll be leaving by the end of the month. She has nothing left for herself here now that I've taken all the money she would have gotten from the divorce. I offered a one way ticket out of here and we've got an agreement that if she leaves quietly, I'll buy her a house wherever she is going."

"None of this feels real," I mutter, resting my face in my hands.

Harlow's hand reaches for my leg under the table, her gentle touch soothing my raging hormones.

"What will you do now? Where do we go from here?" I ask, wondering how we can repair our relationship. That is, if what he is saying is the truth. "And how can I know this is the truth and not your way of being in my life?"

"It's true girl, your dad asked me to be a witness for his will. I read the terms of his contract and I questioned him about copies of the police reports on the car crash. He told me everything and about his suspicions of your mother's involvement. I had a detective do some investigating on the case and we got proof a few days ago that your mother caused the crash. She tampered with the brakes. It's how they managed to get so far out of town before they went."

"Why didn't you ever tell me?" I whisper.

"I didn't want to hurt you, but I can see now that everything I did hurt you so much more."

"So all of the times you agreed with her or stayed quiet, that was all show?"

"Of course," he says snapping his head to mine. His eyes are red and sincerity clouds his eyes.

"And the baby?" I question, wondering if that was all for show.

His eyes soften when he looks at me, a smile tugging at the corner of his lips.

"You my cherub made me the happiest man alive the day you announced you were pregnant. I can't wait to be a granddaddy," he gushes.

"Really?" I ask him choked up, reaching across the table to grab his hand. This is all I've ever wanted. His blessing. I never cared about my mother's, but my dad, I always wanted him to approve. There were times when I remembered him from when I was younger, remembered how much I loved him, needed him, and connected to him. Now I understand why it all changed as suddenly as it did.

My fucking mother!

"Really, and if it's okay with you, can I meet Mason, the father?"

"Yes," I grin, wiping my eyes, feeling excited for the first time in a long time.

"Speaking of, we should get back," Harlow says disappointingly.

"What? Why? We just got here."

"We've been here nearly two hours," Harlow laughs and I'm shocked. The time has gone by quickly. "Malik texted and told me and said to get our asses back, that he needs to speak to us," she shrugs, not meeting my eyes.

I look at her warily and sigh. I know we need to go. Malik hates it when she ignores him and I don't want to be on the listening end of them two making up.

"Why don't you come with us, Charles?" Nan asks, gathering her things.

"I wouldn't want to intrude."

"No . . . No, come. Mason would love to meet you," I lie. I don't know how Mason is going to react to all of this. When we collected my belongings he never stopped glaring towards my dad, cursing under his breath every two minutes.

"I doubt that," he chuckles, but grabs his coat anyway and follows us out to Nan's car.

Walking up to the house the place is quiet and I look over to Harlow, raising my eyebrows questioningly. "I thought you said they were here?" I ask.

"That's what they said," she replies, not meeting my eyes again and I want to grab her face and demand her to tell me what the hell is up. Instead I ignore her blushing cheeks and unlock the front door. I barely make it a step inside the front room when a loud ring of 'SURPRISE' is shouted out from around the room.

I gasp stepping back, bumping into Harlow. Tears spring to my eyes and I look around at the people filling the front room.

Old woman Edna is here with Joan. Mark and all of the Carter brothers are here and a few other people from school. Banners and balloons are hung up around the room. Some in pink saying baby shower and some saying congratulations on the new pad. I laugh when I see them; knowing Max had some doing with the 'new pad' comment. Why he didn't just write 'new house' is anyone's guess; the kid really does think he's a gangster.

Mason's face comes into view, and instead of the smile I presumed he'd have on his face, it's scrunched up in a fierce glare.

Before he can open his mouth and ruin the moment, I rush over to him and crush myself against him.

"Thank you. Is this why you've been acting so strange?" I ask smiling.

His face softens when he pulls away a little to look down at me.

"Yeah babe," he grins. "Why is your dad here?" His voice has lost its earlier softness and now has a hard, rugged edge to it.

"Don't," I plead, grabbing the back of his neck and lowering his head so he's eye level with me. "It's a long story. Really long, but my dad . . . he's a good guy, I swear to you. Please give him a chance."

His face doesn't soften at first and I begin to worry that there will always be a rift between the two, but then his face relaxes. It doesn't soften, but he relaxes and in return I relax against him too.

"I can't promise much Denny, but I promise to give him a chance. The second he hurts you, I'm done and I'll hurt him back," he warns and I melt then and there, wondering how the hell I got so lucky to have him as mine. He would go as far as to hurt my dad just to get revenge on someone who made me sad. That is so freaking sweet, or completely wrong, but hey, I'm a woman and I want my Prince Charming to protect me.

"Thank you," I smile, reaching up to give him a peck on the kiss.

ELEVEN

THE PARTY IS IN full swing and after introducing Mason to my dad, the atmosphere in the room relaxed. It seems Mason wasn't the only Carter brother to step in for my honour. All of them looked warily at my dad, until I walked over and assured them all that everything was good.

We're all waiting for Max to come back so we can open the food Joan happily prepared for the gathering. I'm about to ignore my manners and help myself when Max finally walks in. The whole room erupts with cheers and Max takes a bow before walking over to the breakfast bar where I'm currently standing waiting to eat.

"Brownies?" I question irritated.

"Yep, but you can't have any either. We had to use raw egg or some shit with another ingredient that pregnant women can't eat, so no touching," he warns and I roll my eyes at him. Like I'm going to eat them, they look freaking disgusting and have none of the chocolate icing on them that I like.

Helping myself to the food, I pile up my plate before making my way over to Mason who is sitting on the sofa talking to his Granddad. When Mark sees me he stands up to let me sit down.

"No, it's fine; you can sit there," I tell him, not wanting to interrupt their conversation.

"Sit down Denny," Mason orders and I shake my head 'no' in defiance.

"Calm down, I'm going to get some of that lovely quiche before it's all eaten," Mark says, standing up and moving out of the way. I take his seat and turn to Mason.

"Did you leave anything for the rest of us?" Mason questions, amusement in his voice.

"Yes, but this is for you too. I didn't think you'd go up until everyone had their share, so I got you some," I wink and he grins big taking the egg and mayo sandwich that he knows I can't, and don't eat.

"I knew there was a reason I . . . wanted you," he grins.

"Yeah yeah," I smile back, my heart beating like hell thinking about that one little pause in his sentence. My heart and brain were hoping he would say 'love' but the words never left his mouth.

"We're opening presents after, but first I want to show you your surprise."

"My surprise?" I ask confused.

"Yeah, your surprise. Well . . . it's for both of us, but more for you, kind of."

"Oh God, you didn't get a box of condoms did you? I think it's a little late for that," I giggle, but soon turns into a laugh when I see him blush.

"No. Something much more needed," he grins. "Plus, we won't be using protection, I plan on getting you knocked up in another couple of years," he winks, and I stop mid chew and stare dumbfounded at his comment.

"I'm joking, Denny, breathe," he laughs, and I send him what I hope is my scariest glare and carry on eating my cheese sandwich.

This mama bear is hungry.

His comment still lingers in the back of my mind half an hour later as he walks me up the stairs, everyone else slowly following behind.

"Is this where things start to get kinky?" Joan whispers loudly and I choke, laughing.

"Gram's, please shush and stop talking dirty," Harlow pleads making us all chuckle.

"I like it one on one myself," my own Nan replies and I groan out in embarrassment.

"Nan, please take Harlow's incredible advice and shush it."

"Geeze, lighten up, it was a joke."

I roll my eyes although I know she can't see me as we make it to one of the spare bedroom doors.

"What are we doing in here?" I ask Mason, looking at him curiously.

"Don't get mad, but this is the surprise. If you don't like anything inside then we can change it. Okay?"

I nod my head 'yes,' too frozen and nervous to speak as I watch him slowly open the door. I step inside, my mouth agape and my eyes opened wide.

The medium sized room that was once piled with boxes and other materials and paint, is now painted a pale pink and purple with different coloured butterflies. Up on the farthest side of the room, against the wall, is a beautiful princess cot. The white pine wood with white netting above and pink bedding looks like every baby girls dream come true. Above the cot is a pattern of butterflies, which I stare at for a few seconds feeling like something is missing.

"It's where her name will be when we have a name for her," Mason whispers into my ear. It's then I notice everyone behind me is dead silent, even the two Nan's who haven't shut up for the past half an hour, are silent.

I walk over to the chest of drawers sliding my fingers over the white wood and smiling at the soft teddy bears Mason has decorated the top with. On the other side of the room is a bookshelf, lined with various fairy tales fit for a princess. The place is absolutely magical.

Sat by the window is a white rocking chair. Encasing the adorable rocking chair on one side is a mini table, on the other a changing matt table. The way Mason has it set up, makes it look like the most comfortable place to relax. I twirl around in the middle of the room feeling completely overwhelmed, until I lay my eyes upon Mason.

He's standing over by the door with everyone else, looking unsure of himself, and waiting patiently for my reaction. Ignoring everyone else, I walk over to him, feeling tears fill my eyes. I don't waste any time wrapping my arms around his neck and burying my head into the crook of his shoulder and neck.

"Thank you so much," I whisper choked up.

"So you like it?" he whispers back, his arms wrapped around me, holding me close. His warmth surrounds me like a blanket and I can't help but hold onto him tighter.

"I love it Mason. This is perfect. You're perfect. Our girl is going to love this," I tell him honestly, not realising what I said until it left my mouth.

"You think I'm perfect?" he asks with a smirk when he pulls away from me a little.

"I never meant that," I tell him, punching him lightly in the arm where he rubs looking wounded.

"Yeah, I'd believe you, but your eyes tell me different," he smirks, his voice low and husky.

I'm about to protest, to open my mouth, but my Nan walks in gushing over the room, everyone else following suit until Mason yells at them to get off the carpet if they're wearing shoes. His serious expression has me giggling into the back of my hand, which only earns me a glare from him. His expression soon softens and he moves his head forward to mine, gently kissing me on the lips before pulling back slightly, his lips still only a breath away.

"I'll do anything to keep that smile on your face. Even if it means I have to redecorate our daughter's bedroom again and again," he tells me and the seriousness makes me giggle again, until he cuts it off with another kiss. The kiss lasts longer this time and just as we both become more frantic, hotter, both clinging to each other, Mason pulls away. A moan of disappointment leaves my mouth. We stand there, both breathing heavily. It's then I notice we're alone in the bedroom. I'd been so consumed with Mason that I didn't hear anyone clear out of the room.

I look up to Mason with wide eyes to find him looking down at me with the most intense expression that has me clenching my thighs together.

"I'm going to kill Max," he grunts.

"Um why?" wondering why he's bringing Max up.

"Everyone left because he told them to. Apparently getting a boner watching your brother make out isn't a good thing," he growls.

"What did he say?" I laugh, not even bothered anymore about what he says. I'm so freaking used to him. I'm also glad I didn't hear him say anything because I would never have lived it down.

"He said, and I quote 'Come on ladies and gents, before the rest of you get a boner like me. How uncomfortable would that be in a room full of family?' before he got them all out."

Bursting into a fit of laughter, I have to shove my face into his chest to try to muffle the sound. A few seconds later Mason is following, his chest shaking with laughter which only makes me laugh harder.

Back downstairs chaos awaits us. We've not been gone long and all hell has broken loose.

"I saw you eyeing my man up," Joan yells, shoving my Nan with her index finger.

"Oh please, I was not eyeing him up. Why would I with a room full of hot, young beefcakes," my Nan snaps back and I groan, leaning back into Mason's hard, warm chest staring at what can only be called 'a cluster-fuck.'

"Like you stand a chance you hu-"

"That's enough now ladies, let's enjoy the party and not fight over worthless men," Charlie, our friend from school speaks up from the sofa.

When had she arrived? Charlie used to be Kayla's only other friend, the girl Davis raped, and when Charlie returned the last term of school after being away, her, Harlow and I began to hang out. How it happened is anyone's guess.

"Charlie sweetie, she keeps eyeing my man. If it's not my man then it's one of his boys," Joan tells her, her eyes wide flickering between Mark and Nan. "Did you just wink at her?" she snaps at Mark, stomping over to him.

"What? No! Of course not," Mark defends heatedly.

"You were," Nan grins sending him a wink.

He groans sitting in the chair before giving a helpless look to anyone in the room who was brave enough to make eye contact with him.

"You're such a coward, what, you can't handle me in the bedroom anymore, so you need someone tamer?" Joan shouts, and everyone shuts up looking horrified at what they're hearing.

"Honey, this isn't the time or the place to talk about this, so can we all calm down?" Mark tries again.

"So you're not looking at her?"

"I only have eyes for you . . . " he says sweetly.

"Ewe, I don't want eyes, I don't *need* eyes. Why would you only have eyes for me? Have you forgotten that I love just getting a good ole fashioned box of chocolates and a bunch of flowers?"

"Romance is dead," Nan remarks.

"You'd think they'd use their initiative. In our day we never had Doodle, we only had our brains, but even with that they still don't get it," Joan remarks.

"It's Google honey," Nan smiles. "I disagree. Google is like a woman honey, we have all the answers."

"You saying I'm thick?" Joan asks warily and I mentally slap myself for not warning anyone about my Nan beforehand.

"I feel like dancing, who wants to dance?" Charlie yells fist pumping the air, interrupting what I'm sure would be another Nan fight.

"Ohhhh, I love a good dance," Nan replies at the same time as Joan replies. "Let's shake what our mama's gave us."

When she starts twirling her ass into a seductive hip curl, which I thought would be impossible given her age, but no, Joan has it covered perfectly.

"Anyone else wish her mother taught her the whole 'shake what ya momma gave ya' bullshit expires at the age of thirty?" Myles whispers and Max grunts in agreement.

"Oh, oh, I know, Charlie you can teach us how to twirl," Nan claps excitedly.

"Who gave them the loopy juice?" I whisper to Mason, ignoring Myles's comment, otherwise I'd laugh and draw attention to myself.

"Fuck knows," he chuckles. "But I'm going to need to bleach my eyes out after this."

"You and me both. You and me both," I tell him, frowning at Charlie when she starts twirling.

"That's not twirling," Nan scolds. "That girl doesn't do it like that. You know the one . . . she humps a wrecking ball."

"Oh, you mean twerking?" Charlie asks grinning.

"That's what I said," Nan waves her off making me giggle.

"I'm never going to un-see this. I'm never going to be able to look at either of them in the eye again. What happened to Grandma's staying at home, watching black and white movies whilst knitting and making us tea and biscuits?" Max whines covering his face. "No, now we have to suffer with . . . with . . . I don't even know *what* to call this," he cries.

"I hear you, brother." Mason winces when Joan bends over, following Charlie's instructions and starts shaking her ass.

"Hey Denny, can I talk to you for a moment?" my dad asks looking pale, making sure to avoid looking in Nan's direction, which makes me smile. When he looks up, he notices Mason, his eyes looking weary and uncertain before locking with mine and softening, his eyes avoiding Mason's behind me. I give him a gentle smile and nod my head to follow me into the kitchen so we can have some privacy. Mason follows and because I'm going to tell him whatever my dad wants to say, I don't bother telling him to give us some privacy.

I actually feel bad that I invited dad to the party, not that I knew there was going to be one, and left him alone all evening to fend for himself in a house full of escaped crazies.

Honestly, read tomorrow's headlines . . . **Warning: Crazies on the loose. A mental hospital gets investigated when patients escape from the facility. These patients are unpredictable, but can be tamed with food and sex**

"What's up?" I ask my dad once we step inside the kitchen.

"I need to get going. The estate agent called when you were . . . um . . . upstairs."

"Estate agent? You're selling the house? Why? Where are you going to go? Why would you make up with me then leave me? I don't understand," I tell him, feeling tears fall from my cheeks and Mason's hard chest at my back supporting me, his hands holding me at the waist.

"Calm down, baby. I think you should go," Mason demands in a hard voice; one that sends shivers down my spine. It's deadly quiet and holds so much warning.

"You've got it wrong baby girl, I promise. I'm selling the house, but not moving away," he tells me, pleading with me, his eyes holding so much pain and fear, my chest hurts. I jumped to conclusions. This could have been bad. Mason could have kicked him out and not let him have a chance to finish what he wanted to tell me. I'm such a hormonal idiot.

"You're not?" I whisper.

"I'm not. I hate that house. Who needs an eight bedroom house when there was only ever three used really. We never needed that much space. So I'm going to buy one closer to town and a lot smaller. Maybe a two or a three bedroom house. Maybe we can make up the spare bedroom just for the baby," he tells me, his eyes hopeful.

The music in the front room grows louder and I give a look to Mason that isn't happy. The adults are getting out of control and I need to put a stop to it before something gets broken. What has gotten into them God only knows. I'd think they were drunk, but we don't have any alcohol in the house.

"Yeah dad, that would be nice," I smile then look to Mason. "Wouldn't it?"

"Yeah," Mason replies, but his voice doesn't match the tight smile on his face, instead it's dry and sarcastic. I shake my head, not wanting to get into it with him and look back over to my father. His face has slipped and he nods his head as if he can read Mason's thoughts and is agreeing to them.

I'm not losing him again. Not a chance. I haven't fully had a chance to explain everything to Mason, so when I do, I'm hoping he'll understand and back off from my dad. I might be quick enough to forgive, but the way I see it I could hold a grudge and lose out on having a father for another nineteen years.

"Do you want to go to dinner in the week or something, when you don't have to work?"

"I'd love to," he says sounding both pleased and excited. "I have Thursday off from noon onwards, so give me a call when you know when or where. Or I can arrange something and text you the details?"

"No, that's fine. I'll arrange something then get back to you," I smile, leaning up and kissing him on the cheek. Before I could pull back his arms wrap around me. I'm taken off guard at first so it takes me a few minutes to hug him back, but when I do he tightens his hold on me, like he doesn't want to let go. It feels like I've died and come back to life, and he's afraid if he lets go I'll disappear, the thought has me fighting back tears. "I know I'll never deserve your forgiveness. I'll never forgive myself, but thank you. Thank you for giving me the chance and letting me be in your life."

My eyes water and I hug my dad back tighter before pulling away. The second I leave his arms, Mason has his hands wrapped around my hips and is pulling me back into his warm embrace.

"See you Thursday," my dad chokes out, before turning around and leaving.

I'm watching the kitchen door where he left and jump when my Nan runs in looking horrified.

"What on earth is going on?" I yelp.

"Are you in labour? Are you? Have you eaten? Did I see you eat anything?" she cackles, her giggle high pitched and wild.

"What are you going on about?" I ask at the same time Mason mutters, "Fuck me."

"Did that, and it got me pregnant," I mutter dryly before turning back to my Nan. "Now what is going on Nan? You're acting crazy . . . Okay crazier."

"I'm fine. I'm not crazy, but that Joan woman is. Do you see the way she keeps eyeing me? It's making me nervous and jittery . . . oh, maybe that's her plan. She wants to get me at my lowest, catch me off guard before she strikes," she shouts out.

"Who's striking who?" Max asks strutting in and taking a seat at the breakfast bar.

"He's another too," Nan whispers, her eyes narrowing on Max who just grunts before folding his arms on the breakfast bar and burying his head in them.

"Another what, Mary?" Mason asks amused.

"Another one that can't stop staring at me and it's going to blow my chances with Myles," she says dead serious, which makes me choke on a laugh once again. Mason and Max both collapse into a fit of laughter, the noise gaining everyone's attention from the front room and bringing them into the kitchen. Joan is the first one in, walking beside Mark. Myles and Charlie behind and a few other people, but I can't see Harlow or Malik anywhere.

"Home," Myles mouths and then winces when Nan walks over to him.

"How about that dance now?" she giggles, her hands slapping over her mouth which in turn, makes her giggle louder, Joan following in her own set of laughter.

"Something is seriously going on. Did someone drug them?" I ask out loud.

"Not unless they ate the brownies, then no," Max mutters, clearly bored and disturbed by the whole ordeal.

"Brownies?" Mason growls and I put a calming hand on his arm. His breathing is shallow and I wonder what has him so worked up. "What. Did. You. Do?"

"Me? Why do you always presume that it was me? I'm not the bad twin you know. Myles has his share of bad. Just last night he robbed the last snickers bar out of Maverick's stash."

"You fucker, I knew it was you," Maverick grunts at Myles from the kitchen doorway. "I'm off to work. Denny, it's lovely to see you, but I'm off," and he waves, disappearing out of sight before I get a chance to say goodbye.

"Fuck you Max. You're the one that set the bed sheets on fire when you tried to set your fart on fire, so don't bring me into this," Myles huffs before following Maverick out the door.

"Now you're running all our guests away," Mason growls, and I lean to the side a bit to see that he's right. More guests are sneaking out of the front door, only leaving Charlie, Max, Mason, Nan, Joan, Mark and I in the house.

"I'm pretty sure it was Joan and Mary when they offered to show us men what a real strip tease was," Max snaps rolling his eyes.

I glance at my Nan and gasp, then to Joan who doesn't even look the slightest bit affronted. Instead, they're both laughing their heads off, like Max just turned into *Lee Evans* and told them the funniest joke on earth. I shake my head disappointed, then turn and give Max a glare. Now Mason brought it up, I know he did something to those brownies. If my projections are right, then he's going to get some serious payback.

"What?" he yells holding his hands up, looking around the room for help, but not getting any.

"What did you do?" I grit out. "It better not be weed Max because my Nan has a heart defect. If it slows down to a certain rate she can go into shock, collapse and then die. Nothing will ever save her," I cry out, full on lying to him. He needs to be taught a lesson. What if I was craving brownies and actually had one while I was pregnant? The idiot doesn't think.

"Fuck!" he yells running over to my Nan. "Dance, we need to get your heart rate up," he shouts grabbing her hands and treating her like a ragdoll; he gets her to dance by waving her arms everywhere.

I watch for a few minutes before bursting into laughter, especially when my Nan turns green and throws up all over Max's nice white shirt. Well, now it's stained yellow and an orangey colour, but let's not get into it. I'm pretty sure there weren't any carrots served in the food either, I think when I look at the sick dripping off his shirt. The smell itself has me wanting to hurl.

"Oh my God, she's foaming from the mouth. Someone help. . . . help. . . . fucking hell, that stinks," Max squeals before he starts gagging himself over the kitchen sink. He quickly rids his shirt and being the woman that I am, I can't help but ogle his fine muscles. For a seventeen year old lad, he's got the package, just a shame he doesn't do it for me. He's too fucking much. Too high maintenance and a complete womaniser, plus, he doesn't make my skin tingle or my heart race when he enters a room like his brother does.

"I think I'm going to be sick," Joan moans, and Mark takes her hand and starts walking her to the door. "I've got sick on me. It's all over me Mark. Get it off! Get it off!"

Her voice fades out and I turn to my Nan to make sure she's okay and then over to Max who is grabbing a clean t-shirt of Mason's off the ironing pile. I narrow my eyes at him, but he seems unaffected.

"You . . . ," I point to Max. " . . . can take my Nan back home. I can't believe you would do something like this. What if I had eaten one of those and it harmed the baby?"

"I told you not to touch them," he snaps throwing his hands up.

"Listen mate, when you tell someone not to do something or they can't have something, then they're going to want it more. You're fucking lucky I was craving onion and not brownies because I would have eaten them and that would have been on you," I growl, before stomping off upstairs.

When I get to the top I stop, instead of turning right to mine and Mason's room, I head left and make my way into the nursery, a huge smile lighting up my face.

TWELVE

BY THE END OF the week, I was in a blissful, horny, frustrated state and tonight was the night Mason was taking me out on another date. We haven't had a chance to do much besides stay at home with some kind of takeout and a movie because of my ever growing bump and bad case of heartburn. Never even realised such pain in my chest could exist. So Mason decided tonight, which is Friday, that we'll go out for something to eat before coming back to watch a movie in bed.

Harlow's due back from court any moment. We've planned to go into town and do some shopping as the last time we never managed to get farther than the cafe before we came back for the surprise baby shower/new home party.

After getting up late again this morning, I'm surprised I'm ready and dressed by the time the doorbell rings just gone twelve.

Harlow.

Running down the stairs as quickly as I can, I rush to the front door and open it up to see a sad looking Harlow.

"Hey, what's up?"

"What? Oh . . . um . . . these were at your door," she says handing a bunch of lilies over to me.

"Must be from Mason for tonight," I grin.

"Aren't lilies meant for funerals?" she asks unsure.

Shit! "Yeah they are," I say slowly, eyeing the bunch of flowers like they are poison. I find the card taped to the side and move in to the front room to put the flowers down. Opening the card, I'm drawing my eyebrows together.

What the hell!

"What's wrong?" Harlow asks looking at me.

"It says '*Now may you rest in peace.*' How creepy is that?" My hands are shaking and my mind is wondering what on earth Mason was thinking about writing that. "Let me just call Mason."

His phone rings three times before he answers.

"Awe, babe, are you missing my sweet ass already?"

I grin into the phone, the lilies long forgotten and shake my head. "Yeah, because I didn't see you four hours ago," I laugh into the phone.

"Babe, I barely got a goodbye out of you when I left four hours ago," he chuckles. "What's up?"

"Oh, yeah, why have you sent me creepy lilies?" I ask, hoping not to sound like an ungrateful brat.

"Well, I'd love to tell you babe, but it wasn't me who sent them. Who delivered them? Maybe they can tell you who purchased them. If it's Max or Myles playing fucking games with my head I'm gonna start punching them," he growls and I giggle.

"Unless they wanted to scare one of us then I don't think it's them."

"What do you mean?"

"The note says, '*Now may you rest in peace.*'"

"What the fuck," he growls. "Do you know where they're from? I'll call up the company."

"Hold on," I tell him, tucking the phone into my ear as I turn the card over. No name or company details are located on the card, so I check the flowers and see nothing there either. "Nah, nothing."

"Shit. Wonder why someone would send them," he whispers aloud.

I open my mouth to talk, but then my eyes look over and meet Harlow's sad ones and I know my friend really needs me right now.

"Mason, I've got to go, but I'll call you later, okay?"

"Sure thing, babe. Oh, and let me know if you need me to pick you up from town. I'll be finishing just after three," he tells me.

"Okay, see you after," I tell him then end the call. I immediately approach Harlow, her head is down and her shoulders are slumped so I take a seat on the sofa next to her.

"You okay?" I ask her gently. "How did court go?"

"The final hearing is two weeks from today. You should have seen him Denny. He looked right at me, his eyes burning with so much hatred towards me. It scared the shit out of me," she whispers, her body shivering.

"He can't hurt you," I tell her, wrapping my arm around her shoulder.

"What if they don't believe me? What if they set him free? He's making up lies that sound so believable, even I'm questioning myself and I know what went down that day. I know he was going to rape me. How can they let him go free?" she cries, her tears falling heavily down her face. My hand reaches out to wipe them away, but she's up on her feet, pacing in front of me like a mad woman. "I mean, what's the first thing he's going to do when he's free? He's going to come after me. What will it take for them to do something about him; does he have to actually rape me before he's convicted? It's like they're saying because he never got to go through with it, it's okay. It's not okay. If they let him off, I'll be walking around in my own personal nightmare Denny."

"Harlow, calm down," I tell her, standing up.

"I can't Denny. My chest feels so tight," and to emphasize it, she's grabbing at her chest, rubbing furiously. "I thought I was coping with everything, that I was moving on from what he did, but I'm not. I'm still stuck in that mouldy smelling bedroom, feeling the hard springs in my back and the petrified emotion consuming me. I can't do this. I'm making it all worse," she sobs out, her whole body shaking and her face pale.

"Hey," I snap loudly, gaining her attention long enough to grab at her shoulders and give her a wake up shake. "You *can* do this. You are doing it. He hasn't got the power to take that away from you Harlow. You're strong, you're beautiful, you're independent and you've overcome much worse babe. Don't let him win. Don't let him have the pleasure of knowing he's gotten to you, that you're scared. Because I know you are.

"When I woke up on the ground that night, the first thing I remembered was you, and the fear I felt just before he knocked me out. I had been so scared for you, for everything he'd already put you through and what you had already gone through. But I swear to you Harlow . . . if anyone can get through this, it's you."

"I can't Denny. I just can't. His face today," she shivers. "It held so much promise of retribution. I just wanted to run out of that courtroom. The way his lawyers ripped into me, talking about a sordid relationship that we never had. I felt dirty, ashamed, and it's why I needed to have a hot shower before I came over. He makes me feel like that each night in my nightmares," she sobs, and I grab her shoulders and pull her in for a tight hug. Tears fill my own eyes at the sound of her own desperate silent pleas for the pain to stop.

"Have you spoken to Malik about any of this?"

"No and you can't tell him what I told you. I don't want him to think that I'm weak. I'm just so fucking scared," she tells me, and then pulls away, her bottom lip trembling.

"You need to talk to him before all this consumes you, Hun. You shouldn't have to deal with this alone. You shouldn't be dealing with it at all. You're strong Harlow, remember that. Don't cling to the anger; focus on your future happiness, because that's all you'll get. Davis is the only one going to hell."

"Grhh, I'm being so silly," she tells me, stepping away to wipe her tears and rubbing at the smudged mascara under her eyes.

"No you're not, you're being human."

"I'm just scared," she whispers.

"You wouldn't be human if you weren't," I remind her.

"Urgh, look at me. I look a mess and we need to go if we want to get you an outfit."

"We can stay here if you prefer. I've got loads of clothes, so we can stay in and watch a movie instead," I smile, hoping she confides in Malik later on.

"No. No. It's fine. I'll just go sort myself out then we'll go."

"Are you sure because I honestly do not mind," I tell her, truly not wanting her to do something she's not up for.

"Honestly, it might do me some good to get out and take my mind off of things."

"Alright, you go and sort yourself out and I'll go put those," pointing to the flowers.

"In the bin?" Harlow laughs, and it's nice seeing her laugh after all that.

"Yeah, the bin," I laugh bumping my hips with hers.

Walking into the kitchen, I wait until I hear the bathroom door upstairs close before grabbing my phone and texting Malik.

Me: *She isn't taking the court case as well as we thought. D x*

Malik: *I'm coming over*

Fuck! He can't come over. She'll know then that I just tattled on her, even if this is for her own good. She needs help, but she also needs to know she's strong enough on her own.

Me: *No!!!*

Me: *We're going on a girl's day, don't ruin it. D x*

Malik: *I'm not going to sit at fucking home while she's suffering Den. She needs me.*

Me: *No, what she needs is a distraction. She needs her mind taken off what she went through and going to town will help with that. I didn't text you to go all caveman, I texted you to tell you that when she's back to be gentle with her. Get her to open up. Don't be an ass. Dx*

Malik: *Nice to have you back Denny.*

I grin at the text like a damn fool. It does feel good to be back. I'm actually starting to feel like myself again, and not this self-conscious, insecure, shell of a woman I've become. I'm back to my old, outgoing, bossy self. Okay . . . nearly. I've still got a way to go before I'll ever feel normal again, but for the first time in a long time, I feel like it could happen.

"Who's got you smiling?" Harlow asks making me jump.

"Bossy," I blurt out, before laughing. "Nothing, let's go shopping, and if you're a good girl I might buy you a cupcake," I wink and head out.

Walking down Main Street the weather begins to feel chilly. With the end of August approaching I'm not surprised the weather is cooling down. Sun and heat never last in England. But this year, I'm kind of thankful. I was starting to think I'd need to walk around in a bikini.

"Okay, where to now because that woman in the last store really needed to pop her eyes back in her head? Did you see the way she was staring at my bump?" I ask in disbelief. We'd just been in one of the popular clothes stores in town and were literally followed around by one of the assistants like we were thieves. Then to top that shit off, she eyed my bump like it was infected, looking disgusted and I wanted to rip her eyes out with my nails.

"Yeah I did. For a second I got worried you were going to go Michael Myers on her ass."

"Trust me, if I had a butchers knife I would have used it on the bitch," I laugh.

"Shit you sound scary," she laughs. "Remind me never to get on your bad side."

I'm still laughing when we join the queue for Greg's to get the cupcake I promised Harlow earlier when the old lady in front turns around.

"Ohhh, how cute," she gushes, her hands pressing against my baby bump. I'm frozen at first, my face turning bright red before turning my stunned gaze over to Harlow to see she has the same wide eyed expression as me. "How far along are you? My daughter could never give me Grandkids. They are so precious, babies."

I'm completely speechless. I know she's asked me a question, and I know I should answer, but I don't feel like she's actually asking me. She wakes up bean, and I want to shake the ever loving shit out of her. I've spent most of our shopping trip either being watched, or in a toilet because of bean pressing down on my bladder. Now this lady comes along, whom, may I add is a stranger, not only touches me, but wakes her up.

I'm pissed.

Like, mama bear pissed.

Who in their right mind would think touching a pregnant ladies bump would be okay? Especially a stranger who could flip out and attack them over it. It's like my belly has a sign on it saying *touch me, I'm a baby.*

"Dear, she just kicked," she gushes loudly and I'm about to tell her no shit, I'm the one carrying her, until my mouth snaps closed in a tight lipped expression when she reaches out to grab her husband's hand, placing it on my bump before I can even tell her no.

"Oh yes, how lovely," he smiles at me, obviously not seeing my complete and utter terror. I feel Harlow snicker against me and I give her a warning glare to not encourage them further.

Too late.

"Our daughter could never have grandbabies. We were so disappointed," he tells me sadly and that's when I snap.

"Well you're not having mine so get your paws off my stomach now, both of you," I snap, stepping backwards.

"Watch your manners young lady," the old lady scolds.

The nerve! "Manners? Where were your manners when you just had your dirty mitts all over my stomach?"

"That is no way to talk to your elders," the man says calmly, and I give him a glare, narrowing my eyes at him.

"I'm sorry. Would it have been more polite if I had started rubbing my hands all over your stomach?" then snap my mouth closed when I realise how that sounded. My face reddens further when Harlow spits out a laugh and I turn, grab her arm and stomp away.

"The nerve of some people. What is it with people today? Have I got something on my back?" I ask turning to give her my back, but don't give her the chance to answer. "I cannot believe she stood there, touching me, violating my personal space then acted like I was the one who was in the wrong. Seriously . . . who the hell do they think they are?"

"I don't know, but your face was a picture," she laughs, then holds her phone up for me to see the side profile of my face, looking pissed, open mouthed and wide eyed at the old bag who touched me.

"At least I have a picture of her so I can remember who she is. Shit, she freaked me out," I shudder, and then shudder again when the hairs on the back of my neck stand on end. The feeling of someone watching me starts to freak me out and I start taking notice of our surroundings, not seeing anyone I recognise, out of place, or even the old bag from earlier. I even checked twice for her and her husband.

"What's up?" Harlow asks and I snap my head to hers startled.

"Sorry. It's nothing. Come on, let's go get me an outfit for my date, then maybe we can try to brave the queue again without being mauled," I giggle, but it's forced, my mind still on the feel of someone watching me.

Luckily, by the time we hit the last clothing store, I find what I want. It will go perfect for mine and Mason's date tonight.

Because I'm still unsure of where he's taking me I decided to keep it fancy casual. You know when it's not fancy, but it's not a jeans and t-shirt kind of place either. So I decided to go with a deep green maxi dress that has a white and green patterned scarf around the waist. When I tried it on the scarf came above my bump, so it fit perfectly. It shows more cleavage than I usually like, but to hell with it, they'll probably drop two sizes and sag south once I've had the baby, so I'm flaunting it while I've got it.

I've got jewellery at home that will go nicely with the outfit and some flat shoes that will look perfect as the dress falls to mid-thigh.

"Want to go for a coffee?" I ask Harlow, checking my watch to see I've got an hour and half still until Mason picks us up.

"If you want to, we could actually go to the club if you want, see if Mason is there."

"Come on then. Let's go get them a cupcake each before we go," I smile.

Harlow nods, and once we've purchased a box we start making our way down to the club.

"What is the club called?" I ask her, never having asked until now.

"Malik said it used to be M5C, but Mason changed it to MC5. The rest argued for a while over it."

"Why?"

"Well M and C are their initials, and there is five of them, but Max and Myles said MC5 sounded like a motorcycle gang."

"A motorcycle gang? We have scooter runners, not MC's running around the place," I laugh.

"That is why Mason ignored them, and changed it to MC5. He said M5C didn't go and sounded too much of a mouthful. Then downstairs is called V.I.P."

"Have you ever been?"

"You're joking right? Malik wouldn't dare let me step foot in a strip club," she laughs shaking her head at me.

"What about the normal bar?"

"Oh, I've been in once, but to be honest, Malik doesn't spend much time there," she shrugs.

"I can't wait to see where he works," I gush out smiling.

"How are you and Mason getting along?" she smiles knowingly, her shoulder bumping with mine.

"We're getting on really good actually. He is so sweet and attentive, and has changed so much during the time I've been back. But sometimes I miss his flirtatious personality."

"Have you guys . . . you know . . . ?"

"Had sex? No, we haven't. Not from my lack of trying either. It's not like I don't know he wants to. He has a constant boner that shows me how much he wants it, but he will never take it any further than kissing and cuddling."

My voice sounds bitter, even to my own ears and I have to wince a little. Shit I sounded like a bitch.

"So you're a sexually frustrated, pregnant lady with high crazy hormones?" she giggles and I shoot her a warning look.

"Yeah," I breathe sadly. "It's a shame I can't knock him out and have my wicked way with him," I wink.

"I'm sure he wouldn't mind," she laughs and we step outside the club. The huge MC5 sign is painted on in bright, bold, red letters.

"Let's see if we can sneak up on them," I shush her, opening the door to the main area and sneak to a standing table which is placed near a wooden block that will hide us. Once we're there we both peek around it and my eyes water instantly.

Mason is standing at the bar pulling a drink while a girl in the same uniform as him is rubbing her fake tits up his arm, her fingers brushing against his bicep.

"That bitch," I whisper yell and go to step out, but Harlow grabs my arm stopping me. "Let me go," I snap.

"Shush, look," she points, her eyes on where Mason is.

My heart hurts, it feels heavy in my chest and I can't help the tear that falls from my eyes. When I turn back around he's no longer masking a relaxed expression, but one of pure torture and anger.

He tells the girl something then moves to serve the next person, but he comes back to step around the girl, she sticks her ass into his groin, and rubs herself against my man.

"That fucking bastard," I cry on a whisper, not having the strength to walk away or avert my eyes. I'm about to plead with Harlow to take me home, but then he slams down the customers drink on the bar and turns a furious glare on the girl, who is now looking white as a ghost.

"I've got a fucking girlfriend, a pregnant girlfriend, who I've told you I'm happily in a relationship with," he says, talking slowly when he mentions our relationship. My heart races, but now it's for another reason, it's because he called me his girlfriend and told her we're happy.

"Why would you want to settle down, have a brat that will only end up hating you for running out on it and its mom in years to come? You aren't fooling me Mase, I know you'll have those pants of yours down at your ankles by the end of the week."

Not being able to take it anymore I step out from my hiding spot, and Harlow doesn't stop me. Instead, she follows behind me as I walk up to the bar.

Mason doesn't see me at first, he's too busy giving fake boobs her last warning, but when he turns to talk to the customer he was in the middle of serving, he stops, frozen, as he looks up into my eyes. If I hadn't just witnessed their encounter for myself I'd say he had something to feel guilty about, but I know he doesn't.

"Babe," he grins and the girl working behind the bar swings her attention to us, and I give her a smug expression.

"Hey baby," I coo. "I just wanted to run by and see you at work. We are going to wait until you've finished," I smile sweetly, then give fake girl a condescending smile.

"Well grab a chair and I'll be over. I just need to finish serving," he grins, his face genuinely pleased to see me.

I nod my head grinning, and watch him walk into the back with a food order. I'm still watching his ass walk away when a loud cough startles me, averting my attention.

"Hi, I'm Denny, Mason's *girlfriend*," I smile snidely.

"Well, enjoy it while it lasts," she smirks back, her eyes glaring holes into my head.

"Why do you say that?" I ask sweetly.

"Because Mason doesn't do girlfriends, he does fuck buddies or one night stands."

"Have you been either one of those?" I ask faking a hurt glance.

"Not yet, but I will be," she smirks and I smile inside.

"Did you hear her?" I ask Harlow, smiling, but Harlow just smiles timidly, before lowering her gaze to the floor. "Trust me sweetie, you'll be waiting an awfully long time for that to happen. He's with me and that's how it's staying."

"What because you're carrying his sprog? Sorry *sweetie*, but you're not the first girl that's probably tried to tie him down. Once he sees what a mistake he's made, I'll be here waiting."

"Are you sure about that?"

"Oh yeah," she grins, her eyes hard.

"You seriously are delusional. Everything about me is real; everything he sees in me is real. It's me he comes home to, me he shares a bed and a home with, and it will be me that marries his sorry ass. Now I expect you to get off your high horse and realise what a slut you sound like."

"You need to hear what you sound like. I'd bet my whole months wages that the baby ends up not even being his."

"Well unlike you I can keep my legs closed. Ever thought why he slept around? Ever thought it's because that's all you're worth? He knows he'll never be able to bring you home to his Granddad or his brothers. He knows he'll never make a home with you and that waking up the morning after is enough to put him off you for life. Don't think you're something special. You girls may think sleeping with him once is like winning a gold medal, but it's not. I'm the one who feels like she's won the lottery. I'm the one that gets all of him, not you, so fuck off, do your job, and back the fuck off my man," I snap, my voice rising.

I take a deep breath the same time I hear a tiny chuckle beside me. I look back at the girl who is glaring at me with so much hatred, and I nearly take a step back. Nearly. Then a flicker of movement catches my attention from the corner of my eye and I gasp in horror. Mason is standing by the entrance to the back door, his face a blank mask.

When he starts walking over I start to regret talking back to the bimbo, but then I remember the look she gave me, the words she said and I clench my fists, ready for the fight with Mason if I have too.

"Go take a seat over there, Harlow. Danni, get her a drink of coffee," he orders, his eyes not moving away from mine when he grabs my hand and pulls me over to the other side of the room, to where the exit doors are.

The doors lead to the staff room, the office and other rooms. When he pulls me into one of the rooms not labelled, I shiver, and it's not from the cold, but from the tension coming from Mason.

"Look I'm sorry . . . No actually I'm not. She's a bitch and I'm glad you didn't sleep with her. But, I'm not sorry for what I said . . . " I ramble.

"Shut up," he growls and I snap my eyes up to meet his dark, desire filled eyes. My mouth snaps closed and when it does he takes a step closer, his body flush up against mine. My breathing is coming in deep, fast pants and I can't take my eyes away from his. It's like he has me in a trance.

"That . . . that was the sexiest, most, hottest encounter I have ever witnessed," He breathes out.

"W-what?"

"You heard," he seductively grins. "I think I like you getting all territorial over me." His voice is a mere whisper, his breath fanning across my cheek. My face flushes and I remind myself to keep calm. I don't want to show him how much his proximity is affecting me, but it's proving to be too hard -pun intended- when his hardness is pressing against my lower stomach. "Did you mean what you said?"

My mind struggles to even contemplate his question, and I reply with a short, moaned, "Huh?" the feel of his lips against my neck is doing dangerous things to my mind and body, sending me to a puddle of goo.

"Did you mean it when you told her I was your man?" he chuckles, amusement filling his voice as he kisses a line at edge of my jaw, up to the corner of my lips, where he ends up stopping, his lips hovering over mine, so close, yet, not close enough.

"You tell me, Mason," I manage to breathe out, my eyes fluttering closed as I lean forward. My lips manage to touch his for a brief second before he pulls back, his eyes drawn together in confusion.

"What do you mean?" His voice is husky and I have to tighten my knees together to try and ease the ache he's started, but it does nothing but make me ache more, my body screaming-no, demanding, for him to pleasure me, to touch me.

"*Are* you my man?"

"Of course, just like you're my woman, love," he whispers.

My face splits into a huge grin, love sparkling in my eyes for the first time in a long time. When Mason notices his lips crash down to mine in a hungry, passionate kiss that has me feeling dizzy, disoriented, and feeling completely undone.

I'm squirming beneath his touch, our chests rising and falling and both of us clinging to each other like it's our last kiss.

"Hey Mase, Elliot's here, so you can get off . . . Wow!! Shit! Didn't see you there," Maverick mumbles after walking in and catching Mason pressing me up against the wall. My face flames and I bury my head in Mason's chest, fighting the urge to giggle. Yep, that's right, I've turned into one of those. One of those people, who, when they're nervous ends up laughing over the most awkward, and saddest moments.

I remember once getting into trouble at school, and I ended up laughing in the teachers face because I'd been that nervous, that worried that he'd tell my parents, I could only laugh. It was either that or cry. The teacher didn't think my giggling was amusing, nor did he think it was clever and I ended up getting lunchtime detention for the whole week.

"Bro, seriously fuck off," Mason growls, his chin resting on top of my head. His body is still shaking, and I can feel him fighting for breath. His very impressive erection is still pressed up against me, and I end up biting my lip to stop myself from laughing. Mason must sense something because the hold he has on my hips tighten.

"Yeah, so, I'll just go back to work. Have a good night," he says before closing the door and that's when I hear him burst into laughter and I end up following, but my face still flames with mortification.

"You think it's funny my brother caught us making out like two thirteen year olds in a storage closet?"

"Yeah, um, no, but kind of," I giggle, my face pulling away to look up at him.

"What am I going to do with you?" he chuckles, pulling away. The cold air from the loss of his body covers me and my skin breaks out in goose bumps.

"What time are we heading out?"

"Tonight, so we can be back in time to watch a movie earlier enough so you don't pass out on me."

The crinkles at the corner of his eyes and the dents where his dimples are show he's amused.

"Come on. Let's get out of here," I grin, loving that he notices my issue to not finish a movie until the next day. It's happened every time we've watched a movie together. We'll put it on; I'll fall asleep near the ending and then finish it off the next morning. We've become adept to it.

The first time it happened, Mason had been talking to me throughout the movie and he was surprised at how quiet I was being, but when he looked he found himself cuddled up to a sleeping me.

THIRTEEN

Finally dressed up for the date Mason and I are going on, I begin to feel nervous. Over what, I don't know, because whenever I'm with Mason I feel like I'm being my real self. I don't need to pretend to be a happy, cheerful, go-getter Denny everyone assumes I am.

First impressions of me are always answered differently. Some say I'm too easy going, some say I'm too honest and need to think before I speak, but then, there are the others, the ones that see the happy, smiling, cheerful me, or the ones who think I'm a stuck up brat with rich parents.

Honestly . . . I'm just me.

"You look fucking hot, babe," Mason says making me jump. He walks up behind me and presses his front against my back, his chin resting on my shoulder as his hands slowly-ever so slowly- slip around my stomach. We're both looking in the mirror at one another, and in all honesty, we look kind of perfect together. Big-headed of me, I know, but who cares.

"Thanks," I tell him, looking at his eyes through the mirror. They darken and my breath hitches. I love it when his eyes do that, turn darker, the chocolate brown turning almost black and he only does it when he's turned on. Like he is now.

"Stay right there. Don't move," he warns me before slipping one hand around to the back of his dark jeans. His white buttoned down shirt goes great with them, and with the sleeves rolled up and the top few buttons undone, it looks sexy as hell. I love this look on him.

When he brings back his phone and lifts it up in the air for a selfie, I nearly burst into tears, but instead, what I do, is start giggling. We've not had a picture with just the two of us taken yet, so him doing this makes my heart and belly do funny things.

"Say, *Mason is sexy*," he smiles, his chin resting back on my shoulder and I smile into the camera. "Mason is an idiot," I say through my smile and Mason clicks the picture, before bursting out laughing.

"I guess I deserved that," he chuckles, still standing behind me, looking like he has no plans of moving.

"Let's have a look," I tell him, grabbing his phone. I click on the picture and my heart stops. His one hand is wrapped around me, resting on my large stomach, and his chin is resting on my shoulder, but his eyes, God, his eyes are shining with such happiness it takes my breath away.

"We need to get going," he tells me, but makes no movements. When I feel his hot breath against my shoulder my knees almost buckle and I gasp. His soft, full lips are next and I lean my head to the side to give him better access to my neck, where he places a line of soft kisses up towards my ear. His tongue feels slick against my skin and all of a sudden, the temperature in the room has hit a boiling point.

Reaching around, I grasp his firm, tight bum and press the tips of my fingers in it, pressing him closer to me. His large, hard bulge has me craving for something more than his lips and his touch.

When he finally turns me around I do a mental happy dance, hoping he's going to finally touch me, touch me in a way that I can finally explode, and get rid of the ache between my legs that has done nothing but build rapidly since the day I moved in.

"Yow Mase, can I borrow your *Hunger Games* DVD," Max shouts startling us both.

Mason growls in my ear, his head tucked into my neck before pulling away muttering. "I swear I'm going to fucking kill him if he keeps cock blocking me."

I giggle and grab my clutch off the table and grab the *Hunger Games* DVD from off the shelf. It's up here for a reason. Max, so far, has wrecked nearly every DVD we've lent him, but whenever he does now, Mason charges him double the price the DVD originally cost.

"Where are we going again?" I ask, knowing he's taking me for dinner, but not *where* he's taking me.

"Babe, I know you're hungry, but be patient. You'll be fed soon enough my woman," he grins before giving me a light smack on the ass. I squeal out in surprise and turn to narrow my eyes at him, but as soon as I turn back around to head down the stairs, my face breaks into a huge grin, finally having back the Mason I fell in love with all those years ago.

Oh my God!

He didn't.

He freaking has.

Mason and I walk up the street towards McDonalds and I look down at my outfit in sheer embarrassment. How could he let me dress up for McDonalds?

"Mason, really? I know you love your burgers, but seriously? I could have just worn my pyjamas to eat here."

I don't even bother to cover my disappointment, or the fact I feel like a complete ass that he'd bring me here for a date nonetheless.

"But you've been craving Mc chicken sandwiches for weeks now. I thought it would be romantic," he frowns, with a slight gleam in his eyes.

"Whatever, let's hurry up before I murder and eat you. I'm starving," I snap, carrying on towards the fast food restaurant.

He laughs behind me and I don't bother to turn around to glare, or to even snap at him. I'm too worked up and I know for a fact whatever is going to come out of my mouth will sound bitchy and ungrateful, but most of all, I know I'm on the verge of crying.

Just as I get to the door, Mason grabs my hips and pulls me back easily to his front. "Baby, why do you think I'd take you here? We've got a table there," he chuckles in my ear, his warm breath sending shivers down my spine.

I follow his pointed finger to one of the highest priced restaurants in Coldenshire. It's just a few doors up from McDonalds, which I never really noticed before. My mind was too busy thinking of ways to kill Mason for bringing me on a date here. Not there is anything wrong with McDonalds; I just wanted to have a memory of us in an intimate setting.

"Huh? What? Jesus Mason, why didn't you tell me this before I started cursing at you for thinking you were taking me to McDonalds?" I growl, my anger rising.

"You're so fucking sexy when you're pissed," he chuckles, his arms once again surrounding me, holding me to him.

"Answer me, goddamn it."

"Alright, alright . . . I booked a reservation the other day. I honestly didn't know it was next to McDonalds, or that you'd think *that* is where I'd take you," he grunts.

"Sorry," I tell him honestly, my head bowed to the floor.

"Babe, there's no need to be sorry. Let's go in before they give our reservation to some poor fucker who didn't think to book in advance."

"Okay." A smile lights my face, and I link my arms through his as we make our way inside.

"Hi, can I help you?" a young male waiter greets us, his eyes raking across my body. I'm not sure if it's hormones, or the lack of sleep, but I'm pretty sure he's checking me out.

I'm not going to lie, he looks pretty fit, but he's not my type, that and the fact he's nothing compared to Mason. It also doesn't help his case when he asks if he can help us. *No mate, we're just standing in the middle of the restaurant to get our own food.*

It's like when you go food shopping and the checkout assistant asks if you need any bags. As if you'd say 'No, it's fine I have ten million hands that can help.

"I booked a table for me and the missus. It's under Carter. C.A.R.T.E.R," he spells out and I can't help but cover my mouth to cover the laugh that escapes.

What an idiot!

"Oh here. C.A.R.T.E.R, Carter," the bloke repeats rolling his eyes.

"That's what I said," Mason says proudly, puffing his chest out and I chuckle again. "You okay babe? You seem to have the giggles. You haven't been around Joan and your Nan have you?"

"No," I tell him rolling my own eyes this time and he just smirks giving me a wink.

"Right this way," the bloke tells us and leads us to a table that isn't far away from the door.

"I asked for the best view in the house," Mason tells the bloke.

"Sir, I can assure you this is the best view in the house."

I want to tell him it looks like the only view in the house as it's the only one near the window, but I don't want to hurt Mason's feelings knowing he's excited about this date.

"I like it," I tell them, going to take a seat, but Mason stops me by shouting stop, his voice loud and gaining attention from nearly everyone in the restaurant. "What?" I whisper horrified.

"Babe, it's a date," he says, like that explains it, then walks around to me and guides me in front of the chair. The chair smacks the back of my legs and I hiss out in pain as my ass slams down on the chair.

"Thanks," I snap then squeal when the chair moves forward, nearly knocking my pregnant stomach into the round table. "Jesus, Mase, chill-out and go take a seat," I tell him nervously, worried what he'll do next.

"Sorry, babe, just wanted to do it right. Max said what to do when we got here," he shrugs embarrassed.

"You took advice from your whore of a brother?" I deadpan, totally forgetting the bloke standing over the table.

"Um . . . huh . . . your waiter or waitress will be with you shortly," he says before sprinting off back to his podium.

"You scared him," Mason chuckles watching his retreating form.

"You really took advice from Max?"

"Yeah. He had some really good stuff. He looked some shit up on Google, but you can't blame the guy. He said I needed to woo you to get in . . ."

"Get in my what?" I tease, a smirk twitching my lips.

"Your pants," he sighs, scrubbing his hands down his face. "Honestly, that's not what I want to achieve from all this."

His hands gesture to the room and I blink surprised. He's not lying. He really hadn't taken me out just to get in my pants. Not that he needed to try; he would only need to say the word and I'll agree, but I'm not going to tell him that.

"What did you want to achieve?" I ask him quietly.

"Your trust, and the feelings that you had for me before. The old and new us."

"What do you mean?" I ask him intrigued. We've had heart to hearts a few times since I arrived back in town, but this is the closest we've gotten to an honest conversation about *his* feelings now.

"Just that before I fucked things up, you looked at me like I made the stars move, and that I made your world turn. When you look at me now, you're unsure, your walls are up and you seem so tense when we're together sometimes."

Yeah, it's called sexual tension, but I don't voice that out loud.

"Mason, my feelings for you back then were different. Yeah they were strong, but what we have now is honest, it's real. I still have trouble understanding why you'd want me. And with the baby now involved it makes me wonder if you're only with me for her."

"You know that's not true. This is what I hate the most about what I did to you. You question my motives towards you, and I promise you babe, I have nothing but good intensions towards you. I'd give my life for you."

My belly does a little flip and my eyes soften. He really does mean it. If he can try as hard as he is, then I can try just as hard to push through my childish insecurities. What I feel for Mason hasn't gone, yes it's different, but that feeling, that strong feeling I get when he's around is still just as strong as it was before it all went tits up.

"How about from now on, instead of worrying about what the other is feeling we talk to each other? I believed it when you told me you wanted to be with me, and I believe you when you tell me that you aren't with me for the baby. It's what hurt the most when you did what you did. I knew deep down you felt the same as I did when we were together. I could feel it as strongly as what I felt for you. But what you didn't do back then, but are doing now, is giving us a try. It's more than I ever wanted from you Mason. I would have given you anything, everything, just to be with you, I still would. Even at school, I'd tell Harlow I'd spend one night with you if it meant I could just be *with you*. What I never counted on was the way I felt when I was actually with you," I shrug, my eyes glazing over from the raw emotion releasing inside me. I needed to get it off my chest, to make him understand and I hope now he does.

"Wow! I really don't deserve you, but I promise I'm going to try honey," he smiles and I smile back at him.

The waitress comes over and takes our drink order and because of how long she took to get to us, we had already decided on what to have for dinner, so we give her our food orders too. Once she disappears I give Mason a smirk.

"What?" he asks after taking a sip of his beer.

"You didn't look at her once."

"Who?" he asks confused looking around.

"The waitress?" I tell him, looking closely to see if he's bullshitting me.

"Babe, seriously, I'm with you. Why would I want to look at someone else?"

I'm too shocked to speak. I open and close my mouth what feels like a thousand times until I give up and just keep it closed.

"Did you go through the nursery?" he asks making conversation.

"Yeah," I smile, my mind picturing the amazing nursery he built for our princess. It still warms my heart that he did that as a surprise for me.

"Do we need something else? Did I miss something?"

"We need a steriliser for the bottles-"

"Hold on, don't they suck on your . . . tits?" he says pointing to my ample chest.

"Yes Mason she will, but she might not latch on, or like it. I read it in one of those pregnancy books you'd gotten me."

"Oh, I didn't get them for you. I needed to do some research so I went out and got everything I'd need to know. I read about breast feeding. It also says you might not feel comfortable to do it. It can be painful. Also you may have an infection which can stop the process of breastfeeding."

"Either way I'm bottle feeding, Mason. I'm not going to be up through the night breastfeeding on my own. So I can breastfeed in a bottle."

"Okay, now I'm confused."

"I can't believe we're talking about this here," I chuckle. "You can get a breast pump that pumps your milk into a bottle."

"Like milking a cow?" he chuckles, his eyes crinkling at the corners.

"Yes," I say dryly, my eyes rolling.

"What else then? I was thinking about going pushchair shopping soon, oh and we'll need a car seat. I read online somewhere that some baby shop in town will fit them in safely for you. I think it's worth a shot, at least then they can show us how to do it. Safety is important."

"You've been thinking hard about this?" I tease.

"I have babe. We will also need to get your bag ready for the hospital. I have the list written down at home. I'll give it to you to look over to see if I missed anything."

"WOW! You really have thought of everything," I giggle. "We also need to get her some clothes. I know she won't need a lot, and a lot of people will buy her outfits, but she'll need a lot of various sizes. Then we need to stock up on nappies and baby wipes."

"I don't want to use baby wipes on our baby. I read in one of those books that it burns their skin, so I'm not risking it. I've got a list ready to take when I next go to Kara to get nappies and cotton wool and so on . . . "

My face must look a picture. I'm open mouthed, wide eyed and completely stunned to silence. The only sound you can hear is the chatter from the people around us.

Mason really has thought long and hard about everything, especially if he's already written a list to go to Kara with. Kara is a large store that sells everything in bulk. They sell anything from washing powder, to toilet roll, to nappies to sweets. The place is huge and so much cheaper than buying them separately in a shop.

I open my mouth after taking a sip of my Coke and pause when a large man over at the podium raises his voice.

He's large and mighty good looking. He's holding two car seats, each holding a baby that looks around a few months old, both wrapped in pink and standing next to him is a beautiful woman with a bright red face trying to calm him down.

"This is ridiculous. It's not like they're going to run around and disturb people eating. They're babies. They've already eaten and will be asleep for the next two and a half hours," the scary large man snaps, his eyes looking down adoringly at his twin girls.

"Dante, come on, we can go somewhere else."

"No. This is discrimination. All I could see on the door was a no smoking sign. Nowhere on that door did it say no kids. If kids aren't allowed in here they would have a sign. Like the smoking one stuck on the door outside. They're treating us like we're bringing our own food in. Dude, I haven't, you can check my changing bag if you want," he tells the bloke, not giving him a chance to talk.

"As if," Mason mutters under his breath, so I turn back around to face him.

"I know. You'd think he'd give up and go somewhere else," I agree.

"What? No way in hell babe. The dude is right. Why should he leave just because he's got two girls on his arm? Hey you," Mason shouts across to the bloke at the podium. I wish I got his name, so I could stop calling him 'that bloke.'

"Yes sir?" the podium bloke replies.

"Does that mean my missus and I need to go?"

"What? No. Our policy is strictly no kids. I'm sorry sir."

"Well then, we'll have to go."

The bloke looks as confused as I do and he even looks around the table, then to my pregnant stomach.

"Sir, with all due respect, your girlfriend is pregnant, she doesn't have a child."

"No need to be cocky," the large man at the podium says, shuffling the car seats further up his arms.

"No but she's a mom and has a baby with her, inside her. It's just like their situation. Only difference is, their kids are in car seats and ours is in her stomach. It's not even past nine, so technically the no kids rule is just something you'd prefer, nothing illegal. So why don't you find them a seat, and if their kids start to be a disturbance, then get involved. Until then, do your job and find them a seat," Mason snaps, sitting back in his chair. When he stood up is anyone's guess. I'm too mortified and kind of turned on to even keep up. How he stood up for two kids rights is just . . . just sexy as hell. And no doubt he'd do the same if that was our little girl.

Everyone grunts their agreements and I duck my head, a little embarrassed to have so much attention on us.

"I like you kid," the large bloke grins at Mason and Mason grins back. "Come on Kelly, we got steak to eat."

The blonde woman shakes her head, amusement showing on her face. If I had to guess, the woman was used to her bloke's interactions. I give her a smile when she gives our table a glance and she gives me a soft smile back before following her bloke over to the table they're being directed to.

"I cannot believe you just did that," I whisper yell across the table to him. I'm also proud he got the podium dickhead to change his mind, but Mason doesn't need anything more adding to his enormous ego.

"Believe it babe. I'm a fucking God," he chuckles then breathes in when the food arrives at our table. "Ahh, about time, I'm starving," he grins, giving me a wink and I shake my head and the waitress just gives me a small smile and a girly giggle. Now that her eyes are off my man, I'm actually glad we've got her as a waitress. She doesn't seem hard headed like the others I've come to know when I've gone out to dinners with my parents.

We ate our dinner and dessert before leaving the fancy restaurant. After much discussion during our meal we both decided a KFC would have been much better. Just because a place is fancy and has high prices, doesn't mean the place is high quality. Even the waitress who had waited on us gave us a discount, saying she felt bad with the little food I consumed.

I'd asked for a well done steak, but what I got was a medium rare and with the baby, I didn't want to eat it, or risk seeing the blood seep out and pass out. So bless her heart, she knocked off the price for my meal and gave us the desserts for free.

Mason had been ecstatic.

I decided to wait outside under the shelter of the restaurant while Mason ran halfway down the road to the parking lot to retrieve the car.

The door behind me opens and the couple from earlier walk out, both car seats held by the large bloke.

"Hey, I know you. You're the chick with the kid," he tells me grinning.

"He's not a kid and yes that's me."

I try to smile, but the bloke kind of freaks me out. Even with his easy playful attitude, his size and height give him a dangerous edge to him.

"Suppose not," he mutters, before looking at his wife. "Wait here, I'll get the car."

He runs off down the street and I stand awkwardly under the shelter until the woman next to me speaks.

"How far along are you?" she asks sweetly.

"I've got just over eight weeks left," I tell her, my hand rubbing affectingly over my pregnant belly.

"Your first?"

"Yeah. How old are these two?" I ask her, bending down at the knees to touch the little ones hand. Her hand immediately opens and latches onto my finger and my heart races. This is going to be me in over eight weeks and the thought has me excited and nervous. "They are adorable," I tell her standing back up.

"They're only four months old," she answers proudly, just as my little girl decides to kick me in the bladder. I double over and clutch my stomach and the woman rushes over to me, her hand on my back.

"Are you okay? What's wrong?"

Before I can answer a car door slams and Mason is in front of me. "Babe, what is it?"

"It's just a kick. It took me off guard," I tell him, straightening up. The woman backs off a little, her nose scrunching up.

"Let's get you home," he tells me, wrapping his arm around me.

"Can we wait a second for her husband to come back?" I ask him, gesturing to the woman alone with two kids next to me.

"Hey, sorry, I didn't see you there. No problem," Mason replies just as another car pulls up behind Mason's.

"It's nice to meet you," I tell the woman.

"I'm Kelly and that large Ogre is my husband, Dante," she replies smiling.

"I'm Denny and this is Mason, my boyfriend."

"Nice to meet you," Kelly smiles then Dante puffs his chest out grinning.

"Dude, be prepared," is all he says to Mason, before Kelly smacks him on the chest.

"What do you mean?" Mason asks confused.

"The birth? It's like watching the goriest horror movie."

"What?" Mason snaps, looking horrified.

"Yeah," Dante nods his head. "First time for me was the worst. I had nightmares for weeks mate. And it was over my best friends wife's pussy," he tells Mason, earning another smack from his wife. "It was a disaster man. Her hole was like this," he says, his hands spread out showing how big and I chuckle.

"It wasn't," Kelly says, smacking Dante on the arm. "He passed out, so don't ask him anything," she giggles.

"I did not. I was just taking a breather. I had just delivered a baby Kelly. That shit was scary as fuck and you can talk, you didn't do anything," he teases, a huge grin upon his face. The dude isn't as scary as I originally thought. He's kind of like a big bear. A big bear that's huge and has muscles that looks like *The Rock's*.

"I'll be fine. I can handle anything as long as they're both safe," Mason replies and I smile softly up at him.

"The kids got game," Dante chuckles before picking the car seats up. "It's nice meeting ya both, but we need to get going before the old lady at the B&B locks us out," he grunts, running over to the car shielding the babies in their seats.

"Old lady?" I ask confused, wondering if I really want to know.

"Ignore him," she laughs. "He's just scared because she didn't fall for his charm or jokes when we arrived. We're only here for one more night before we head back home, so good luck with the pregnancy," she tells me, before turning to Mason. "And make sure you don't faint. Be a man about it," she chuckles, tapping him on his chest once before following her husband and rushing over to the car.

"Take me home?" I grin up at Mason and he grins down at me.

FOURTEEN

Arriving back at home, the sky completely opens and rain pours down, soaking the both of us as we rush as quickly as we can through the garden to our house.

Mason opens the door as the first crack of thunder booms through the night sky. The sound forces me to jump, nearly biting my lip off in the process.

I'm shivering by the time we make it inside, and I run my hands up and down my soaked, bare arms.

"Let's get you out of your wet clothes," Mason tells me huskily, his face inches away from me. We haven't put the lights on yet, but I still manage to see his eyes rake down my chest. It's then I realise I'm not wearing a bra, and the wet material is clinging to my bare breasts, my erect nipples showing clearly through the material.

"Ah-hum," I nod, agreeing, but no words leaving my mouth.

Mason chuckles and takes another step closer to me, not bothering to turn on the lights.

His hands reach my waist and although we were both out in the rain, his hands feel like they're on fire when they touch me and I sway forward into him, my stomach blocking me from getting any closer.

"Hmmm," Mason grunts, his hands sliding up over my ribs to under my breasts and my body arches towards his touch. His thumbs, ever so slightly, swipe over my erect nipples and I let out a quiet moan.

Wetness pools between my legs and all the pent up sexual frustration that I've been gathering since being back with Mason threatens to erupt.

His phone rings, but he ignores it as his head leans in for a kiss. My mouth meets his in a heated explosion, my hands clinging to the back of his head, running my fingers through his wet hair. My moan reaches my ears when the ringing stops and Mason pulls away, leaving me a panting mess.

My legs threaten to give out when his lips reach my neck, placing light and hard kisses as he kisses a path all the way down to my chest, then down between my breasts, before finally, finally sucking a nipple into his mouth.

The sensation is overwhelming and I cry out in pleasure. The material from the dress, his heated breath has me close to cumming.

His phone rings again, and we both groan, but mine turns into a cry of pleasure when he takes my nipple in his mouth while rolling the other one between his thumb and forefinger.

"Ahhh, please," I pant breathlessly.

"Hold on babe," he grunts, his voice heavy with arousal.

Another call ends, but then it starts again, but this time with a different ringtone and I stiffen under Mason.

"Shit!" he grunts pulling away, his face looking pained and pissed. "I need to answer that," he whispers, sounding regretful. I nod my head, unsure if I can manage to talk.

"Hello," he answers, and then listens to the other person on the phone. "What the fuck? I'm with Denny, can't you handle it? Fuck! Yeah. Okay. I said okay Mav."

He ends the call standing with his back to me, his breathing heavy. I can feel the tension rolling off him and I take a step towards him.

"Is everything okay?" I ask softly, worried about what has gotten him so worked up.

"No. I need to go babe," he says, regret filling his eyes. "That bitch from earlier, who worked at the bar, tried setting fire to the bar."

I gasp horrified. As if the crazy bitch did that. "Oh my God, is everyone okay? Are you sure it was her?"

"Luckily no one was hurt and the damage is contained to the one office. We have her on camera, but Mav needs me to go down. The police want to question me about her or something and as I run that part of the business, I need to be the one to answer them."

"Go! Go! Sort it out," I urge, completely shocked someone would do that. Not only have they put people in danger, but they nearly burnt down someone's livelihood.

"I don't want to go," he groans, grabbing me by my hips.

A shiver runs down my body and now that his warmth is gone, my teeth start chattering. I hear him curse into the darkness before grabbing my hand.

"Let's go get changed and then I'll go sort this mess out. Hopefully it won't take too long."

I head up the stairs, switching lights on as I go with Mason following behind me.

Once we reach the bedroom, Mason's gaze doesn't leave mine; I can feel his stare burning into my skin, and my arousal returning. Taking off my wet dress is difficult at first, the material has tightly clung to my skin and when I try to get it over my head, I get it stuck.

Mason's laughter pisses me off, but half of me can see what he finds amusing. I'm soaking wet with a dress stuck over my head, bare breasts, only a black thong covering my lady bits and a pregnant stomach. I must look a picture.

"You're beautiful," Mason whispers close to my ear and it makes me jump. I hadn't realised he had been that close.

His hands reach above me, my breath hitches and then I can see. My back is to Mason, which I'm half thankful for and half hating. When his warm fingers run down my side, then back up to lightly brush against my breast I shiver. My whole body breaks into goosebumps and then embarrassingly, I moan loudly when I feel his erection at my bottom, his hands sliding down to cup my ass cheeks.

"Hmmm . . . you have a great fucking ass," he hums in appreciation, his touch setting me on fire.

"Thank you," I cough out. "I'm going to take a shower to warm up," or cool off, but I'm not sure which is winning.

"Right. Yeah. You go shower and I'll be back in a bit. I'll text you when I'm on my way back," he tells me, and then sweetly, he places a kiss on my shoulder before turning me around. His gaze never leaves my face and for that, I am thankful for. If he took one look at my body, my breasts, I'd probably jump him and right now he needs to go sort his business out and I need to cool my libido down.

I lean in to give him a kiss, hoping it will be a quick one so he can get going, but then his hands come around me, cupping my ass cheeks, and brings me flush against him, my bare breasts against his bare chest and I moan in approval. God he feels so freaking good.

"I won't be long." His voice is husky, filled with so much built up sexual tension.

"Okay," I whisper back, then give him another peck on the lips before grabbing my dressing gown hung on the back of the chair.

MASON HAS BEEN gone for over two hours and it's now getting really late. I'm bone tired, but ever since I came up over an hour ago, I've been restless, tossing and turning. My body is frustrated, begging for the release it craves so desperately, the release Mason left me begging for earlier tonight.

Frustrated, I kick the covers off my feet and half off the bed and slide my feet out. Since unpacking all my stuff, I've managed to give everything a place. Even the dildo I secretly bought when I moved into Nan's after the first month of living with her. Oh, and it's not for reasons you'll be thinking of, but right now, this second, I'm so fucking thankful I bought one.

Grabbing the chair from my vanity desk, I drag it across the bedroom to the wardrobe, open the doors then drag the chair in as far as it will go. It's a walk-in wardrobe, but not like the ones you see on the television. You know the one where it's as big as your whole bedroom or the whole downstairs? Yeah, mine is literally like a broom closet you'll find at an old church school. Either way, it's still big enough to fill all my clothes and I do have a lot.

Up on the top, there are three shelves and on the second shelf are my hidden boxes. Boxes I told Mason to secure and to never look through as they hold my most inner, most personal items.

A dildo and all of my diaries.

Grabbing the box I know it's in I slide it across until I've securely got it in my hand and make my way back to the bed.

I gasp when I bring it out of its packaging, forgetting how bloody big it is. I'm also confused as to why you can pick a colour. Seriously, it goes up your doo-dah and it's a wham bam, thank you ma'am. I'm confused to the vibrations set on it, but then I'm blonde, so hey, what the hell do I know?

Not having used it since before moving back home, I quickly think of something to use as lubricant. My mind runs wild, and I nearly squeal in triumph when I think of the lip balm I have in my handbag downstairs, but then choke it down.

Nearly tripping back over the blankets, I lob the bright pink dildo on the bed and rush over to the nursery. Mason or someone had put all the essentials on the changing mat. Talcum powder, baby shampoos are lined up with other bottles, so I grab the one I want . . . the baby oil.

It doesn't take me long to switch out the lights, remove my pyjama bottoms and knickers, and lubricate the dildo.

That's when I switch it on and no vibrations happen. Shit!! Maybe I need a new one. It has been sitting in a box for months on end with no one to play with it.

Switching the light back on I roll to the side and grab the remote. I'm hoping it carries the same batteries as the dildo because there is no way I'm calling Mason and asking him if he has any spares lying around. That would seriously be awkward.

Finally changing the batteries and placing the dead ones into the remote I roll to the other side, switch off the lamp and lay back down.

I'm breathing heavily and have to give myself a minute to relax.

All this trouble just to have an orgasm that only lasts a few seconds.

I lightly rub the vibrator across my already wet slit, the vibrations making me feel crazy. *Now I know why they added the vibrations,* I think as I run it across my clit.

I'm drowning in pleasure in just a few seconds of having it near me, so I gently run it back up and down once, before coating it with my arousal, making it more lubricated.

It feels uncomfortable at first as I enter and pull it back out, the rubber feel of the vibrator rubbing harshly against my sex. Grabbing the baby oil I pour some more on, making it slide in easier, bit by bit.

Once fully in I begin to relax back down on the plush cushions, the blanket now down by my feet.

The light flicks on and I let out a startling scream, my hands grabbing for the blanket to cover myself up. Once I'm covered I look towards the door, hoping to God it isn't Harlow or any of Mason's brothers, but when I turn and see Mason's face, I start to wish it was one of them.

"You need a hand?" he says quietly, quirking an eye.

"Um . . . no," I stutter, my face flaming hot and most likely bright red.

"Are you sure? You looked like you were struggling."

"No. Not struggling. Why don't you go um . . . take a shower," I suggest, really needing him out of here.

Just my luck he walks in when I'm finally getting myself some, not that I used it for that previously.

Mason walks around the bedroom to my side of the bed, before turning the lights down low by the switch next to my side of the bed, leaving the room lit in a dim glow.

Sitting next to me he puts one arm over me, and the other one symmetrical, but on the side nearest to us, the move making it feel like he's caging me in.

"What . . . w-what are you doing?" I ask when he brings his head down lower, and for a second I nearly forget about the dildo still half inside of me. It must have fallen out when I grabbed the blanket in a hurry to cover myself up.

"Denny . . . why do you have a dildo between your legs?" he asks, and he makes the question sound so normal, like it's asked every day. I'm completely mortified and I duck my chin as low as it can go, but he only removes the hand nearest us both and uses it to prop my chin up. "Answer me."

"Because . . . because . . . fuck sake Mason, just because," I snap, my hand reaching down to switch it off. The vibrations are starting to send me dizzy and the heat from embarrassment and the heat from the vibrations are making it hard for me to breathe.

"Oh no you don't," he says, stopping my hand from reaching down between my legs. "Now tell me."

"Mason, you know what is down there," I snap again, showing him I don't find any of this funny. Not that I think he's finding it funny, not at all, he's had a serious, deep, dark expression since the second he walked through the door.

"Now tell me, *why*? I can sit here all night Denny," he smirks, so I smirk back.

"The batteries won't last that long."

"Want to bet I change them? Now start talking."

"Fuck sake. I do it because of the baby?"

"Because of the baby?" he smirks, looking and sounding amused.

"Yes. After I had my first scan and Nan took me to get some pregnancy book it got me thinking. I have only had sex twice Mason and most women who get pregnant are usually more experienced, you know . . . down there-"

His laughter cuts me off and I give him a glare, smacking him lightly on the chest, the movement causing me to let out a quiet moan. His laughing halts to a sudden stop, and his eyes blaze close to the colour black. His intense gaze burns into my already heated skin, setting me alight.

"Carry on," he tells me hoarsely.

I give him another glare; this one I'm hoping gives more warning. "As I was saying . . . it got me thinking. And because I'd only slept with you, I was literally giving birth to a baby a virgin. So I bought the . . . um . . . vibrator so I can . . . you know . . . stretch my doo-dah," I explain, not wanting to tell him the other real reason. He only asked me why I had a dildo, not why I was using one.

"And that's why you're doing that . . . now," he smirks, his lips twisted into what I can only describe as delectable.

"Yes," I lie, averting my eyes to the other side of the room, the vibrations tightening my core.

"Liar," he whispers. "I bet you've been waiting for me to go so you can have your way with it."

"W-what, don't be so stupid," I scoff, my face burning brighter.

"Lying really doesn't suit you. If you're so worked up you only had to ask, babe."

"You've been freaking busy," I snap, before opening my eyes wide.

I cannot believe I just admitted to that.

He grins at me, his face calculating something from the way his smirk twists into a sexy grin. My pulse picks up and I start to wriggle, wanting to both turn the vibrator off and turn it on faster.

"Let's see what I can do," he whispers huskily, his fingers grabbing the edge of the blanket before I can reach out to stop him. My chest is still covered by a thin white tank top, my nipples visible through the light material and Mason lets out a pained groan.

Slowly, he lifts the thin fabric up my body, the material covering my face and forcing my arms to be raised above my head.

"Hmmm, I think I like you like this," he chuckles, his fingers running between my breasts at a torturingly slow pace.

"Mason, please, I can hardly breathe," I half lie, because I do feel a little suffocated. The word 'breathe' barely leaves my mouth before he has it up and over my head and thrown across the room. His smiling face and dark penetrating eyes bore down into mine; before he leans down to kiss me.

The kiss sends every nerve ending into a frenzy, my body feeling light and my head feeling dizzy with lust.

God, he's a good kisser.

He pulls away and I moan disappointed, but he just places a quick kiss on the tip of my nose before kissing down my neck.

He manages to manoeuvre his body so he's settled between my legs, the blanket still bunched up against my waist, but that doesn't stay like that for long. He grabs the edge and in one hard tug, he has it off the bed and onto the floor.

I gasp, completely bare and vulnerable to him as I lay here completely naked with a vibrator between my legs.

"Pink," he murmurs softly, before tracing his finger across my clit and through my slit. I buck moaning, my stomach tightening and I grasp at the bed sheets on either side of me.

"Take it out," I moan wanting to feel him inside me.

"Why?" he asks, stopping to look up at me.

"I want you," I groan, especially when he starts his torture with his skilled fingers.

"Oh baby, this is all for you, but we're not having sex yet, but I'm going to taste you," he says before moving further down the bed so his face is level with my sex, and I swear, I don't need to have a mirror to know how red I am right now. I can feel the flush on my chest, rising up my neck to my face.

"Mason," I plead, for what I'm not sure.

He chuckles, his warm breath fanning my sex and I buck again, my sex moving closer to his awaiting mouth.

When he doesn't make a move for a few seconds, I lift my head, but with my bump in the way I can't see what he's doing which just makes me wetter. I'm about to ask when I feel the vibrations become harder, stronger, and I squeal out in surprise, the pleasure something I never felt before when I used one.

Maybe it's because Mason is in control, my mind wonders.

His breath is against my clit, but his one hand is between my legs, holding the vibrator as he starts to thrust it in and out. I cry out, my hips bucking so wildly that Mason has to use his other hand to press down on my hips, but it only causes me to cry out louder.

"Oh God," I moan loving the feel of him, but the moan soon turns into another cry of pleasure when his tongue reaches my clit, flicking it once, twice before I feel myself tighten.

"Touch yourself," I beg, needing him to be pleasured by this too. It's the one thing I've always fantasised him doing, but he never did. We skipped most of the foreplay, too desperate to get each other's clothes off.

His moan against my clit sends a new wave of pleasure and I have to grab onto the sheets to try and keep myself grounded, wanting to wait for him.

"Are you touching yourself," I gasp out, needing to know so I can picture him.

"Fuck! Denny, you're killing me," he groans out, but then he moves into a kneeling position, I gasp in pleasure seeing his hand wrapped around his meaty, thick erection and I lick my lips wishing I could get my taste of him. It's only fair since he tasted me.

"Stop looking at me like that Angel, I'll end up blowing my load," he breathes out, his hand on the vibrator twisting a little to give it a new angle, the thrusting picking up along with the speed of vibrations.

"Oh God Mason," I cry out, wanting him. "I want to touch you."

Thinking he'd refuse, I'm surprised when he moves, not removing the one hand from the vibrator as he moves closer towards my head, lying on his side.

He gives my belly a light kiss before his fingers touch my clit and I moan out, wetting my lips when I turn my head, his cock near my mouth. I don't hesitate, although I should because I've never done this before, but something inside me is begging to do it. So I take his cock in one hand and run my tongue around the tip, the saltiness hitting my taste buds.

I have to quickly remind myself of what I read and when I do, I try taking, but with the way I'm laying, I'm not able to take him all the way. I'm lucky if I get halfway before I start gagging.

With my lips wrapped around him and the feel of his fingers torturing my clit and the vibrator between my legs, I can feel myself building up, ready to explode.

"Fuck, I'm going to come soon, are you close?" he asks, his voice ruff and husky.

I moan around his cock which causes him to groan. "If you don't want me to come in your mouth let me know now, babe."

I don't bother answering; I just take him a little deeper, ignoring the cramp in my neck. As soon as he realises I want him to cum in my mouth he groans, exploding. The taste isn't as horrible as everyone makes it out to be, it's gone as soon as it's swallowed, and that's what I do, swallow. I'm also trying to focus on licking it all up, another thing I read in one of my smutty romance novels. Only it's not as erotic as they made it out to be. I try my hardest to concentrate, but with his fingers, the vibrator and him cumming in my mouth, I'm ready to explode and all it takes is Mason to pinch my clit hard for me to explode, my mouth pulling away from his cock, crying out it in pleasure. My back hits the mattress properly and I cry out in pure pleasure and ride out my orgasm.

Just as I begin to recover, Mason's mouth is yet again on my clit, his lips sucking hard and I scream out again, my mind completely blank, my eyes clenched shut, and my whole body locked up tight as wave after wave shatters through my body.

I barely feel him pull his lips away or turn off and remove the vibrator. And I certainly don't recall him leaving the room for a washcloth, but I feel him when wetness wipes between my legs, and Mason gently kissing my thigh.

I feel like I must have dozed off when I feel the bed shifting and the blankets pulled up and across my naked body.

"I can't move," I moan. "You've paralyzed me."

Mason chuckles, curling my body to his front, his hands resting on my naked belly, and his fingers caressing gently over my bump.

"Go to sleep Angel," I hear him whisper and I pass out, but just before I do, I swear I hear him say the words 'I love you' but it could all just be a dream.

A very *good* dream.

FIFTEEN

It's been four days since Mason and I had our 'sexual' encounter and I'm starting to think he regrets it. I've tried everything in my womanly power to seduce him, but he always disappointingly pulls away.

I've had to suffer throughout the pregnancy being horny. Then he gives me a taste of the relief he can offer me, but then takes it away. It's like he enjoys torturing me.

I even hinted to him what I wanted by showing him a book that states that most women get horny or hornier during their pregnancy, but the twit just isn't reading between the lines. I swear, at the rate he's going I'll be making a billboard advertising what I want him to do to me.

"What is up with you?" Harlow asks, sitting next to me in the front room. She came over earlier while Mason went to work to watch some show she wanted to check out about space people. To be fair, I'm getting pretty into it and I've even got a soft spot for one of the characters called 'Finn.'

"It's Mason," I sigh, feeling sadness seeping through my veins.

"What's the idiot done now?"

"Nothing and that's the problem," I sigh feeling deflated.

"Explain," she says, moving so she's sitting cross legged on the sofa facing me.

"I huh . . . we . . . we . . . fooled around. We fooled around and it's like it repulsed him that much -although at the time he seemed pretty into it—that he can't stand to want to touch me like that *ever* again," I sigh, falling backwards against the back of the sofa.

"Usually, I'd know what to say, but I don't. Maybe you need to come right out and ask him yourself."

"Did you know he even took dating advice from Max? From Max of all people," I huff, not knowing why I'm really feeling this frustrated, this angry and this upset. It's not like he's breaking up with me, he still kisses me, hugs me, and holds me when I'm asleep. It's just when I try to take things further, like when my hands roam his hard chest, he ends up grabbing my hands stopping them going farther south.

"Okay, taking advice from Max wasn't one of his best ideas, but make sure you give him a chance to explain. He's due back soon isn't he?" she asks looking at the clock hung on the wall.

"Yeah, any minute now."

He left hours ago and it wasn't until Harlow mentioned him due back that I realised how long we had been watching 'the 100' show. And as if on cue, I hear his footsteps outside the door.

"I'll go, give you both some space," Harlow whispers, grabbing her shoes from off the floor.

"You don't need to go, we have two more episodes on this disc."

"Nah, its fine. I'll come over when I've had my college interview Monday," she tells me.

"Yes, then we can celebrate you getting in," I grin.

"Right, I'll see you later," she smiles, getting up and leaving the same time Mason walks in.

"Hey Harlow, are you going?"

"Yeah, Malik should be back from getting that new bike part he needed," she shrugs and waves goodbye over her shoulder.

"How's your day been babe?" he asks genuinely interested.

"Funny you should ask. I need to talk to you about something. Can you sit down a sec?"

"Yeah, sure. Is everything okay?"

"Yeah, and no. Just sit down a second," I plead, and relax when he does, sitting in the same spot Harlow just vacated. "Why won't you touch me?" I blurt out.

"W-what? I do touch you. I touch you all the time, Angel," he tells me wide eyed, a faint blush to his cheeks.

"No Mason, not like that. I don't mean in passing or giving me a hug, I mean sexually. After the other night I would have thought you wouldn't have been able to keep your hands off me, but you've barely even let me touch you. What is up with that?"

"W-what, you're reading into things babe, we're all good," he says, not looking me in the eye and my heart stops. Is he going to break things off again? I wait for the harsh words to escape his mouth, and to feel the pain of my heart breaking into two, but nothing comes, but the tension of waiting for it is making my body ache.

"You seriously aren't going to tell me, are you? If you don't find me attractive Mason then just fucking say it."

"You're just being hormonal," he tells me, standing up and pacing.

Oh no he didn't just say that to me!

"Yes Mason, it's my fucking hormones. Not the fact that I had mind blowing orgasms from someone I lo . . . someone I thought was on the same page as me, to find out I'm so far off line, I'm on another track," I snap sarcastically.

"No. Fuck! I didn't mean it like that. Look, just . . . I don't know. Just relax. I do find you attractive babe, I've proved this to you more than once. Why are you getting so worked up over this?" he asks, a faint blush to his cheeks, and his eyes still not fully meeting mine. He's hiding something and it hurts knowing that.

"I'm going for a walk," I snap, slipping on my Converse.

"It's dinner time babe, just stay, please," he begs, but it falls on deaf ears as I grab my cardigan, thankful the pregnancy makes me hot all the time now that the weather is cooling down.

"Fuck off Mason and you stay and relax," I bite out. "I asked you a simple question, one you couldn't even answer honestly."

Tears fall from my eyes and I ignore his pleas for me to stop and think about it. Instead, I just keep walking, not bothering to look back as I slam the door behind me, needing to get out of his way.

For the longest time I just walked, I don't know how, or when, but I ended up in the centre of town, the streets silent and void of any other people.

For the first time since leaving Mason earlier, I start to feel the night's cold air and let out a tiny shiver, wrapping my cardigan tighter around me. It's just then an all-night open cafe comes into view. Walking in I make my way up to the counter and order a hot chocolate.

I'm not waiting long before I've paid and it's given to me. I make my way out of the cafe, heading back towards home, thinking about what will happen between me and Mason. I really need him to be honest, to tell me why he's being the way he is. If he's hiding something from me then it must be serious.

Groaning, I shake my head, my eyes still diverted to the floor, not watching where I'm going. Which is what I should have been doing, especially as I'm a female, and walking alone during the night.

A noise from not too far away startles me and I whip my head up and scream in horror before calming my racing heart down.

"Mom! What are you doing here? Dad said you left?" I ask, rubbing my overbeating heart.

"Your dad," she says distastefully. "Is an idiot thinking he can get rid of *me*. I made him who he is today, he should be thanking me. He was useless and a lovesick puppy when we first met. He's a fool if he thinks I'm going quietly, whatever the threats," she laughs, but the laugh is hollow and kind of sounds like Cruella De Vil when she laughs.

"I don't understand. What are you going on about mom? That doesn't explain what you're doing here. Have you followed me?" I ask, and jump when I hear the same noise from earlier. It's coming from the alleyway my mother is standing near and I wish I could get her to move somewhere else, but I know it will only egg her on to stay where she's standing. She's stubborn like that.

"Did your father tell you I didn't really want you? That I got pregnant just so I could have his money? Because he's right, I did. I never wanted a child. Not a child that did nothing but cling to me, vomit on me, and demanded too much attention. You were such a burden to me, Denny. Now it's time to kill two birds with one stone. Hurt your father and get rid of you like I should have done years ago," she sniggers evilly and I look at her wide eyed. She's clearly lost her ever loving mind. I always knew she was psychotic, but this . . . this is something far beyond psychotic; I don't think there's a medical term for it.

"I . . . I don't understand mother. What are you saying?" I ask feeling a little panicked. Looking around the area, the panic doesn't subside and the urge to flee just intensifies. There's no one around to help me if she does something equally alarming as her odd behaviour right now.

I've never felt any sort of love from my mother, so her telling me she never wanted me doesn't even sting, nothing could have surprised me about her feelings towards me. I guess I've always truly known, but it still never stopped trying to gain her approval over the years, to make her proud.

Now I can see why dad was so scared to leave her, why he distanced himself from me during my childhood. She really is a raving lunatic.

"Well, I want you gone. It will kill your father, but also get rid of you. My all-time embarrassment. My biggest failure. Your father will never recover from losing you. You were always his main concern, the reason he stayed with me. Even when he acted like he didn't care about you, I knew. I knew he still kept a close eye on your grades, had someone record your school plays, but the man was weak, he still is. I can't wait to see his face when he gets the call to say he lost you," she grins. Her grin disarming and disturbing to the eyes.

Slowly, I put my hand in my cardigan pocket, silently pressing the buttons to what I know to be Mason's mobile number. I don't want to risk it dialing the last person I called as I'm pretty sure it was my Nan. She'd probably be out somewhere with friends on a Saturday night. And knowing her, she's probably either at bingo drinking the rest of her buddies under the table, or in a bar chatting up someone thirty plus years younger than her, and don't think I'm joking.

Not long after moving in I got a call from a local bar asking me–okay pleading with me- to pick her up. When I walked in I had to pry her off a twenty something year old lad who looked like he was going to be traumatized for the rest of his life.

And something tells me I'll need someone sober for what's about to come. I can feel it in my bones, that fleeting instinct there, not too far in the back of my mind. It's screaming at me to 'go,' to 'run,' and not look back.

"Mother, you're scaring me," I shiver, hoping the next button I press on my phone is the call button, but I don't have too much time to dwell on it when Craig Davis's brother suddenly walks around the corner, coming from out of the alley with a smug, evil, smirk on his face. My face drains of colour and my whole body goes on high alert.

What the hell is he doing here?

I look towards my mother, and back to Carl, and it occurs to me, my mother knows him, she's not at all the least bit intimidated or scared of his presence and the thought scares me more than I'd care to admit.

Taking a step backwards my mom begins to laugh, the high pitched sound screeching in my ears, but it's Carl's amused expression while he shakes his head that has me freezing on the spot. That's when I look down to see a huge butcher knife held firmly in his left hand and my whole body locks up, freezing in fear.

"I'm going to have fun with you," he snarls then lunges at me, a scream roaring from my throat.

This cannot be happening.

SIXTEEN

MASON

WHERE THE FUCK is she? It's been over two hours and I'm about to lose my fucking mind over it. I've gone out once, driving around the area not believing she'd go so far, but I've seen no signs of her.

Dialing Harlow's number again, I'm about to give up and just call Malik when she finally freaking answers.

"Jesus, who set a light up your arse?" my brother greets me, and I growl into the phone.

"Where's Harlow, jackass?" I snap, not having the patience to deal with him tonight. I need to know where Denny is, my stomach is all up in knots and something inside my head is screaming at me that something is wrong. I can feel it. I can feel it right down to my bones.

"She's in the shower, where I just was before you rudely kept ringing every two seconds," he snaps back.

"So Denny isn't there?"

"Bro, I think I'd notice a pregnant chick in that tiny shower with me and the missus," he teases, trying to make light of my dark mood, but it does nothing but piss me off more.

"Shit! Don't fuck with me Malik; I'm not in the fucking mood. Go check downstairs with Joan. I'm going over to see if she's at the house."

"Where are you then? She could just be at home in bed asleep," he laughs sounding amused at my paranoid, erratic behaviour.

"Cause I didn't think of walking upstairs you twat. We had some sort of fight. I think it was a fight anyway and she stormed out and she hasn't been back, Malik. I'm scared something's happened, I can feel it," I tell him, my voice breaking towards the end.

"Well shit. Maybe she's just walking off some steam?" he offers softly.

"She's fucking pregnant wearing only a pair of jeans, tank top and a cardigan Malik, she wouldn't risk hers or the baby's health."

"Yeah, you're right. I'll go downstairs then head next door if she's not here. You call her Nan and see if she's heard from her, if not call her dad. Call me if you find her. I'll be over in a second," he tells me before ending the call.

My body should have relaxed, that somehow saying what I'd been thinking for the past hour and a half would somehow make it all sound ridiculous, but it only makes me feel more anxious.

"Fuck Denny! Where are you?" I groan, pulling at the ends of my hair.

When her Nan answers and assures me she's not with her I call her dad, who sounds just as worried as me, unlike her Nan did.

"Have you gone and looked for her?" he asks sounding pissed and worried. I want to bite back at him, telling him not to give out fucking advice when he's treated her like shit her whole life. Instead, I bite my tongue and just tense my fists.

"Yes Charles, I did. I'm fucking worried. I can feel it," I croak, the feeling of loss suddenly hitting me.

All of a sudden my phone beeps with an incoming call and I look down at the screen.

"It's Denny, I'll call you back," I rush out, not entirely sure I finished before answering her call. "Denny? Denny? Where are you? I've been so worried. I'm so, so, so fucking sorry," I beg, the tightness in my chest not releasing.

"Denny, babe, talk to me," I plead, but soon shut up when I hear the sound of manic laughing.

"I'm going to have fun with you," a muffled voice snarls, and it sounds vaguely familiar, but I can't figure out where. A woman's laughter rings through the phone just as a loud scream rings through. All my blood drains from my face, leaving me dazed and weak.

Malik chooses that moment to walk in with Myles and Max, a startled look on his face when I start shouting into the phone.

"Denny? Denny? Baby, answer me," I roar down the phone, breaking down when the call ends suddenly. "Fuck! Fuck! Fuck! Fuck!"

"Bro, calm down, what's going on?"

I ignore Max and dial the police on my phone, my eyes watering, a lone tear sliding down my cheek before I have the chance to wipe it away.

"999, What's your emergency?"

"Hello, my name is Mason Carter," I explain, rattling off my address before going into the whole argument we had earlier, to the phone call I just overheard.

"Sir, I've sent uniform out to take your statement. They will be with you shortly. Please hold tight until then," the woman on the other line tells me, and I want to scream at her to calm down, but my temper flaring isn't doing anyone else any good. Plus, I need to get her back and I can't do that if I'm arrested over disturbing the peace or some shit.

"What the fuck bro? What's going on?" Malik asks once I end the call.

"She called when I was in the middle of talking to her dad. She didn't speak, but I listened. A male voice said 'I'm going to have fun with you' while another voice, a *woman's* voice, laughed. It wasn't even a laugh you hear when someone's told a funny joke, it was cold, menacing and dark," I shiver just remembering the sound. "Then she screamed. She sounded so fucking scared guys," I croak out, falling to sit on the armrest of the sofa.

"Fuck!" all brothers say in unison.

I nod my head in agreement, then nearly drop my phone when it starts ringing again. All brothers jump to attention and I'm so grateful that they're here right now.

"It's her dad," I whisper, and all boys relax their postures, Myles grabbing his own phone out to call someone, who, I don't know.

"Charles, you need to come to the house," I whisper, my voice clogged up from wanting to scream, cry and smash things.

"Oh my God. What's happened? If something's happened to her," he chokes out, and I can hear the tears in his voice. "I'll . . . I'll be there soon."

The line goes dead and I stare numbly at the phone. For how long I don't know, but the next thing I know is Harlow running into the room and wrapping her arms around me.

"She's going to be okay," she whispers softly, tears running down her own face.

"Yeah, bro, we'll find her," Maverick says on my other side and I look up dazed, wondering when the fuck he got here.

"I can't lose her," I choke out, not caring if I look like a wuss.

"You won't Mason. The police will be here any minute, and they'll find her, we'll find her. I promise," Mav tells me, his voice filled with honesty, so much honesty my heart hurts.

"It's my fault. I couldn't just tell her I was scared; scared if we went further than fooling around she'd leave me, or that we'd lose the baby. I couldn't risk it. Now, I'm going to lose everything. I can't lose her Mav, I can't, I love her. Fuck! I haven't even told her that. Did ya know? I fucking love her so much that when I try to feel it, I mean really feel it, I can't breathe, that it hurts that much I just want to hold her and squeeze the ever loving shit out of her and not let go. Now she's gone and she could be hurt," I choke out, more tears running down my face.

"You'll be able to tell her yourself once she's back home, bro."

I look up at Mav at the same time Joan and Granddad walk in followed by Denny's dad and two police officers.

I quickly stand up to greet them, wondering if they are already looking for her. "Have you found her?" I croak out, my voice hoarse and dry.

"We have a few questions. First though can we get a description? We usually don't report a missing case until twenty four hours after they've been missing, but according to the phone call, your girlfriend screamed?" he asks.

I nod my head confirming. "Yes, she screamed after someone said I'm going to have fun with you," I tell them. "She must have pocket dialled my number, so whatever happened she had enough time to do that. She must have felt safe at one point before she started to dial me."

"Can you give us a description so we can have other patrol cars on the lookout?"

"You can't miss her," I reply harshly, not meaning to. "She's just over seven months pregnant, she has blonde hair to here, and is stunning. She's wearing a pair of grey jeans, I know because we bought them yesterday, her other clothes were getting too tight. These were maternity jeans," I croak out. "She's got a white tank top with her cream cardigan."

"Does she have any tattoos? Scars?"

"No," I shake my head at them, feeling more and more dejected with each question they throw my way.

"Right. Is there anyone you can think of who would want to hurt her?"

"Her mother," her dad scoffs and I whip my eyes to his in alarm.

"Her mother? You think her mother would hurt her?" I ask utterly shocked.

"Wouldn't put it past her, son. She's been sending me crazy messages all day," he tells us and gets his phone out to show the police.

"What about the break-in? Could the two be connected? That was about my case," Harlow whispers, but loud enough for the one officer to hear.

"I'm sorry. What break-in?" he asks looking between us.

"Denny, she stayed at her brothers before we moved in here together. One night there was a break-in. Nothing was stolen, but a picture was shoved under her locked bedroom door. The picture showed one of the witnesses to the Davis trial, dead."

"Oh, yes, I've been informed of the case. So Denny is another witness?"

That's what I fucking said asshole. "Yes."

"I'll call this in. If it's the same person that has Miss Gittens, then we will need a bigger team."

"You should have everyone searching for her anyway," I sneer, standing up.

"Don't do something stupid, son. I don't want to have to arrest you, but I will if you push me."

I nod my head sharply, barely registering anything they're saying to each other over the radio. Walking into the kitchen I grab a bottle of vodka and pour myself a decent amount.

"Don't take that too far boy. She's going to need your head straight," My Granddad's voice cuts in and I slam the glass back down after downing the glass. I run my fingers through my hair before frustratingly pulling at the ends.

I need her.

I need her here so goddamn much it's slowly killing me from the inside out.

"Granddad, I can't do this. I can't lose the only good thing I've ever had walk into my life. I spent so long pining after her, thinking she'd never see past a good time, or the real me, but she did. Then I went and let my fears consume me and I fucked everything up. I just got her back," I choke out, the tears falling as another sob tears from my throat.

Granddad walks up to me, pulling me into his beefy arms and slapping my back.

"She's going to be okay," he assures, his voice choked up just as mine is.

I feel like this is karma. Karma for letting such light into my dark soul, but I'm selfish enough to never let her leave again.

I need to find her.

I need to get her back, where she belongs.

SEVENTEEN

DENNY

WAKING UP, I groggily try to roll over, but something pinching my wrists stops me from moving.

If Mason is trying to do something kinky I'm going to fucking throttle him. My bladder is bursting to be relieved and I'm freezing, no doubt Mason is also hogging the blanket.

"Mason, I'm freezing," then cough when I smell the most rancid smell I've ever smelled. I can't even begin to describe just how bad it is. It's burning my nose and when I open my eyes I startle awake. I'm not in my bed, at home with Mason, in my nice clean, warm house. No. Instead I'm in a dingy, black, burnt out basement, with rain water puddles in various little holes around the room. I sit up blinking, noticing my hand is attached to a long metal chain that is attached to a concrete wall.

"Help," I croak out, suddenly remembering what happened. Images of flashbacks skitter through my mind and I struggle to make sense of some, until they start flashing in order.

Mom and Carl, Davis's brother were there, he had a knife and went to attack me. I tried to run, but didn't get far when he put an awful smelling rag across my face. No wonder my brain is all foggy and confused.

"No one is going to help you," a cruel voice whispers and my head shoots to the left, the movement making me nauseous. My hands run over my belly, making sure nothing is wrong, that they didn't hurt my baby when I was knocked out, but everything seems fine. I mean, I would bleed if something was wrong, wouldn't I?

"Mom, please, mom, let me go. I promise I won't tell anyone, just please let me go. I'm having a baby, your grandchild," I beg, tears falling rapidly down my face, now just realising how dangerous of a situation I'm in.

If only you didn't run out on Mason, my mind screams at me and I want to scream back 'fuck you' but keeping quiet wins out.

"Grandchild?" she laughs and I want to puke. How can this woman be my mother? I'd never treat my kids like this, let alone put them in a dangerous situation like the one she's put me in. "Stupid girl. When will you learn? You and that sprog mean nothing to me. What made you think I'd care if I've never cared about you to this point?" she sniggers, the sound feeling like a kick to the gut. I can handle her not loving me, but her grandchild? I've read stories where some people who sucked at parenting always end up being better grandparents, fuck was that wrong.

"There has to be something inside you that knows what you're doing is wrong? That a part of you wants to be in your granddaughter's life? Please mom. I've never asked you for anything. Not even as a kid did I ask for anything, but I'm begging you, please don't leave me here. Please," I cry.

"Weak, weak, weak girl," she mutters looking at me like she's looking at something disgusting.

My head bows down, my body going completely numb.

She's not going to help me.

Clapping has my body jumping on the grimy, too thin foam mattress on the damp floor.

"What a beautiful escape speech. But your mother made me a deal; I get you in exchange for making your dads life a living hell. Making sure he couldn't sell his house has been fun so far, so seeing how he reacts to me killing you? That is going to be even better. First though, we have a matter to discuss."

"What matter?" I snap out, my body shivering from the damp, cold room.

"Craig. You gave your fucking statement after I warned you bitch," he sneers, his yellow teeth glowing in the dull lit room.

Seriously, does his whole family brush their teeth with butter? I cringe at the sight.

"Oh, this is my queue to leave," my mother laughs, stepping over what I can only presume is burnt wood. "Oh and Carl dear, you really should get some air freshener down here, it smells awful," she gripes and I want to laugh. The place needs more than just air freshener, it needs rebuilding, and fucking heating.

"Bye, Viv."

"Vivian," she states sharply before leaving me to defend myself with a complete and utter psychopath.

"Now," he says, clasping his hands together. "Where were we? Oh yes, your betrayal. You gave your witness statement against my brother after I so kindly gave you a warning, which is more than I gave the other one, he gestures, using his thumb to point behind him. I look around him but see nothing but darkness. He snickers when he sees the direction I'm looking in and it makes me want to vomit all over again. Something feels really wrong in this room. Something other than the fact I've been kidnapped.

"You killed Hannah?" I squeak out, the picture of her lifeless body flashing through my mind, making me whimper.

"Ahh, I see you took notice of the picture," he chuckles, using his knuckles to lift my chin, but I brush him away, turning my head.

"Don't touch me," I spit out. I cry out sharply when it earns me a backhanded slap across the cheek. My right cheek burns with fire and stings where the ring he's wearing has cut into my cheek. The notion makes me feel sick and I have to focus on steadying my breathing before glaring back up at him.

"I've already given my statement. What are you planning on achieving by kidnapping me, other than a prison sentence?"

He laughs loudly, leaning down to get in my face, his breath knocking me back with its foul odour and I have to swallow back bile that's threatening to rise up my throat.

"Oh, I have something much, much better than your statement. I've been watching you and your group of misfits for a long time," he snarls and I scoff at the word misfits. He's a delinquent, who has killed, kidnapped and God knows what else. "The girl, the girl fucking with my brother's future, she's going to help me."

"Your brother's future? He was going to rape an innocent girl, and not for the first time either. He's done it before, but do you care?"

"No, bitch probably deserved it. From what I heard, the first one he raped would be her one and only experience, she's that fucking ugly. He was doing her a favour breaking her in. Plus, it won me hundred quid him banging her," he chuckles and bile rises in my throat.

"You're sick."

He shrugs, not looking bothered one single bit, which makes me hate him even more.

"Anyway, back to my plan. Harlow is going to retract her statement, stating that what my brother is saying, is in fact, the truth."

"And what makes you think she will agree to that?" I snarl, venom hitching in my voice.

"Oh, this is where you come in. I'm going to make sure she knows how you'll end up if she doesn't. Oh and, I'm not stupid, I'm going to want proof before releasing you," he grins, thinking he's got it all worked out already.

"Let me go?" I ask, hoping filling my voice. "But my mom . . . you said-"

He laughs loudly interrupting me and I cut my eyes into tiny slits. "I'm not really letting you go. I'm going to have my fun keeping you alive, to suffer, and if you don't cooperate with me, then you'll go the same way she did."

"She?" I ask, wondering who the fuck he's on about now.

"Yeah, *she*," he grins then gets up, moving to another lamp to turn it on. What I see will be forever burnt into my brain. I scream so loud that my throat feels red raw. I keep screaming and staring at the scene in front of me, praying it's not real, but deep down, I know there is no way that the sight in front of me could be faked. My back is pressed hard against the wall and I begin to get hysterical.

Another slap to my face has me heaving and I lean over as far away from the ratty mattress as I can and vomit all over the damp, burnt floor. The burnt wood startles me, and then hope seeps into my pores for the first time since waking up. I'm at the old Gunner's house, no wonder there is hardly anything to the stairs. How ironic is it that he brings me here?

"Please, please cover her back up," I plead, crying out.

"Pleasure honey, after all, the bitch fucking stinks," he laughs then covers her back up with the dirty sheets.

His phone rings, playing a new rap song and I want to roll my eyes, but after seeing Hannah's dead, bloody body, I don't want to provoke him.

"Yeah? So the pussy phoned the police," he laughs to whoever is on the other line. "You sure they're all gone? Good. Send me the girl's number, let's get this going. I have shit to do," he tells them before ending the call. Not seconds later a message alert tings.

"Now, let's get one thing straight, yeah. You'll do as you're told. I'm going to ring your little bitch of a friend, and you're going to tell her to drop the charges. I don't care what you have to do, just fucking do it. If you try anything . . . and I mean anything to alert them to where we are, I will fucking slice your throat open," he growls, holding up a shiny, silver butcher knife that I saw him holding earlier. I nod my head, wiping tears from my now dirty smudged cheeks.

He dials a number and I can hear it ring, just as he turns it around I get a glimpse of the screen and notice it's on video call, not a normal call. Fuck!

"Hello? Oh My God! Denny? Denny? Oh my God. Guys," she screams and I hear footfalls stomping towards her, but whoever pushes her out of the way I don't see because my eyes are filled with thick tears.

"Shut the fuck up," Carl roars, quickly putting the knife to my throat. I squeal completely startled, and fix my eyes on the screen and notice Harlow and Mason on the screen. Both expressions look pained, sad, and angry.

"Are you okay, babe?" Mason asks, his voice sounding hoarse.

I nod my head yes, too scared to speak, but then Carl pushes the knife sharper into my neck and I cry out.

"Harlow, Harlow, I need you to . . . I need," I cry out, not able to say the words. It's not right.

"Fucking speak to her now you bitch, or have you forgotten that I'll slice your throat? Maybe I'll cut that baby out of you first," he sneers and I cry out, completely scared out of my mind. My whole body is quaking with fear, my body shaking uncontrollably now.

"Harlow . . . I need you to go to the police and tell them what happened here was a lie. Say that you didn't know how much trouble he would get in, please. I'm begging you," I cry out and hope like hell I get out of here alive.

"Times up, bitch. You have until tomorrow morning at nine to have the charges dropped otherwise she dies," he snaps into the phone before ending the call.

"Why are you doing this?" I cry.

"Because you bitches deserve it."

"Oh, so if your brother ass raped you, would that be okay too? Would that mean you deserved it? Can you hear how fucking stupid you sound? You're asking a victim to drop the charges of attempted rape all because he's your brother."

"Shut your fucking mouth," he growls, his fingers squeezing my cheeks together, the pain hurting me and no doubt already forming a bruise.

"Why? Is it because I'm hitting a nerve?"

"The only nerve that is going to be hit in a minute is the one up your cunt if you don't shut the fuck up," he yells and I cower back against the wall, a small whimper escaping my lips.

I DON'T KNOW WHAT time it is when I next wake up, all I know is my bladder is killing me. I've been dying for the toilet ever since I woke up the first time, but looking around I can't see him having a clean toilet in the place.

Bending forward to rub the pain away, it only makes the pressure on my bladder worse. It also wakes my princess up, and she pushes down hard onto my bladder and I'm ashamed to admit I leaked a little.

"Carl?" I croak, my voice sore. "Carl?" I shout louder.

"What?" he snaps walking down the steps.

"I need the toilet," I tell him, hoping he takes pity on me and not expect me to piss myself.

"So fucking go, or do you need me to hold your hand, darling?"

"Can you release me? Take me to an actual toilet?" I ask, holding up my tied hand.

He laughs throwing his head back and I slump forward. I should have known he wouldn't let me go to the toilet, or even a clean fucking bush.

"There's an old paint bucket right there darling."

"I can't piss in that, I'd never reach," I tell him, standing up. My legs leave the mattress and they're wobbly, I steady myself on the wall, but then squeal when I feel something crawl across my hand.

"Not my problem," he shrugs watching me with an amused expression.

Noticing a plank of wood, I use it to try getting the bucket a little closer. After five minutes of manoeuvring I finally get the bucket close enough to hover above.

"You can leave," I tell Carl dryly.

"Nah, this is the most you've done, and I'm gone in an hour," he smirks and my stomach sinks. I've still not figured a way out of here, and now I've got an hour until he ends my life. Would he kill me before or after?

"Can you turn around please?"

"Nah," he smirks and I want to cry out. Arrogant jerk!

I'd rather not go through an hour of pain or piss myself. I remove my cardigan using my teeth to keep it in front of me to cover my lady bits the best I can. Slowly, I slide my trousers and knickers down, but not far enough that if he tries something I can't pull them back up.

He's watching me with amusement, but I take no notice. I still keep a close eye on him, watching in case he does make a move. If he's raped Hannah, what the hell is he going to do to me?

My cheeks redden as I take what seems to be the longest piss in the world and although I'm hovering over a bucket, I still manage to get it dripping down my leg. I shake off remains the best I can, but I don't care. I feel dirty, used, violated, and disgusted in myself, so the quicker I'm dressed the better.

The cold starts to bother me, so I put on my cardigan, once again closing it tightly around me. Carl laughs and I look at him with so much disgust.

"I'm off to meet your fucking friend. I best scope out the place first just in case she decides to get the pigs involved. I'm glad I waited until now to tell them where to meet me with the proof. I want a signed statement stating the charges against my brother are false. Let's hope the bitch cares enough to get you back."

"I hope they arrest your ass. Then you can rot in jail with your brother," I snarl, and he storms over pinning me up against the wall. His fingers feel like they're squeezing in the same spot as he did before, it hurts that much. I cry out with pain and clench my eyes shut.

"Yeah? Maybe I'll let you fucking rot down here with that dead bitch. See who fucking suffers the most then, bitch. I'm going to kill you fucking slowly. I'll make you scream so loud you'll pass out. You're going to regret fucking answering back to me," he growls, spit flying in my face when he talks.

"Drop dead," I cry, hating the fact I'm showing enough to let him know I'm scared and he's hurting me. My face is going numb, and my hands are itching to wipe the spit off my face.

He shoves me harder into the wall and luckily I sort of prepared for it and made sure only my head and the top of my shoulders made impact, not wanting to cause harm to my unborn baby girl. When he's gone I'll try finding a way out, until then, I need him to think I'm stuck here.

Which, I most likely will be if I don't get out of these chains.

EIGHTEEN

MASON

THE NIGHT HAS gone so fucking slow; I don't know how I've not managed to beat the ever loving shit out of someone.

They arrested Vivian, Denny's mom, not long ago and have had her in for questioning. She was found with Denny's purse and phone, but so far the bitch isn't talking. The only thing we know for a fact is she had Denny's purse and phone, two suitcases full of clothes and a plane ticket out of the country.

I've begged and pleaded to have five minutes alone with the woman, but the police won't let me. I've never wanted to hurt a woman in all my life until now. It should scare the shit out of me; that this anger, this hate is boiling up inside of me to the point I'd actually follow through with strangling the life out of that woman. She's supposed to be her fucking mother. I know I can't be surprised, look at my own parents. But for Denny, she doesn't deserve parents like that, especially not a mother who has put her life in danger.

A phone rings in the background and I lift my head up, listening to see if it's the police with more news.

"Hello," I hear Harlow answer, before her breath hitches. Even in another room I can hear the fear in her voice. "Oh My God! Denny? Denny? Oh my God.

Guys," she screams and I fly off the stool and into the front room, the rest of the boys behind me. I push Harlow out of the way, not really meaning to. I settle us both until we're both staring in complete horror at the screen.

"Shut the fuck up," a male voice roars, and I watch as Harlow clicks record to tape the video chat. A knife shoots out, pressing against Denny's throat and I go to grab it, before realising that I can't.

"No," I whisper, feeling my eyes harden. I'm going to fucking obliterate whoever this fucker is. My heart aches not being able to hold her. She's covered in dirt, her face looks red and her cheeks are bright red, tears coursing down them like a stream. I'd do anything right about now to save her, to trade positions.

"Are you okay, babe?" I ask, wishing my voice didn't sound so dry, so clogged up.

She nods her head yes, fresh tears running down her face and the knife presses harder into her neck, a red line marking how much pressure he's using and she cries out. Her cry has me stepping forward, and I cry out with frustration, running my hands through my hair.

"Fuck baby, it's okay. It's going to be okay," but she doesn't hear me over her own cries.

"Harlow, Harlow, I need you to . . . I need," she cries out, her breath hitching like she's struggling with what to say and that hurts more. Knowing he's forcing her to say something she clearly doesn't want to say.

"Fucking speak to her now you bitch, or have you forgotten that I'll slice your throat? Maybe I'll cut that baby out of you first," he sneers, and I make a growling sound, my fists clenching into tight fists. She looks so scared, so petrified, it's killing me. My whole body is shaking with adrenaline and I wish the fucker was standing right in front of me.

"Harlow . . . I need you to go to the police and tell them that what happened here was a lie. Say that you didn't know how much trouble he would get in, please. I'm begging you," she sobs, her eyes darting above the camera, to the camera then to somewhere in the room. For some reason it's like she's trying to tell us something.

"Times up, bitch. You have until tomorrow morning at nine to have the charges dropped, otherwise she dies," the voice snaps from behind the camera, not once does the pussy show his face.

"What the fuck?" Maverick says, speaking first. The room has gone deadly silent and I move back, my eyes not blinking, my body locked up tight. My fist lifts with its own accord and all I can focus on right now is pain. Inflicting it, receiving it and needing it. I punch the kitchen door, the wood splintering and breaking around my knuckles, neither the pain nor blood are registering. No one tries to stop me, not even when I raise my bloody hand back up and punch it again.

When I still don't feel any better, I grab the nearest thing to me which happens to be a cup and throw it across the room, the sound of the smash not deterring me from grabbing another and doing the same.

I feel glass crunch under my feet. I don't know how much I've smashed or what I've broken, I just know it's a hell of a lot, and no one tried to stop me. They obviously knew I needed this, needed to feel something other than pure rage and fear.

I can't lose her, I whisper in my head, the same mantra I've repeated to myself all night as my knees fall to the floor in a heap, the glass crunching under my weight.

"Call the police, get them here, tell them that Denny has made contact and who has her," I hear my big brother tell someone. His words are background noise to me. That is until I repeat in my head what he said, then I stand up, getting in his face.

"Who the fuck has her?" I yell, standing toe to toe with my brother.

"Calm down bro, we'll get her. I recognized the voice as Carl, Carl Davis. This just makes sense. The only thing that doesn't make any sense is why her mother has her stuff."

"Probably sold her out, the sick fucking bitch," Max growls, looking as pissed as I am.

"Let's go then. We know where the fucker lives," I tell them, feeling hope flare in my veins.

"No, don't," Harlow shouts rushing back into the room. "He just sent me a text message saying no police. If we do . . . ," she chokes out, not able to tell us the rest. Malik gently takes the phone off her, reads the message, then his hard eyes look back up at mine. It's then I know that it's something seriously sick.

I grab the phone from his hand before Mav has a chance to stop me. He's standing close behind me, reading the message himself from over my shoulder.

Unknown number: No police. If I even get a whiff of a pig, you'll be receiving your child in a box . . . oh and make sure the bitch brings a signed statement.

I'll text you in a few hours where to meet. If the bitch doesn't bring me what I want then you'll never find the bitch or the baby again. As soon as I have what I want, I'll tell you where I have her.

"I'm going to fucking kill him and his fucked up brother," I growl. "This is why I pushed her away. I can't fucking protect her; I'm fucking useless like dad always said I was. Only ever good enough for one thing," I snarl, pacing along the kitchen. Everyone stares at me, but I don't care; I just fucking need her back. "You all told me to give it a chance, that it will be worth it, but look at her now. She's hurt, scared out of her fucking mind and the sick bastard is threatening to kill our baby," I shout out, throwing another punch to the kitchen cabinet.

"Calm the fuck down now, bro. If anyone deserves happiness in their lives it's you, brother. Denny loves you. She really fucking loves you and she's going to be in that room scared out of her mind, thinking about coming home to you. She's relying on you," Myles shouts, tears pooling in his eyes.

"He's right Mason. She loves you and she's going to need you to get your fucking head together. You can't help her feeling sorry for yourself. None of this is your fault. No one could have predicted this happening," Mav tells me, clapping me on the shoulder.

"I still think we should go torch the fucker's house," Max grumbles, looking seriously pissed.

"You okay?" I ask, realising I'm not the only one struggling here.

A manic laugh leaves his throat, his head thrown back until he drops it forward, his eyes hard and boring into mine.

"She's one of my best mates, dude. She's the only chick apart from Harlow I actually like and not want to stick my dick in her. But worst of all, I hate seeing you so fucking messed that you're throwing punches at walls that can't fight back. You're being a pussy," he snarks, his sarcastic tone trying to lighten the mood. I give him a small grin, knowing he's not comfortable with all this touchy, feely shit. He's never been one to express his feelings, or really show when he's upset. He only gets happy, over happy, or angry. There's never really anywhere in between with him.

"Okaaay," I say slowly before leaning against the kitchen work surface. "What are we going to do? If we can't go to the police, then what the fuck are we going to do? I'm not risking her or the baby's life."

"I have an idea," Harlow pipes up, tears still staining her face.

"Babe, let us try and sort it out," Malik tells her, wrapping his arm around her and bringing her flush against his chest.

"Fuck off Malik and let me talk. Just cause I'm a girl doesn't mean my ideas won't work," she snaps glaring at him. Then she turns to me and gives me a sad smile. "I reckon we call the police- just let me finish please," she begs when I go to interrupt her.

"Go on," I nod for her to continue.

"I think we should call the police, explain over the phone about what is happening, and that he must have someone watching us or his house or something for him to know if we do call them. He said he'll tell us where Denny is if we bring him what he wants. If I write a forged statement giving him everything he wants then it will work."

"No Harlow. He tried to rape you, he can't get away with this," Malik growls.

"I know babe, but you're not getting it. It doesn't matter what I give him because we'll be telling the police what it says. We can also call my lawyer and see if there is a clause or something that will get it dismissed. It's either that or we try to figure out where he has her on that video," she says, pointing to me where her phone is still held in my hand.

"Let's call the police first and see what they suggest," my Granddad replies looking tired as hell.

Mary, Denny's Nan rushes into the room like her ass is on fire. "I'm so sorry. After bingo we went for a drink and I passed out on the sofa. I didn't hear my phone. I woke up to get a glass of water," she cries, her hair a wild mess and crinkled clothes loose on her body. "I'm so sorry. What's happening?" she asks and it's Denny's dad, Charles who answers.

"She's been taken by some thug who's brother attacked this little one," he says gesturing to Harlow.

"Yes, Denny told me all about it when we left," she says looking confused.

"Well the attacker's older brother has taken Denny so he can blackmail a written statement off Harlow to release his brother from all charges. He won't tell us where she is until he has what he wants."

"So if we know who he is and why he has her then there is not a thing the courts will do. Give him what he wants because it won't stand up in court. Harlow only has to stand up in court and tell them it was forced, that Denny was kidnapped and threatened. It won't get used. Give him that and he gives us Denny

... unless..."

"Unless what?" I ask, staring at the crazy lady with wide eyes. How is it we've all been running this around in our heads for the past how many hours and she turns up and makes more sense of it all?

Like I said, crazy lady.

"Unless he's not planning on releasing her," she whispers, holding a hand to her chest.

"Fuck! Someone call the police again, I'm going to watch this video again and see if I can tell where she is."

"What can I do?" Mary says and Joan walks up to her wrapping an arm around her.

"You can help me make everyone something to eat and drink."

I'VE REPLAYED THE video call of Denny over and over again to the point I had to get Harlow to run over to hers to get her charger.

A message alert beeps on Harlow's phone making me jump.

Unknown number: Meet me by the fishing pond down by Green Day in an hour. Don't forget, I'll know if you've got the pigs involved.

"Guys, he's contacted," I shout, getting everyone's attention. Harlow wakes up from the sofa. She fell asleep an hour or so ago. Joan fell asleep too, but it seems everyone is now awake.

After calling the police they told us they were sending someone out, that they were short staffed. After that I told them to fuck off, that my girlfriend and baby's life are in danger, so if they wouldn't do their job, I would. We're still hoping someone makes it here before we leave.

"What's he say?" Maverick asks walking in from the kitchen. His eyes have a dark shadows under them, he looks as tired as I do.

"He wants us to meet him at the fishing pond down on Green Day in an hour. Do you really think this will work?"

He opens his mouth to reply when banging starts up at the door, stopping all of us in our tracks. We all look to each other before looking back to the door. When it's clear no one is expecting anyone we all move towards the door.

Charles is the first one to the door; he opens it looking pale and drawn as the rest of us.

"Son?"

"Dad," Evan nods. The badge on his trousers has me looking up at him wide eyed. I remember him from some of the parties we used to crash at school, but other than that I don't think we ever really got on. My feelings for Denny had always gone unnoticed by everyone, including Denny, but her brother, Evan, knew and warned me away from her.

Like that happened.

"What are you doing here?" I ask him impatiently, not having the time. I need to watch the video again, I know I'm missing something and it's there. I just need more time.

"Can I come in?" he asks and I nod, moving out of the way and directing him into the front room.

"Take a seat," I gesture, the phone squeezed tightly in my hand.

"No, I'm good. Look, I know Denny's missing. I know who has her. The station radioed in a few hours ago saying you called in with more information? I need to know what that is?"

"How about you start from the fucking beginning?" I growl, stepping forward. "You knew your sister who is fucking pregnant had been kidnapped, and you hadn't bothered to come and check in?"

"Look, I'm not allowed to go into specifics. I can tell you that I've been working undercover to bring down the gang that Carl Davis is involved in. We caught the last gang member today outside watching your house. I'm taking a good guess here in saying he was outside watching to report back to Carl about what's been going on. All we need now is Carl. I need to know what he gave you in terms of ransom or whatever it is he wants?"

"He wants Harlow to give him a signed written statement stating that his brother is innocent and that what he's saying is the truth. He wants us to meet him in an hour, but we don't believe that he's going to give us, Denny," I tell him, trying hard not to punch him in the face right now.

"I know you want to punch me right now, but I needed to stay off the grid so I could do my job. I'm not the bad guy here. I'm here to help. If I could have gotten here sooner, I would have. Believe me."

"Does she even know what you do for a living?" I ask him before turning to Charles. "Did you even know?"

"No, son, I didn't," Charles answers, turning to look at his son in awe, or maybe hurt? I'm not sure.

"No she doesn't, but it doesn't fucking matter. What matters is getting her back. After talking to my mother at the station I don't believe we will be getting her back."

"What did the crazy bitch have to say for herself?" I ask him, my muscles tensing at the mention of her.

"She's completely lost it. She didn't even know who I was at first. She kept talking about Denny, how she ruined her life, bla bla bla," he snaps. "Dad, is there something I need to know? She honestly didn't know who the fuck I was, or acknowledge who I was. She kept saying she wasn't my mother."

"Son, I'll have this conversation with you another day, but right now, let's get your sister home," he smiles sadly.

I watch in fascination as Charles gives Mary a helpless look. Whatever they need to talk about is something I don't want to be in the same room as when it's revealed. By the look Mary gives Charles back it can only be bad news.

"If it's about her not being my mother, I already know. But you, you I'm not sure about," Evan says like he has all the time in the world to have a family discussion.

"As interesting as this is, I want to get Denny back," I growl.

"Yeah, sorry," he nods.

"I'm going to look over this video one more time, there has to be something on here that I missed. You guys work with Evan a second while I watch this."

"What's the new plan then? I take it you came with one, otherwise you're wasting our time," Max bites out, obviously not happy with the new presence in the room.

"I can't go to the pond, but I already have men there," he replies, ignoring my brother's tone.

"You do?" Harlow asks, a bit of colour returning to her cheeks. I didn't even think how she would be feeling. After all, she would have to be the one to meet up with him to give him the statement.

"Yeah, we knew something big was going down before he took Denny. We weren't sure what it was going to be. It's where they do most of their dealings, thinking no one can see them, but they're wrong. I have four non-uniformed officers fishing, I'll have two more using the running trail and then police will be nearby and ready to strike. . . . "

He rattles off giving them signal instructions in case the wire they are sticking to her doesn't work. She'll be going in alone, but will be surrounded by plenty of officers.

I start the video again, this time plugging in the headphones so I can block out everyone's voices in the room.

The video starts mid-sentence, and I watch, my heart still splitting in to two until I get towards the ending.

"Harlow . . . I need you to go to the police and tell them what happened here was a lie. Say that you didn't know how much trouble he would get in, please. I'm begging you."

I re-watch the scene again; listening to the words, *tell them what happened here was a lie*.

"Fuck!" I shout, grabbing fistfuls of hair and pulling. "I know where the fuck she is," I shout, yanking the earphones out of my ears and running for the door.

"Wow bro, hold up," Maverick shouts, grabbing my shirt to pull me back.

"Get the fuck off me now, I need to go get her," I snap trying to twist his hand off me.

"Want to clue us in first? What if someone is there with her? This could be dangerous and you might not even be right," he snaps, and I know he's right, but I'm too concerned about getting to her more than anything else.

"I don't know how we missed it," I hiss out, again running my fingers through my hair, my scalp burning from when I pulled at it earlier. "She said in the video where she was. Whether she meant to or not, she said it. If she fucking did mean it then we have been sitting around here like clueless bastards all night."

"Said what, son?" Granddad says stepping closer.

"She said '*tell them what happened here was a lie.*' What happened *here*? Here, as in the Old Gunner house. That's what she was trying to tell us without letting Carl on to it. We need to go," I hiss out, getting ready to bulldoze my way through all of them if they don't move out of my fucking way.

"Right, I'll go with Mason," Evan speaks up. "Maverick you come with us and Malik stay with Harlow. You drive her so it doesn't look too suspicious. He'll know something's up if you let her go on her own."

"I wasn't planning on it," Mal grunts, looking at Evan like he's lost his mind.

"Let's go. Dad, my partner will be here any second to go over everything with you before you leave. Just make sure you all listen to him. If you fuck this up he'll only get off scot-free."

We rush out of the door, making a dash for the nearest car which just happens to be Evan's black Audi A4 S Line.

Posh git!

NINETEEN

DENNY

Another ten minutes passes before Carl actually leaves. I heard him arguing to either himself or to someone on the phone just before he left. It sounded more like it was to himself, because he was ranting on about no one answering their *'fucking phones'* (his words) anymore.

Hope the fucker gets run over by a lorry on his way over to meet Harlow.

I'd already managed to take stock of everything in the room when I first woke up, but it seems without the lighting over where I know Hannah is lying, there isn't much I can see now in the room. The place is dark, even with the beams of light streaming through the cracks in the floor above.

To the left of me where the piss bucket is still stinking the place out, not that the smell from Hannah is any better, I notice a metal pole sticking out of the wall. Maybe if I can reach it, I could use it to whack at the chains and break them. If it doesn't work then at least I can take Carl by surprise when he comes back and hit him over the head to buy me more time. Hopefully I'll hit him close enough to me so that when I knock him out I can still reach for the key. Not that I've seen him with one.

It's just one of my many wild guesses tonight.

Stretching my leg over, keeping my hands firmly placed on the wall for balance, I try to grab the metal pole with the toe of my foot. It's loose like I guessed, so I use all the strength I can to wiggle it back and forth to loosen it. It's difficult when it's only the toe part of my foot that can reach.

Finally it clatters to the floor, the sound echoing loudly in the small confided room. It's then I squeal jumping back.

"Oh my God, I want a holiday after this," I snap, looking frozen at the woodlice, worms and whatever creepy crawlies slithered out with that pole and onto my foot. Just my luck, the biggest part of the light is shining on bugs.

I hate woodlice; hate them with a freaking passion. My brother, Evan, he used to stomp on them and the noise, my word, that noise when he stomped on them was disgusting, and it made me wince every time. Do you know what I'm on about? That crunch when they press their big feet on them and you hear the woodlice back crunch? Yep, I hate that sound, really bad.

I'm not even going to mention the ants. I've tried to ignore those little fuckers as soon as I realised there were loads of them running around. How something so tiny can scare someone so much bigger is beyond me. It's not like they can eat me. It's just that they can get every-fuckin-where.

And this may or may not have something to do with the ant's nest I sat in when I went on a school trip. I'm just saying, ants and me don't have a good experience.

"Come on," I growl, trying to use the tip of my toe to roll the pole across, trying to avoid the crawlies, but all I manage to do is push the pole away a little. "Fucksake, please, if anyone can hear me, then please, for heaven's sake, get me that pole."

Not seeing any other option I slide onto the grubby mattress and slide myself as far as the chains will let me go towards the pole. Once my arm is pulled as far as it will go without popping my shoulder out, I use my left leg to get at the pole. My bare toe touches it and I want to squeal with delight, but then something crawls across my feet and I scream out.

I grit my teeth knowing it's either let a little ant or woodlice scare me or be murdered and God knows what else he has planned for me. There's no question, I need to be brave, suck it up, and get on with it so I can get out of here. Taking in a much needed breath, I push myself to move back into position.

"They can't hurt me, they can't eat me, and as soon as I have the pole all I have to do is shake my leg and they'll be gone," I grumble to myself.

My foot touches the cold, metal pole again and this time I manage to bring it towards me some more, making the strain on using my toes relax a little. I work it closer, and closer, till finally I get up out of my position, shake off my legs before brushing everything off with my hands, not wanting to miss a crafty crawly. There's bound to be one that sticks on through my shake. There always is.

Reaching down, I lean over and pick up the pole, hoping like hell I didn't just waste my time and strength getting it. Already I want to fall back to sleep, the little I got last night was not nearly long enough. Plus, I was freezing cold, being held hostage by a rapist and murderer and betrayed by my own mother.

All in one day.

Using all my strength I tug at the chains again, hoping to see some kind of weak link, but there isn't any. It's tightly bolted to the wall and as much as I need a spanner or screwdriver right now, I've only got a metal pole.

Giving up trying to weaken the chain, I begin to use my last resort and smack the metal pole against the chains bolted on the wall. I try to aim for where it's attached, but all it does is ricochet off the bolts, pain racing from my hand all the way up my arm from the harsh vibrations of the hit.

Not wanting to give up I try again and again. I try until my face is dripping with sweat, mixed in with tears and until all my strength is gone. Once all my energy is spent, I fall to my knees on the mattress facing the wall, shame and failure consuming me. I place a soothing hand on my stomach, silently telling my baby girl how much she means to me already and how much I love her father. He's the one person apart from her that I've ever truly loved, and I never got to say those words to him. I never got to tell him how much he means to me and that the only reason he hurt me the way he did was because I always felt like it was me pursuing him, and not the other way around. Just for once I wanted him to come on to me. Now I'll never get the chance. And if I did, I wouldn't care who started what or who chased who, just as long as I got to have him and my baby girl in my arms.

I sob against the wall, creepy crawlies be damned. I feel like my heart has been ripped out of my chest and someone, most likely Carl, is squeezing the life out of it. I don't want to die. I want to see my daughter grow up. I want to see her be born safely, and healthy, but it seems like it's not going to happen given the shitty circumstances.

I cry until my voice is hoarse and my sobs turn strangled, my chest heaving.

Then car tires crunch from outside and I begin to panic. The only plan I have is to hurt him enough that I knock him unconscious and get his keys.

My main priority is to get me and the baby safe, away from him and away from this building and the rancid smell of Hannah's body.

In a robotic daze I grab the metal pole and drag it in front of me, gripping it in one hand so tightly my knuckles turn white. With my other hand I lean it against the dirty wall to steady myself for when I need to strike.

Blood rushes to my ears along with panic, not able to hear anything past the buzzing. Footsteps sound above, more shouting. He's brought people with him. Will they help me? Will they help him? My mind is in overdrive and my panic turns into more sobs, tears clouding my vision. I can hear a voice shout my name from close behind, sounding frantic and panicked, or maybe I'm imagining these things and it's really just in anger.

All I know is that when I hear them moving closer, I find the strength to grab the pole tighter, and stand up, swinging wildly in front of me. If I'm going to die anyway, I'm not going to do it sitting down.

"Denny . . . Denny!" A voice roars sounding broken and strangled, and I have to blink back the tears pooling my eyes.

I gasp loudly, a loud sob roaring from my throat and I would have followed the metal pole falling to the floor had it not been for Mason catching me in his arms.

"Am I dreaming? Are you really here?" I ask, my heart praying like hell this is real.

"I'm here Angel, this is real and we're going to get you out of here," he says softly, tears falling from his own eyes. He tries to hide them, wiping them off with the back of his hands, but it's too late, I've seen them.

"We?" I ask in a small voice, desperate for a drink to soothe my sore throat.

"Yeah, we, darling," another voice says and I look up to find Maverick and . . ."Evan, what are you doing here?" I cry.

"Long story, sis, first, let's get you out of these chains, yeah?"

I nod my head, my arms flying around Mason's neck, my tears not drying for anyone. "You came for me. I didn't think you'd find me. I'm so sorry for walking out on you," I sob.

"Angel, please don't cry. I'll always find you. I'm never letting you go. Ever! Where you go, I go."

"Okay," I smile then watch as my brother rushes back down the stairs with bolt cutters.

"What the fuck is that smell?" Maverick grunts unhappily.

"Mason. You need to call the police."

"Why? What's wrong? We know who had you and we've got it covered, babe."

"No. The smell, it's . . . it's Hannah," I cry, sadly.

"Hannah?" Maverick asks confused, looking around the room.

"She's under there," I whisper. "He showed her to me," I tell them, never wanting to see that again. "Please don't uncover her. I can't take it."

The chain falls to the floor with a loud clang, and I feel the pressure lessening when my wrists are released. As soon as I'm free I lift my hand up to my chest, rubbing my wrist from where the chain cut into me.

"The police and ambulance are on their way," my brother tells us and I look at him confused.

"Why did mom want me dead, but not you?" I ask, and then feel bad about asking. "Shit! Not that I'd rather you be here, or for me to be here for that matter, but why just me?"

"I don't know sis," he sighs. "All I know is dad has some explaining to do when it comes to that woman."

I take in his hard face when he says woman, and I know I'm missing something important. I ignore it and finally move my legs, nearly falling from the weakness in them.

"Whoa, whoa, hold up there. Let's get you out of here. Here, let me help," Mason rushes out. He places my arm over his shoulder for me to lean my weight on him, and then continues to place his other arm around my waist to support me further. He slowly helps me over to the stairs and a feeling of relief and security monopolizes me.

"I'm so tired," I yawn as we hit the morning air outside.

"Are you hurt?" he asks moving to stand in front of me. He takes in my face and I know now that we're in the daylight he will see the bruises that are on my cheeks and face. Not only has Carl backhanded me, he's grabbed me, shoved me and even had a kick at my legs. I don't even want to go there and tell him I had to pee in front of him. The fact I managed to cover myself up doesn't seem important, it's the fact that he was still there, staring at me like I was on display.

"I'm fine."

"What about the baby? Is she okay?"

"I'd know if something was wrong, right? I mean, I haven't felt her move since earlier, but I haven't bled or had any pains," I tell him truthfully, but I'd still rather be checked over. Better to be safe than sorry.

The ambulance sirens echo across the field and I've never been so glad to be another step farther away from this place. When Mr. Gunner finds out about this I'm unsure what he'll do next. When Harlow got attacked by Davis he burnt the place to smithereens, but now that I've been attacked and kidnapped at the same place, along with a murder and rape, I'm unsure what he could possibly do next. I suppose only time will tell.

"She's my girlfriend; she was taken and has been down there with a dead body. She needs to see someone," he says to the paramedic. I'd been so focused on the burnt down building that I didn't even hear the ambulance come to a stop.

Just then Maverick rushes out of the building in time to throw up in the long, overgrown weeds.

"Shit!" I hear Mason whisper and when I turn to look up at him, he looks down at me with concerned eyes. I know immediately what he's thinking. If Maverick threw up over what he saw down in that basement, then what was it like for me? I wish I could reassure him that I'm fine, but I don't think I'll be fine again. Not really. My mind will always remember and imagine her lifeless, bloody body. Nothing will ever be able to wipe that image from my mind. Hopefully in time I will learn to cope, but I've not thought that far ahead.

I sway a little, Mason holding on to me tighter as Evan walks out of the building barking orders into his phone.

"Is he a police officer?" I ask Mason on a tired whisper, feeling my eyes droop.

"An undercover cop, babe."

The paramedic walks over to us, guiding Mason on where to take me. Once I'm lying down on the soft cot bed, I close my eyes feeling safe, ignoring the hushed whispers of Mason and Maverick before finally feeling the rumbles of the ambulance starting up.

WHEN I WAKE UP the smell of disinfectant hits my nose, the smell strong and I know I'm at the hospital. My body aches and I long to turn on my side, but then remember my bump sometimes prevents me from doing that. At home I've got a pillow that Mason bought me that tucks under my bump. He got it from Mother Care. I'm actually wishing he had brought it with him.

Opening my eyes, the first person I see is Mason. He's sitting next to the bed, his eyes still black from the dark circles surrounding them, and I know it's from lack of sleep.

"Hey," I croak, my throat still screaming out for water.

"Angel," he breathes and I notice his shoulders relax. "Are you okay?"

I nod my head. "Can I have some water? Is the baby okay? Did they get Carl?" I shiver, firing off loads of questions.

"Here you go," he says, bringing a cup of water with a straw up to my lips. I greedily drink it, but when Mason warns me to slow down, that I don't want to be sick, I reluctantly remove my lips from the straw. "The baby is fine. They don't need to do a scan, they checked for a heartbeat and it's strong and steady. And yes, I just got a call from Malik, they got him. They should be here any second," he tells me and that's when the door to my room flies open and everyone rushes in surrounding the bed.

"Oh my God Harlow, what happened to your face?" I ask, struggling to sit up. Mason notices and puffs the pillows up behind my back so that I'm sitting up. I'm still a little tired, I must not have slept long enough for my tired body to be satisfied.

"Carl," Malik growls, his face hard as he takes in the big, angry, purple, and red bruise swelling on Harlow's left cheek. Her face is all puffed out and my eyes start to water feeling guilty. She got hurt saving my ass. I didn't want anyone to get hurt.

"I'm so sorry," I whisper, feeling the first of many tears fall from my eyes.

"Hey, it's not your fault. He took me by surprise, but they got him. He's not going to be bothering us for a very long time," she tells me softly.

"What happened?" I ask, needing to know.

Harlow looks to Mason and gives him a look and when I look to Mason to see his expression he gives her a nod.

Weird!

"Your brother split us up into two groups. He, Mason and Maverick went for you, and Malik and I went to meet Carl."

"On your own, are you mad?" I shout, wincing when my throat protests.

"Calm down babe," Mason soothes, sitting next to me on the edge of the bed.

I nod my head then look over to Harlow, nodding my head for her to continue. "We met him at the fishing pond, the one on Green Day. I wrote a fake statement to keep up appearances, but someone moved in the bush nearby and set off alarm bells. We had both turned our heads in that direction so when I was turning my head back to see if he had caught the movement, a fist connected to my face. He ran off in the opposite direction from where the noise had come from, but he didn't get far before one of the other officers pinned him down on the ground. Everything is going to be fine. The hearing for Davis is in a few days, and according to the officer earlier, his sentencing will be a well-deserved one."

"That's great news," I tell her, happy that she's finally getting the justice she deserves, plus for Kayla too. Harlow wasn't the only person Davis hurt; only he hurt Kayla a lot more.

"Did the doctors say when you can come home?" she asks and I turn my head to Mason who shakes his head.

The door to my room opens again and my Nan, dad and brother walk in.

"Hi," I say, feeling more tears falling from my eyes again. Damn waterworks.

"I'm so glad you're okay," my Nan tells me crying, pushing through everyone to come up to my side, opposite Mason. I smile softly, and then give her a tight hug when she leans down.

"I didn't think I'd see any of you again," I tell her and the rest of the room when I pull away.

"It's over now; don't think like that," Mason growls and I look at him in concern. He's obviously not left my side, or even left to get himself a drink or even fall asleep. I've never seen him this worked up before.

"I know, but down in that basement, I honestly didn't think I would make it. I wished for so much when I was down there, and . . . "

"It's okay, shush," Mason whispers, putting his arm around my neck and rubbing circles on my shoulder blade as a few more silent tears fall down my cheeks.

"The police need your statement, sis. First, Dad, Nan and I would like to talk to you alone for five minutes. There is something you need to know," he tells me, and then looks over to Mason. "The doctor said she can go once she's ready. The nurse will be around shortly to take her drip out, and bring the discharge papers."

"Okay."

Everyone clears the room after giving me a huge hug, a pat on the leg before leaving, telling me they're going home to get some sleep. Mason refuses to leave the room, but looking at my brother he doesn't seem that surprised by it. I know whatever they are going to tell me is going to be bad, so I grab Mason's hand in a tight grip, needing some of his strength.

"I don't know if I should be the one to tell you," Evan says and my dad nods his head at him before looking down at the floor. "When I turned eighteen I looked into mom, Vivian. I knew the way she treated us wasn't right. She was always shoving me in your face, making you feel worthless, and I hated it. I also hated the way she would look at me and shit like that. I found out that she isn't my mother; she wasn't even my adopted mother. She was only my mother through marriage."

"Dad?" I speak after a few minutes of trying to absorb the information. When I look at him in the eyes they are filled with shame, and although words are unspoken, I know what Evan has just said is the truth. "How? Why? I don't understand," then a thought occurs to me. "You never mentioned Evan when we spoke in the cafe. I didn't even think anything of it. Why? What is happening?"

"Katie, the woman I loved, the woman your mom took away from me had a secret. When we first met at school we were sixteen, both in love, with our whole lives ahead of us. She went away for a year to an overseas school in France. It was a lie though. I didn't know that she was actually pregnant and her parents had her keep it quiet, that if I was told they would move her away from me. When she returned she acted different, I could feel it. I just presumed it was because she was missing her friends in France. I never questioned it. Years later your mother set her sights on me. She blackmailed Katie about the baby, and Katie being scared didn't want to ruin what we had. She thought I'd hate her, like your mother drummed into her. But I wouldn't have, I don't hate her. She left and I thought it was at first, but it seems your mother is more deviant than we gave her credit for."

"I don't understand," I whisper, running my hand over my stomach. "Why was she nice to him? How did he come to live with us? I'm so confused."

"Evan was six when his grandparent's died. He was still so young, but when he came to live with us I didn't even know who he was. I think she had it planned all along. I always wondered how she managed to get it processed so quickly, but I never questioned it. Once I got better after the accident and got to know the kid more, I loved him. He had something inside him that was impossible not to love.

"I think that was another cruel, twisted plot with your mother. She constantly favoured him and I always wondered why. Not that I thought more of you than him, I just presumed a mother would have more in common with her little girl.

"It wasn't until Evan had turned fifteen that I started to become more and more sure that he was mine somehow. I don't know if it was wishful thinking on my part or what, I just knew that something about him reminded me of Katie and myself. He went to school one day and I used his toothbrush to get a D.N.A. test done. When it came back and confirmed my suspicions, I treaded carefully with Vivian. She was so vindictive. She manipulated all of us, she used us against one another and I'm so sorry I never told you guys, but to me, nothing had changed. I am, and will always be your dad. Nothing Vivian could do could ever change that for me."

We're all quiet, our heads bowed, the only noise in the room is from one of the machines next to me, beeping.

"Why bully me though? Why? I don't understand?" I whisper, kind of jealous Evan doesn't have to share blood with the witch.

"Honestly? I don't know. I believe she thought I'd never find out about Evan or who he was. She used you as a pawn in her game. Never, and I mean never doubt that I had always planned to leave her once you were of age."

I nod my head not knowing what to say and exhaustion hits me once again.

"I think that's enough for one day," Mason tells them, looking at me with concern. My eyes close to prove a point. I need time to process everything they've just told me. I just didn't expect for exhaustion to overcome my body.

I wake up some time later, the sky outside darkening and a hot body sitting next to me. Opening my eyes, I find Mason sleeping next to me. He's in an awkward position when I look up at him, his head at a weird angle against the bed guard. His body is leaning against one of the five cushions on my bed and his one arm is wrapped around the back while the other is hanging loosely on my chest.

This is the first time I've seen him sleeping, one where I get a real good look at him without feeling embarrassed or caught staring. His full bow lips are puckered, hanging open a breath. His facial features are soft, relaxed and the hard edge that he usually carries is long gone. His eyes scrunch up in his sleep making me smile.

The door opening startles me and I'm glad to find it's only a nurse. My startled movements end up waking Mason up and the nurse looks at us apologetically.

"I'm sorry. I've come to remove your drip. When I came by earlier I found you both asleep," the middle aged nurse tells us with a smile. "You both looked so adorable and I was finishing my morning shift when you arrived and you were both so tired."

"Thank you," I croak out, my throat feeling dry.

My body feels grungy, my hair feels greasy, both in need of a good wash. Maybe two with the way I'm feeling at the moment, especially being in a clean, disinfected hospital.

"How are you feeling babe?" Mason asks groggily, rubbing sleep from his eyes and moving back into his chair.

"Okay. Ready for a shower and bed," I smile teasingly.

He laughs shaking his head before he turns his attention back to the nurse. "Are our family still here?"

"They came back a few hours ago. I told them I'd call them once you were awake, but if you'd like you can use the phone in reception to call them. You'll be free to go once I've done this and Denny's signed these forms," she informs us and for some reason, I feel at ease in her presence. After the bad experience I had when I was brought in after Harlow's attack, I promised myself never to step foot in one again unless really necessary. And although this is necessary the option has still been taken away from me. I hated it. The nurses all stuck their noses up at me. They were sharp tongued, disapproving towards me and just plain mean. I'd wanted to cry. I'd been so alone, on my own, without anyone who could sit by my bedside to tell me everything would be okay. They had me attached to a machine, monitoring the baby's heartbeat because of the fall I had taken and the knock to the head. Thankfully everything with the baby had been fine. Obviously.

"Can I? I haven't got my phone with me or my car, so I'll need to call for a lift."

"Honestly, just say Lorna sent you and they will be okay," she smiles to Mason.

"I'll be back in a minute," he says getting up from his chair, but he looks back down at me with his face scrunched up in concern. He doesn't want to leave me. I can understand. A part of me doesn't want him to leave either.

"Go, I'll be fine. Make sure you ask them to bring food, I'm star-ving," I sing, rubbing my large belly.

"I'll see what I can do," he chuckles before leaning down to give me a kiss on the head.

"Oh, he's such a looker," the woman grins at me.

"He is, isn't he," I grin back.

"I thought I was going to have to fight off all the other nurses at one point. They've been dying to come in and catch a glimpse of the young hottie all day, especially when they heard how protective he was of you when you first came in."

"Huh?" I ask, and then wince when she slides the IV out of my arm, the sting startling me.

"When you first came in he was funny with people around you. He kept asking us to be careful, to double check everything when we gave you the all clear. It was so sweet. In all my years of nursing I've never seen a man worried the way he was. It's rare, but rarer to find one his age that loves someone the way he does."

"I huh . . . I don't know what to say," I tell her completely dumbfounded.

"Nothing to say my lovely, just make sure you take care of each other. So many couples your age break up because they expect too much from the other person. They expect them to be who *they* want them to be and not who they are. With you and that young man, you can tell neither of you expect anything but being yourselves to each other."

"That's kind of poetic," I whisper.

"Nah, I think I read it in a magazine once," she teases giving me a wink. "The police still want to talk to you, but they left ages ago. I'm sure they'll get in touch soon enough."

Opening my mouth no words come out, my eyes and mouth flicker to the door, my heartbeat beating far too fast. When it's Mason that walks through my body visibly relaxes.

"Are you okay?" the nurse asks, keeping her voice down.

My eyes look over to her to see her looking over at me with concern and worry. I nod my head yes, not really sure. I'm fine physically, but mentally, I'm still waiting for Carl to jump out and try to take me again.

"Maverick is going to pick us up. He's nearly here."

"Already?" I ask shocked.

"Yeah, he was coming over to check in on us and to let us know Hannah's parents have been informed about her body, and that Carl has been arrested for murder, rape, kidnap, and some other charges. The list could go on."

"So he won't be out? There's no chance he can get bail and come and get me? Or go to court and have people after me again to stop me from being a witness?" I breathe out, my heart beating rapidly against my chest that it starts to hurt.

"No baby," he tells me, running his hand over my hair.

"Thank God," I tell him, and then feel my eyes water once again. "Sorry. God, my eyes are leaking again," I moan.

"It's okay. Little bit of tears never hurt anyone," the nurse tells us handing me a tissue. "I'm glad they have the bloke. I'm friends with Hannah's mother. She hasn't been to work for a while though and can't say I blame her. I wish you all the best," she tells me then looks over to Mason. "Look after her, you've got a special one here."

"I plan on it," he smiles, his eyes fixated on me.

"Good. I'll let you get changed in privacy. You can leave whenever you're ready."

"Thank you."

She nods her head giving us one more smile before leaving the room, leaving Mason and I alone.

"Your Nan and Dad brought you some spare clothes. You can shower now or you can wait until we get home. I already told Mav to tell everyone to go home, that you need to shower and rest."

"Hope they didn't take it badly," I cringe. "I honestly just want a shower, get all this grime off me and then have a relaxing bath."

"Then a shower and bath is what you shall have," he bows, making me giggle.

"I want it hot and with lots of bubbles," I grin.

Back at the house Maverick walks Mason and I up to our door. Turning around as Mason opens the door, I look up at Maverick.

"Thank you for being there for Mason," I whisper not able to look at him in the eye.

"Hey, I wasn't just there for, Mason, Denny. I was there because I wanted you home safe and sound. Don't ever think that just because you're carrying our niece that, that is the only reason we want you here with our brother. You're good for him. We love having you in our family. Please take care of yourself," he tells me, leaning in to give me a kiss on my forehead. Mason comes up behind me as another tear slips down my face.

"Come on; let's get you in the bath," Mason rumbles, nodding his head to his brother. Maverick gives me another soft smile and although we've not gotten to speak like I have with the others, I still feel like we've connected. I'm lucky to have been brought into the fold so quickly and so lovingly. I don't feel like a burden to them like I have my whole life with my mother and father.

I feel like things are finally going to change.

"Okay," I nod, giving Maverick a small smile before turning and heading inside. Mason talks to Maverick for a few more minutes while I make my way up the stairs, my feet carrying me right into the nursery. My eyes drift over to the cot as more tears spring to my eyes.

Strong arms wrap around me and I lean into his strength, loving that I got to have this chance.

"Want to talk about it?" he whispers.

"Mason, I was so scared. So freaking scared and the whole time all I could wonder was if I'd ever get to see you or our baby girl, would I be able to keep her safe. What if I had died, if he had killed me? You would have been sitting here saying goodbye to both of us," I choke out, finding it hard to breathe.

"Baby, there is nothing that would have stopped me looking for you. I'm just sorry I didn't find you sooner. Sorrier than you'll ever realise, Angel. You and our girl mean the world to me."

"You both mean the world to me too," I tell him, turning my head to look at him. "When I was down there I realised we haven't even spoke about girl names. I sat there and I realised if I died our baby wouldn't have a name. We could have died and you wouldn't have had a name on her grave," I cry, turning and using Mason to lean on.

"Hey, please don't Denny. Please, don't ever think like that."

"What do you think of Hope?"

"Hope as in . . . "

"A name," I smile. "It's all I had to hold on to when I was locked up. Either that or Faith, but for some reason, throughout the whole pregnancy I've seemed to grip onto hope like a lifeline. Hope that everything turns out okay, hope that you will be okay with the pregnancy, and hope the baby will be okay."

"Hope," he says, testing the name on his tongue. "Hope . . . I like it. Hope Sophia Carter," he grins.

"Sophia? You aren't naming our daughter after the girl you lost your virginity to are you?" I tease.

He rolls his eyes not pleased by my sarcastic comment. "No. It's my Nan's name."

A giggle escapes before I can muffle it with my hand. He looks so cute when he's trying to be serious. His lips do that twitch thing and I want to groan and bite his lip at the same time.

I yawn and Mason rolls his eyes again and I want to say his face will stick like that if he keeps doing it, but I'm too tired and really do need a bath. I can still smell the basement on me. The thought makes me stifle a shiver.

"Bath, I've already got it running," he says, leaning down to shove his face into my neck. "God, I'm so happy you're home."

"Me too," once again becoming emotional.

The shower did me the world of good and I felt fresh once I had finished up, but getting in the bath is just pure heaven.

Mason leans on the side with a washcloth, cleaning my back and I blush knowing he's seeing me naked with the light on. He accidently knocks a bruise I sustained from being with Carl and I wince slightly.

"Fuck! Did I hurt you?"

"It's okay, just a little bruise. Why don't you join me?"

"Um . . . in the bath?" he asks swallowing hard.

"No . . . on the toilet," I tell him dryly, nearly laughing when his face turns to horror. "Of course I meant the bath."

"Okay . . . yeah, I can do that. Scoot forward."

I scoot forward a little making sure to cover my breasts under the soapy water and wait for Mason to strip out of his clothes.

His t-shirt is first, his ripped stomach coming into view and making my mouth go dry. When his hands go to his jeans button I have to squeeze my legs together. The movement was quick and I didn't predict the water sloshing everywhere making Mason chuckle. I look at him sheepishly, not able to admit why I just nearly lost half the bath water.

The trousers slip from his muscled legs, his calves tightening and my whole body tenses up, the arousal turns thick in the air. Then his thick member comes into view and I find myself staring in open shock, my mouth hanging half open.

He steps into the bath behind me, the hairs on his legs brushing against my sides. He slides down behind me, reaching around me to pull me against his bare front, his now hard erection pressing against me and it has me gasping.

"Relax," he whispers, his voice hoarse and husky. I do as he asks and relax into him and watch his hands in fascination as he picks the washcloth back up and starts cleaning over my bump, skimming lightly over my breasts. The simple touch has me arching my breasts towards his hands, and my eyes clench shut and

I stifle a moan.

The sponge disappears and is replaced by his rough hands. His hands cup my ample breasts, my body humming in anticipation. But then his fingers graze and rub at my hardened nipples.

"Hmmm," I moan arching into his touch.

"Shush, I got you."

As much as I trust his word, I know he's going to torture me slowly and right now I need him, I need this, now.

"Please," I beg, not feeling an ounce of shame.

His fingers slide down my stomach and my legs open on their own accord. His fingers brush through the little speck of hair between my legs. My gut reaction is to close my legs, to be embarrassed that I haven't been able to wax between my legs in a while. I dread to think what it looks like down there. Trust me, there have been perks to the pregnancy, one being gifted with a growing life in my stomach and the huge boobs, but it also comes with cons, the swollen feet, not being able to bend down to see your toes, and another, not being able to shave.

Oh and let's not knock out the worst one. Coffee. You can't drink coffee. It sucks balls.

Speaking of balls.

His fingers rub over my clit and I moan loudly, the sound echoing in the small bathroom and I arch again, this time rubbing myself against his hard erection.

When he inserts two of his fingers I know I'm not going to last long. The feeling is so good that I can't keep still. My legs quiver and tighten and my whole body heats up and shakes.

His skilled fingers don't stop their probing and neither does my body rubbing against him, his rock hard erection getting harder behind me.

My orgasm hits me by surprise, my cries of pleasure filling the bathroom and I turn my head to the side, resting it against Mason's shoulder and lean up to give him a soft kiss.

"Let's get you dry," he grins.

I nod my head lazily and grin back at him. We get out of the bath and my eyes glue to Mason as he dries himself before coming over to dry me. The white fluffy towel does nothing to cease my arousal. When he dries between my legs wetness coats between them and I bite my lip from moaning.

Heading into the bedroom wrapped in the towel I turn to Mason, needing to keep being brave like I promised I would be down in that basement. Dropping the towel from my body Mason freezes, his eyes glued to my body with so much desire, the lust burning in his eyes. I know he wants me; I can feel it and see the evidence currently pointing proud and hard towards me.

Yep, definitely aroused!

"Make love to me," I tell him, nearly cringing at my own choice of words. Even so, it still sounds better than 'Please fuck me' or 'have sex with me' that's for sure.

"W-what? But you just got out of the hospital," he curses looking pained.

"No Mason, don't do this," I beg him, stepping closer towards him. "I know you want me, so why do you always push me away? You can touch me, but whenever it goes any further you push me away."

He looks pained and he takes a hesitant step forward. "Denny, I don't want to have sex with you because-"

"Oh my God, you really don't find me attractive," I cry, bending down to grab the towel, thankfully not struggling on my way up. Covering myself, I look up at him through my watery eyes.

"No, no Babe, it's not like that. I'm scared. I'm scared that I'll hurt you and the baby."

"What? I don't understand," I tell him confused, my body relaxing somewhat.

He groans looking to the ceiling before his head drops, his eyes focusing on mine. "I'm scared that I'll ruin what we have by having sex with you again. Look at what happened the first time Denny? I got so scared, and panicked that I would turn into the one person I always promised myself that I would never become. I can't risk losing you again; it nearly killed me the first time. Then there's the whole baby topic. Can we even have sex?" he rambles, pacing back and forth with his hands flying around. "We've never talked about it and it's not like I can ask anyone or Google that shit. The boy's would have a field day if they looked at the laptops history. What if I poke her Denny? What if I give her brain damage, which I could? I read that their head at this stage is positioned downwards."

"Take a deep breath. One, you can't hurt the baby, I asked the midwife the day after we got intimate. Secondly, do you really think you're that monstrous that you'd do that kind of damage?"

He looks down at his dick in a 'what do you think' look and I giggle loudly. He snaps his head up giving me a glare before he sighs looking defeated. I take the first steps towards him knowing I need to make the next step clearer, after all it's me taking the biggest risk here giving him my heart.

"And as for the first topic you brought up, you could never hurt me again, you know too well what it feels like to not have me. As for me, I'm big enough to make my own decisions. I want you Mason, I've always wanted you, but you need to start putting some faith in yourself. How will we ever work if you're always second guessing yourself? If you feel that strongly towards me then you wouldn't second guess yourself so much over hurting me. If you cared the way you say you do then you would know yourself you'd never intentionally do that to me. I love you Mason, I love you so goddamn much, but if you don't make love to me right fucking now I'm never going to forgive you or let you touch me sexually again," I growl causing his eyes to raise.

"You love me?" he whispers looking completely surprised. "After everything I did?"

"Yes you big doofus."

He picks me up scaring me and I let out a loud giggle as he swings me around. When he puts me down he has to keep a hold of my waist, my head dizzy from him spinning me. He reaches down and grabs my face in his hands and kisses me forcefully for a minute. Just as I'm getting more into it, he pulls away breathing hard, staring right into my eyes to my soul.

"I love you Denny. I've loved you for a long time, I've just been too much of a coward to admit it," he says and my eyes water again. He doesn't let me absorb his cherished words, he picks me up and immediately I have to put my arms around his neck.

He places one knee on the bed before laying me down on my back, his hard, rugged body looming over me.

"Tell me again," he whispers.

"I love you."

"I love you too Angel," he tells me before reaching down and taking my lips against his.

TWENTY

MASON

MY BODY LOOMS over hers, settling between her legs, and even pregnant she's still tiny and fragile looking. I make sure to keep pressure off her belly, not wanting to hurt either her or the baby. She tastes so fucking good. I can't get enough of her kisses. I groan into the kiss, my dick painfully hard still covered in the flimsy towel. Denny lost hers in the madness of me spinning her around. Feeling her skin on mine is a pleasurable feeling, one I'll never get enough of.

God her skin is so fucking soft. It's like feeling silk teasing the rough pads of my fingers and the feel has me groaning again.

"Please, inside me now," she begs and I swear I'm about to cum before I've even entered her.

"Fuck, Babe, you feel so good," I groan into her neck, raining kisses down to her breasts before taking one of her erect nipples into my mouth.

God, I love it when she moans, when her body withers beneath mine. I flick my tongue across her taunt nipple, her back arching and bringing her breasts closer towards me. I scrape my teeth, bringing her more pleasure and I groan when she runs her fingers through my hair, pulling at the ends.

"Goddamn-it Mason, please, now."

Her pleading voice undoes me; I lift myself up her body at the same time hers drift down my chest, her fingers flicking the towel open. An animalistic groan escapes my mouth when my dick falls with a slap against her sex.

Denny reaches between us surprising the shit out of me, my body jumping when her hand wraps around my hard length and poises it at her entrance. Without much thought I press my hips forward, the tip entering her wetness painfully slow. She's so tight, so wet and warm that I have to grit my teeth together to stop me shooting my load.

The heels of her feet dig into my ass and before I can stop her she pushes me into her in one painful stroke. Holding her one hand in mine and pinning it to the bed, I use my other to hold her hip down to stop her movements. If she moves right now I'm most likely to shoot my load and I want to ride out this pleasure as long as possible.

"Please don't move," I grit out, finding it hard to keep my calm.

Her body struggles beneath me and I groan, loving the feel of her muscles clenching around my dick.

Once I've gained a bit more control I pull out before sliding all the way back in to the hilt. Her mouth opens slightly, and I look down mesmerized by how beautiful she is. No one could ever compare to her. Ever.

"More," she moans when I pull back out before slamming back in with a little more force, not wanting to hurt her.

She wiggles her hand beneath me as I keep my thrusts at a safe pace, the feeling is the most erotic feeling I've ever felt and I can feel my balls tighten in anticipation.

"Harder, please harder," she begs, her teeth sinking into my shoulder and my control all but snaps and I slam myself harder inside her, her muscles contracting around my dick.

Her hands reach down my body, the feel of her soft touch against my burning skin has a shiver running up my back. My dick throbs when she places her hands on my hips and pulls me into her, the thrust causing us to both cry out. My movements quicken and I can feel her driving closer and closer towards her climax, her walls tightening around me.

"Oh my . . . I'm going to . . . " she doesn't get to finish her words, her back arches, her eyes close tightly and she cries out her orgasm. My orgasm hits me just as quickly and my body collapses against her, but I still manage to find the energy to keep any pressure from off her.

We're both breathing heavily by the time we ride through the waves of our orgasms.

"Was I too rough?" I breathe out moving to the side and bringing her naked body with me.

"What? God no! That was . . . that was amazing," she grins lazily, her eyes half open with a content, pleased, satisfied look on her face.

"Good," I smile and move up so I can grab the towel to clean up, first myself then Denny. Once I'm finished I chuck the towel behind me onto the floor and grab Denny's hips and bring her back to my front.

"Do you want to talk about what happened?" I ask gently, still unsure on what happened down in that fucking basement. Just remembering her being taken is making every muscle in my body tense and for the anger to simmer back to the surface.

"Not a lot to say. My mom set me up. When I was out I bumped into her and it didn't go so well. She wanted me dead Mason. My own mother wanted me dead," she whispers, and from the tone in her voice it sounds like she's still struggling to come to terms with what happened with her mom.

"She doesn't deserve the title of *mom*, Denny. What she did is unthinkable. I know what it's like having a shitty parent, but I had my brothers and Granddad, and hopefully in time that will be enough for you to fill the void that she's left," I tell her gently, hoping I'm not being too presumptuous.

"You're right, I know you are. I guess it will just take time. When I think of Hope, the thought of ever doing what my mother did to me is just unthinkable. I'd rather kill myself before I hurt her."

"You're too good of a person to even contemplate doing that, baby."

"Hhum," she mumbles sounding tired and drowsy.

"Sleep. We'll figure the rest out tomorrow."

I feel her weak nod and smile to myself. This time yesterday I was smashing up the kitchen freaking out over whether we'd find her or not.

Speaking of kitchen I was glad to hear everyone stepped in to help get it cleaned up. The only thing I'll need to do is replace a few cabinets and the kitchen door I punched a hole through. I'm just praying Denny will understand why they are wrecked.

Closing my eyes I let the exhaustion of the past twenty four hours consume me and drift off to sleep with the love of my life snuggled safely against my chest.

Later I'm woken up by a blood curling scream that startles me from my sleep and I fly up in a sitting position when I see Denny hunched over screaming in pain.

Fuck no!

"Denny? Denny? What's wrong? Is it the baby? Did you have a nightmare?" I panic; my hand flying to her shoulder. Fuck, I'm shit in a crisis. My palms are already sweating and my leg is twitching from nerves.

"The bab- ARGGHHHHHHHHHH," she screams and I jump from the bed to turn the main light on.

"What's happening? What shall I do? Fuck! It's not time," I shout, grabbing my phone that's on charge by the bed side table.

"H-hello," a male voice croaks.

"Max, get your ass over here. Something is wrong with the baby," I yell through the phone, really wanting to do something as I sit in front of Denny, her breathing becoming laboured and heavy.

"What? Shit. Be there in two," he shouts disconnecting.

"You. Called. Your. Brother," Denny breathes shooting me a glare as she holds her stomach. Sweat is pouring across her forehead and down her neck. Her hair is sticking to her face and I reach out to move it across as she catches her breath. "And Max. Out of. All your brothers," she pants out between breaths.

"I'm sorry, I'll call Mav. I don't know what to do," I shout, not meaning to yell. "Shit. I'm sorry, I didn't mean to shout."

The door downstairs bangs open and a herd of footsteps stomp up the stairs. Thank God Max thought to call Maverick.

"ARRGGGGGGHHHHHH, MASON," she screams. Her face turns bright red and angry looking and I stand up taking a step back. Shit, what did I do? "We need a doctor, a hospital." She speaks so fast I can barely understand her. Max and my other brothers rush into the room and that's when I realise we're both naked. I quickly shove the blanket over Denny covering her up. When she goes to complain I grab her shoulders and lean in closer to her to whisper.

"You're naked. Let me get you a t-shirt."

She nods her head panting and I hold my hands up to my brothers to wait a minute and to turn around which they all comply. I rush over to the chest of drawers and grab a clean t-shirt of mine and then a pair of her knickers and joggers.

"We need to get you to the hospital," I tell her softly, hoping the panic isn't too evident in my voice. The baby isn't due for over seven weeks. It's too soon. Something's wrong and I know I need to be strong for her, which is what I will do. For her I'd do just about anything.

"Denny, you need to breathe," Max says once I've dressed her and she's sitting on the edge of the bed.

"I am breathing Max," she pants out through gritted teeth.

"You're doing it wrong. It's, hee hee hoo." He shows her how to take in quick breaths and if I wasn't shitting myself over her being in so much pain, I'd laugh at how ridiculous he looks right now.

"Fuck-sake Max, shut the fuck up and will someone get my stuff together. NOW!"

Shit! I rush out of the room to the nursery, grabbing Hope's hospital bag I packed at the beginning of the week. I made a list for other items, but I know I've got the essentials we'll need in here. Once I reach it, I run back into the bedroom, shocked when I find Myles rubbing Denny's lower back, Maverick holding her up so she's standing and Max . . . I'm not sure what Max is doing, but it sure doesn't look like it's relaxing Denny if her pissed off, angry glare has anything to say about it.

"I need fucking drugs Max. Drugs that will knock me out, that will stop this from hurting so . . . argghhhhhh. . . . goddamn much," Denny screams again.

"Not to point out the obvious love, but in your condition turning to drugs isn't wise, Denny. It's not going to change anything, or make life better. You'll get through this."

"I swear to God Max, if you don't get out of my fucking face. . . . Arrrgggghhh MASON!"

"Fine. I'm only trying to help," Max snaps stepping back. "Just didn't want the mother of my niece being a druggy," he mutters.

"Druggy? Someone get him out of my face right now."

I ignore them and grab her hospital bag, hoping like hell I've got enough for her as I shove some clothes in for her. We hadn't gotten around to ticking off the checklist, but with her screams of pain getting louder and seeming stronger, I need to hurry up. Her notes she takes to her midwife sit on the side in a folder, so I quickly grab a hold of those, shoving them into the bag before moving over to Denny.

"I'm ready. Come on." Taking her hand we walk slowly out of the room before she collapses in pain again, her screams echoing around the room.

"Denny . . . what can I do? I don't know what to do," I tell her hysterically, my chest aching at seeing her in pain and not being able to do anything about it.

Making my mind up, I chuck the bags at Max and Myles then bend down and scoop up Denny in my arms. She cries out, but still manages to wrap her cold hands around my neck, clinging onto me tightly.

"It's going to be okay baby," I tell her into her hair. When we get to the front door, Maverick runs ahead to open the door, his phone to his ear talking to who I presume is her Nan or dad.

"Please no," I beg closing my eyes before looking down at Denny who is staring at me with wide horrified eyes.

"Bro, has she pissed on you?" Max snickers, as Harlow and Malik coming running up the path.

"*She* has a name and is in labour. Now move, Mason, NOW!" she screams as another contraction hits her. Well, I'm presuming that's what they are, but I'm still a little unsure with the whole 'it's too early' matter.

"Why are you still here?" Harlow asks us out of breath.

"I've been asking the same thing," Denny cries out.

"She pissed on Mase," Max chuckles.

"That was my fucking waters breaking, you asshole," Denny cries out before another blood curdling scream rips from her throat.

We move quickly through the garden and down the side of the house onto the street and get Denny into the back of my car.

"I'll drive," Maverick yells out as I jump into the back with Denny. She grabs onto my now soaked t-shirt and screams into my chest.

The midwives rushed Denny through the maternity ward doors not long after arriving at the hospital. Maverick went to park the car after dropping us off at the entrance.

"How far along are her contractions?" one of the midwives ask as they start prepping her.

"Close," I tell her quickly before attending back to Denny, wiping the hair out of her eyes.

The nurse looks at me for a second longer, I can feel her stare on the side of my head like she's waiting for me to say something more. I turn giving her a funny look, but then ignore her as another scream rips from Denny. The sound of it pierces through my heart.

"Give me something to stop the pain. No one told me it would hurt this much," she cries again her screams piercing through the air.

"Put this in your mouth and suck in deep when another pain is coming," the midwife tells her and I look at the offending object horrified. Could she have worded that any dirtier? I'll have to remember to use that line when she's recovered after having the baby.

"She still has over seven weeks of her pregnancy to go. Hope shouldn't be coming yet," I tell her worried.

"Let's see what's happening," she says. The rest falls on deaf ears as I'm completely frozen watching Denny removing her joggers and knickers from her body, a body I had only a few hours ago embedded deep inside. The nurse's head disappears between her legs and I all but cringe at the sight. When Denny hisses out a startled breath, I finally let go of the breath I'd been holding.

"What the hell is this place?" I all but yell pulling at my hair.

"Excuse me?" the other midwife asks, lifting her head from where she's standing on the opposite side of the bed. She's an older nurse, one that looks like she's been doing this job for far too long. I'm just glad she has someone experienced helping her.

"It's fine," I dismiss, waving her off, not coping so well with the labour. I don't even know which is left or right at the minute I'm that worried with what's going on.

The sound of her screams will haunt my nightmares for the rest of my life and with everything that has happened over the past twenty four hours, nothing could have prepared me for this. I thought I had another seven weeks to prepare, but no, as fate would have it, they decided to fuck me over.

"Oh, it seems you're ready to push Denny. Can you try on your next contraction for me?" the nurse between her legs says and I look down completely blown away by what I see and I have to cling to the bed to stop myself from swaying. Denny sees the look on my face and starts to sit up.

"What? What's wrong?" she asks panicked.

"Nothing, nothing calm down. I guess I wasn't prepared."

"You've seen it before Mason, now talk," she snaps. Even pissed, bright red, and sweaty as hell she is still without a doubt the most beautiful woman in the world.

"It just looks sore down there is all, and I don't mean from when we . . . um . . . you know," I tell her, leaning in to whisper the last part so the midwives don't hear us.

Twenty minutes of excruciating pushing and I'm ready to pass out. God it hurts, it hurts so much I'm actually willing to bet I've been put off having sex for the rest of my life.

"I NEED DRUGS," I shout when another contractions hits Denny. Her body is weakening, but it hasn't stopped her from screaming out bloody murder every time the urge to push comes. Without thinking I rip the gas and air the midwife gave her when we first arrived out of her mouth and into my own. The first suck of the stuff and I feel on cloud nine. Shit this stuff is good.

"I can see a head," the nurse calls up from between Denny's legs and I start sucking the life out of the gas and air until Denny snatches it back from out of my hand.

"Arrrggghhhhh," she cries from the back of her throat, her head into her chest and her knees up as she pushes again.

Once it's over, her body relaxes back on the bed, her breathing heavy and tears falling down her face. I had gotten her a cool washcloth not long ago, and I wipe her forehead trying to cool her down.

"I should have used a bigger vibrator," she cries drugged up. "It hurts. I should have gotten one of those over the top thick ones. Mason, I hate you. I really hate you. You did this," she screams just as another contraction comes and she starts to push.

Jesus Christ! I can't take much more of this.

"That's it Denny, keep going, just a little harder, come on . . . that's it, one more," the midwife encourages. "Dad would you like to come and see?"

I look at her confused, wondering what she's going on about, but then as I walk down the end of the bed I nearly pass out. I go dizzy and grip the bed for support with my eyes clenched shut.

"What? What's going on? What are you looking at Mason?" Denny yells at me before bursting into tears. "You don't love me. You don't find me attractive," she whines crying. "I knew you would leave me. Don't leave me Mason."

"I'm not leaving you, baby," I tell her, tears in my own eyes from seeing my girls head being born. "You need to give us one last push, Denny. You need to be strong okay?"

She nods her head as another contraction begins and her face turns a bright shade of red and purple. It's that bright I start to panic she's going to pass out, but then I look down between her legs, which was half a mistake because it gave Denny the chance to grab my sore hand again.

After ten minutes into her pushing I learnt not to give her my hand, but words of encouragement. She nearly broke it, and if it wasn't for the one midwife taking a look at my hand I would still be complaining it was broken, it throbs that much. So when I feel her fingers grip around my hand in a strong, tight squeeze I howl in pain.

"MASON," she yells the same time I shout, "DENNY."

Then the whole room erupts in a baby's cry and my whole world stops. I snap my head over to the midwife to find her holding Hope.

My baby girl.

She walks over to Denny keeping the baby in one hand as she lifts the flimsy nighty we changed Denny into over her head, placing the baby on Denny's bare chest. My eyes don't move from Hope, not even when the midwife starts to speak.

"Mason?" Denny calls snapping me out of it. Her voice is tired and soft and I know she's feeling just the same as I am, if not more.

"Sorry?" I ask, wiping my face and feeling wetness coating my cheeks.

"Do you want to cut the cord?" the midwife asks again and I nod my head, my throat clogged up with a ball of emotion.

I grab the scissors she gives me and cut into the rubbery umbilical cord. Hope gives another loud cry, her lungs obviously in good working condition.

"Look what you did," I whisper amazed to Denny.

"What we did," she whispers back, her eyes still filling with more tears.

"I love you," I tell her, leaning into give Denny a kiss on the forehead, then down to do the same to Hope. Her little fists fly out, followed by her chubby little feet. More tears fall from my eyes as I take everything in about her. She's got a cute little podgy belly, and little button squashed nose and has a head of fair hair, obviously taking after her mother. I can't tell who she looks like the most because to me, she looks like Hope Sophia Carter. I can't see yet what colour her eyes are because they are too dark to be able to tell.

"I love you too," she chokes out, then leans up as I meet her halfway down to give her another kiss.

The midwife walks up explaining she needs to weigh the baby and check her over, so I stay by Denny's side knowing Hope is in good hands.

When Denny turns tiredly to look at me, her smile lights up my world, she truly is the most beautiful woman I have ever had the pleasure of being with.

"Thank you. Thank you for never giving up on her or us and for giving me another chance Denny. Without you in my life I don't know what I'd do. I know I completely fuc- screwed things up in the past, but I promise you with all my heart I will try everyday to be the man you deserve. You and Hope mean everything to me and nothing or no one will ever come between that. I can't picture spending my life without either of you in it."

"Mason I-"

"Let me finish," I stop her, watching tears fall from her eyes as she watches me. "I love you. I love you so goddamn much, and being without you for all those months destroyed a part of me I thought I'd never get back, but then you came home and I knew, even before then, that I had to find a way to get you to trust me again, because there was no way I could spend another day without you. You've always been mine, but now I want to show you how much I am yours. Denny Smith, will you marry me?" I ask, and then pull out the loose ring I quickly grabbed before we left the house. I didn't bring the box; scared someone would notice it and ask questions.

"Are you serious?" she asks looking at me wide eyed in shock.

The midwife brings Hope back over interrupting us, but it's the best interruption I've ever seen when she places Hope back in her mother's arms. Denny looks down at Hope, stroking her finger across Hope's cheek.

"Denny, I'm serious. Hope is going to have my last name, and so will you," I tell her, holding the ring out again, my heart beating wildly in fear she will turn me down. I don't think I could handle the rejection right now with all my emotions up in the air.

"Are you asking because I just gave birth or because you love me?" she asks taking me off guard. I sit on the bed, my finger running along Hope's cheek, the same way Denny was doing, liking the fact her eyes flutter closed.

God she's already beautiful.

Looking back up at Denny, I give her a sheepish smile, not sure how she's going to take all of this. "I bought the ring for you four months ago," I tell her honestly.

"But that was . . . that was when we . . . " too lost for words she gives up and I send her a grin.

"I know. I've still got the receipt somewhere at the office to prove it too. I wanted the moment to be perfect and I honestly don't think there is a better moment than this," I tell her, feeling my eyes water again.

"Yes."

"Yes?" I ask confused. Is she saying what I think she's saying?

"Yes, I'll marry you," she smiles giggling. "I love you Mason; I want to spend the rest of my life with you."

She doesn't get to continue her sentence; I cut her off by putting my lips on hers. When she gasps I take the opportunity to slide my tongue into her mouth, the sweet taste making me groan. When a loud cry echo's around the room, we pull away slowly and look down at Hope with gentle faces.

"Would you like me to take a photo of you three?" the midwife who delivered Hope asks, now finished with her notes.

"Yes," I tell her the same time Denny groans. "I look a mess."

"Trust me sweetie, in a few years' time you will look back on this moment and wonder why you cared. You'll want to remember this," she gestures to the room and Hope. "as it is now. Not something you changed by looking good," she smiles and Denny smiles back at her.

"You're right, I don't care how I look," she says while looking down in awe at Hope.

"Do you have a camera or phone?" she asks holding her hand out.

"Oh, we have a camera in the bag, hold on," I tell her and rush over to the bag and grab the camera. Once I've shown her what to do, I look down at both my girls with a huge smile on my face. The camera goes off making me jump.

"Hey, I wasn't ready," I mumble.

"No . . . maybe not, but that picture was just too precious," the midwife smiles, her smile reminding me of my Nan's. It's kind and gentle. "Now shift in closer," she advises us.

Denny scoots over a little, giving me space to place my ass on the bed, and then she shifts Hope so she's somewhat between us, our heads bent together. Before the picture is taken I turn my head over to Denny, who does the same when she feels me shift.

"I love you so much, Mrs. Carter," I grin, liking the sound of her soon-to-be new name.

"I love you too," she says, her eyes soft with love shining through her eyes. Then we both turn our heads, both wearing huge grins on our faces as the flash clicks.

EPILOGUE

DENNY

THREE WEEKS OF being at home and you would have thought everyone would have gotten used to there being a baby around the house. But no! Max comes round hourly, if not more to come see his favourite niece. Myles comes by daily, not wanting to become a pest like his twin brother and Malik and Maverick come between working.

Harlow has been here the most helping out. After having stitches after giving birth, I was finding it hard to manoeuvre around the house. It also meant she missed out on going to the court hearing, but thankfully her lawyer called when it was over and told her that Davis got fifteen years in prison and was found guilty on all charges.

We also found out that his brother Carl would be in prison for life, not ever having the chance to get out on parole, because when they tried transferring him from one precinct to another, he caused problems, attacking one of the guards who ended up dead. The list of crimes he had been charged with just kept getting added along the way.

I'm just glad I won't have to attend court. I'm not ready to leave my baby girl, especially since they let my mom off with a warning. She's meant to have left, but I don't trust the woman as far as I could throw her. My Nan has even hired some private investigator to try and find her. As soon as she knows where the wicked witch of the west left to, she will have her checked on regularly, wanting to know where she is at all times, so that if she does show signs of returning we will have a heads up.

Mason . . . now Mason on the other hand has shocked the hell out of me since I gave birth to Hope three weeks ago. I never expected him to be so hands on. When I first came home I was still recovering, and he offered, well jumped at the chance to do night feedings every time Hope woke up. I could understand his need to do this; I wanted to be around her all the time too, even if it meant just holding her sleeping in my arms. But Mason, he jumps up ready when she needs her nappy changed, or if she stirs.

Like earlier, he had been leaving to go check in on the club and ended up being an hour late because every time he got to the door he swore he could hear her. She never made a peep, I should know, she was in her moses basket right next to me. He left after I threatened him with bathing Hope by myself tonight. Don't get me wrong, I felt his anxiety; I didn't like the thought of leaving Hope for a second, let alone for a few hours to go to work, so I never gave him too much shit.

Now he's back and brought Maverick and Myles with him. Max was already here trying to get me to give in and let him hold her.

"Max, I just got her to go to sleep, wait until she wakes up then you can hold her," I scold, feeling like I'm telling him off like a mother would, and every day the feeling increases.

"She's right. For some reason Hope was hard to settle down last night and she needs her sleep," Mason pipes in, walking into the room looking D.E.L.I.C.I.O.U.S as hell in his black work shirt and his tight ass hugging jeans with his black shoes. My God I love him in a shirt. Especially when he has his shirt sleeves rolled up to his forearms and has the top three buttons undone showing off his hard chest. The veins in his muscled arms show when he lifts the moses basket off the floor from where Max had moved her and I have to discreetly wipe my mouth to make sure I didn't drool. Ever since the night we had sex it's been all I can think about. When the doctors told me we couldn't have sex for a long time, I nearly cried.

"Hey, if I can't hold her then leave her there so she knows I'm here," Max whines watching Mason move Hope back on her stand. He moved Hope when he first arrived and I scolded him for trying to pick her up. So instead of picking her up he picked up the moses basket and carried her over to the armchair, placing the basket on the floor by his feet so he can stare at her.

"I doubt she thinks you leave," Myles mutters chuckling.

"You're just jealous that I'm the best uncle," Max throws back.

I shake my head at their antics, knowing exactly how this will play out. They've been doing it since the day she was born and my ears can't take any more.

"Well it's lucky she's got a mommy and daddy she loves a lot more," I rub in, hoping to shut Max up for a little bit. He just scoffs rolling his eyes, when the front door knocks.

"I'll get it," Maverick speaks up, getting up off the side of the sofa from where he was looking down smiling at Hope.

He leaves and a second later returns with a frantic looking Joan. She breathes heavily as she comes in and kneels on the floor in front of where I'm lying down relaxing on the sofa, after only have two hours sleep last night.

"I'm so sorry," she whispers, her eyes watering and her eyes filled with guilt.

"What are you sorry for?" I ask, looking at her confused. I'm struggling to figure out what she has done to warrant an apology.

"I'm the reason for all of this. For all of your troubles and why you left."

"Joan, what are you talking about?" I ask her again, sitting up a little but keeping my legs tucked under me.

"I'm the reason Hope is here today," she gasps.

"I'm pretty sure you're not Joan," Mason grunts.

"Kinky," Max mutters chuckling and earning a slap and a glare from Mason and I.

"Joan, get to the point, you've kind of got me worried."

"Denny, for you to understand I need to go back to the beginning a little. A few years ago Max and Mason were at the worst with their hoochie ways, so Mark and I decided to teach them a lesson and we went with Max first because he was the youngest and could be helped the quickest. We knew Mason would need more work," she says dryly, looking at him with disgust making me bite back a smile.

"And?"

"And it worked. But I'm so sorry. If I knew the simpleton wouldn't have thrown them away, I would have done so myself," she says giving Max a death glare.

"What are you talking about Joan; we're going to be here all day at this rate? Hope needs her sleep," Max tells her dryly, obviously not liking where the conversation is heading.

"Oh, yes, right. Well, I had a plan. Mark had told the boys they weren't allowed to bring their lady friends around, or that Malik, Max, and Myles weren't allowed to keep sleeping around. Max, thinking he could do as he pleased didn't listen. So one morning, after the girl left I walked in as Mark distracted him with the third degree while I ran upstairs to poke holes in the condoms," she winces.

"What does this have to do with me or Hope?" not clicking on to what she is trying to say and by looking at Mason's face he has no idea either.

"Denny, you and Mason courted each other in that very room. You used those condoms. We were just cleaning out the room and three were missing. Two of those missing I knew had holes in them."

Then it all clicked into place and I sit back completely shocked and overwhelmed. Everything, and I mean everything, had happened because of a prank, but then I look over to Hope's sleeping form and relax.

"It's okay. As much as I wanted kids when I was older with a steady job and a husband, I wouldn't trade Hope for anything. She's my world and the best thing to ever happen to me," I tell her, but my eyes search for Mason's and when we lock eyes I know he feels the same way.

That moment, the moment she poked holes into the condoms brought me here. I've got a fiancé, a little girl, a home, but most of all, I have a huge ass, wild, crazy family who I love very much.

"You're not mad?"

"Are you mad, Mason?" I ask after shaking my head.

"If it had been anyone else, yes, but it got me you and Hope, so no, I don't care."

"Hold up! What are you doing cleaning out my drawers?" Max pipes up outraged and we all laugh at his expression.

"Max, I'm sure the boys have all seen your collection of porn and *High School Musical* DVD's under your bed," she snaps rolling her eyes, and I watch and listen as all brothers give him shit, laughing at him which just makes me laugh along with them. I love this. Love the banter they share together, it's what a family should be like. It's what I want for Hope.

"This isn't fair. It's invading my privacy. Does Granddad know you've done this?" Max asks completely outraged, thankfully keeping his voice to a low hiss.

"It was his idea to clean your rooms and the rest of the house. The place was starting to stink the street out. Having all you boys in that one house under no supervision was a bad idea. I'm hoping we can convert the two houses as one."

"Are you serious right now?" Max asks.

"I'll be back there soon Joan and will have them doing their chores," Maverick pipes up.

"Well that would be great dear if it wasn't for the fact I'm still doing your dirty laundry. And Max, I'm deadly serious. You either keep that house spotless or I'll be looking in to having it converted someway, one that will still allow Mason and Denny to get out. If that doesn't go through, your Granddad and I will be moving in with you and letting Harlow and Malik stay at our house."

"This is . . . this is just wrong," Max throws out, getting up to the door and leaving.

"Well now that's settled and everything is okay, I better get back to working," Joan says before giving me a kiss on the forehead and checking in on Hope sleeping in her mosses basket. "Such a darling."

We all grin watching her walk to the door. When she opens it Malik is holding his hand up in the air, his knuckles ready to knock on the door. He passes Joan with a nod, and walks into the front room.

"I'm going to put Hope's name on her wall," he tells us.

"Is that safe? She's still only a baby," I ask Mason concerned.

"It's fine. We double and triple checked that we could use it. Plus, it's fast drying so the paint will dry before she goes up to bed," Mason tells me making me relax.

"That's good," I nod, and groan when the door knocks again. This time it's Harlow and she's walking in with some shopping bags full of food and stuff that she left to get us earlier.

"Ahhh, thank you," I gush, going to get up, but she puts her hands up to stop me.

"I got it, you stay there and I'll put them away."

"Thank you so much," I tell her, truly thankful that I get to call her my best friend. She truly has gone fabove and beyond with our friendship the past few weeks.

I hear the shopping bags hit the kitchen floor first before I hear the front door knock again.

"Bloody hell, it's like Piccadilly Circus in here," I groan, really needing some freaking sleep.

Maverick gets up from the floor and answers the door when Myles refuses to get up again after answering the three times. I can barely see the front door from where I'm sitting, but Maverick's huge frame is covering the door way, blocking me from seeing who is on the other side. From the sound of the voice, it's a girl. When he pulls back his expression is wary when he looks at me to Myles.

Wondering what has him on edge I sit up a little straighter in my seat, and gasp when Kayla's tiny frame walks out from behind Maverick's large frame.

Holy shit!!!

"It was you wasn't it, the other witness?" is the first thing I blurt out jumping to my feet.

"Yes," she whispers in a small voice, before looking around the room with wide frightened eyes. It's then I look at everyone and see what she's seeing and can't help but want to cuddle her close. Although all the Carter brothers are soft as teddies, to an outsider they are a bunch of strong, muscled alpha males. With what Kayla has gone through they most likely look like The Hulk to her.

"I'm sorry. Are you okay?" I ask, feeling like shit that the first thing that comes out of my mouth is to question her that. I'm just so surprised to see her. When she moved away I never expected to ever see her again. I've missed her. It's then that tears fill my eyes and I struggle to keep them at bay.

"Yes, can we talk?" she asks looking around the room unsure. "Alone?"

"Um yes, of course," I tell her then look to Mason and give him a look to clear off and take his brothers with him. He nods his head getting what I'm silently telling him, but when my eyes drift to Myles, his face is completely pale, his eyes wide and mouth agape staring at Kayla. I notice Kayla giving him sideward glances and I try to figure out what's running through her mind, but it seems since the last time I saw her she's perfected hiding her emotions. Well, most of them anyway.

"Myles, bro?" Mason calls standing next to him. Myles shakes his head, looks at Mason then back to Kayla and nods his head getting up. He follows Mason out of the room, but not before giving Kayla another one last backward glance.

I knew he said they spoke a few times in the library and once after her attack, but it feels like something else is going on that he totally forgot to mention. The tension in the room was thick enough you could cut into it.

"How are you?" I ask again, feeling awkward about what to say. I gesture for her to take a seat and she does, so I take one down next to her.

"I'm okay, better than I have been in years actually. I needed to come and see you, to explain about why I left things the way I did."

"I understand Kay. You don't need to explain anything to me-"

"I do. I pushed you away. You were my only real friend apart from Charlie. I shouldn't have done that to you, I realise now that I needed you more than I let on, and for that I am sorry. I was so harsh to you, for no reason."

"I understand why Kayla. What happened is not your fault. You did what you did to protect yourself. Did I get upset I couldn't be there for you? Yes. Did I hate you for it? No. I knew you wouldn't have done it maliciously, so please don't threat over it."

"You've always been too kind," she smiles, tears in her eyes.

"So they say," I grin, but then lose it when she looks up at me with so much guilt and sorrow.

"Is the girl . . . " she starts, but then takes a huge swallow. "The girl he . . . is the girl here?" she asks, twiddling her fingers on her lap.

"Harlow?"

"Yes," she nods, her face losing colour, and I can tell she's scared and nervous as hell.

"Hold on I'll go get her," I tell her. "Would you like something to drink?"

"No thank you, I can't stay long," she tells me sadly. I smile sadly back, not wanting her to leave again. Hopefully this time we will remain in touch.

I leave the room and rush into the kitchen where everyone is standing around and waiting. Mason walks up to me first, wrapping me up in his arms. The feel of him has me wanting to cry, to cry for the broken girl that she now is, for the girl she used to be but lost.

"You okay, Baby?" he asks.

"Yeah, just emotional," I whisper. "She wants to see you?" I tell Harlow, who is now standing in Malik's arms. He must have come downstairs when he heard her walk in and looking by the tense expression I can see he's unsure about letting her go.

"Me?"

"Yes, please," I beg her, my eyes pleading with her.

She nods her head before turning to give Malik a kiss, I think more to relax him than anything, and then follows me back into the living room where Kayla nervously awaits.

"Hey," Harlow says, ever the loving person.

"Hey," Kayla replies, trying to smile, but she's so nervous all we manage to get from her, is her bottom lip wobbling before she bursts into tears. Before I can walk over to her and wrap her in my arms Harlow is there pulling her into her arms on the sofa, whispering something into her hair. Movement near the door catches my attention and I turn to find Mason holding Myles back. My curious look matches Mason's, but once Myles sees Harlow has her his shoulders slump and he walks back out of the room without catching Kayla and Harlow's attention.

My attention turns back to Kayla and Harlow on the sofa. Both pull away, but Harlow keeps her hands holding Kayla's and I think it has more to do with giving her strength that she obviously needs at the moment.

"Are you okay now?" Harlow asks softly, while I watch silently. I kneel in front of them, making sure I'm close enough to reach out and grab Kayla's other hand. She flinches when I do, but then realises it's only me and relaxes.

"I'm sorry. I'm so sorry for what he. . . . what he did," she chokes out.

"You have nothing to apologise for," Harlow tells her sternly.

"I do. If I had stood up to my mother none of this would have happened. It happened because I'm too weak to stand up for myself."

"What you did was survive something unthinkable. Kayla, never and I mean never apologise for something *he* did. As for your mother, if she's anything like Denny's then you have every right to be wary."

"Huh?"

"Long story," I butt in, giving her a small smile.

"What I'm trying to say is, you were young. You trusted your mother to know what was best for you. For that you only have your mother to blame, no one else. She's just as bad as him in my eyes."

"I knew what he did was wrong though, it's why I kept all those clothes, why I held onto them and the nightmares for so long. Each night I went to bed and closed my eyes I could feel them, taunting me, laughing at me, but I knew I'd need them. I knew I made a mistake in not going taking action with the police, for listening to my mother, but I was just so scared. After he . . . after he . . . " she chokes out again, her tears falling from her eyes.

"Hey, it's okay, slow down, breathe," I encourage her, not wanting her to have a panic attack. She's been through too much already and from Myles reaction to her crying, I'd say her having a panic attack would give him an aneurism.

"After he . . . raped me, I was in so much pain it killed me to have a shower or a bath. Then when I went to the hospital they did an internal examination which hurt just as much, I didn't want to go through any more pain, I just wanted it to stop. I could have prevented him from harming other girls."

"He didn't get that far," Harlow says softly, her tears falling down her cheeks.

"You don't know?"

"Don't know what?" Harlow asks her warily.

"After the sentencing more victims came forward. Our lawyer seems to think it's because they knew he wouldn't harm them. One girl was nine at the time and lived next door to them. Her mother had complained about the noise coming from their house, so one night he did it to punish her," she tells us, her voice sounding regretful, and sickened.

"Oh my God," Both Harlow and I gasp horrified.

"How old was he?" I ask, regretting the question as soon as it escapes my mouth.

"According to the girl I met, he was twelve."

"You met her?" Harlow asks.

"She asked for me, so when the lawyer asked for my permission I said yes, needing to see if it was my fault, but she was his first victim and was always too scared to tell her mom and when she did, her mother was so scared of the family she moved away."

"But still . . . she was a little girl," I cry out, my eyes immediately wandering over to Hope, who is safely sleeping in her moses basket still.

"I know. She must have been terrified too."

"She was," Kayla tells us sadly. "But it still doesn't help the fact I gave him free reign to rape another three, nearly four girls," she sobs out, her breath hitching.

"Oh my God," Harlow gasps, a sob tearing from her mouth. She reaches up to cover it with her hand, but it's too late, Malik rushes in and is by her side. Kayla sees him and flies out of the chair, landing on the floor with a thud, her hands cowering over her to protect her head. We all stop and stare, and my mind goes into overdrive watching her fear for her life when there is no danger.

"Hey," Malik says gently, moving slowly away from Harlow. "Kayla, do you remember me?"

She slowly moves her hands away from her face and looks around wide eyed and horrified. Her face is bright red, before it drains of colour and more tears fall down her cheeks.

She nods her head 'yes' before looking at me with shame in her eyes. She gets back up, making sure to stay clear from Malik and sits back down in her seat, her fingers clinging to the sofa.

"Then you know I'd never, ever, hurt you, or my brothers. I promise you that with everything I am. Harlow is my girlfriend."

"You are?" She asks, looking to Harlow and seeing her in a new light. "Does he know?"

"He saved me," Harlow tells her sadly.

Kayla nods her head slowly, her expression seeming to look like she's thinking that information over.

"Will those other girls go to trial too?" he asks, obviously listening on the conversation. I turn and notice the other brothers standing with concern in the doorway, Myles further into the room than the others looking at Kayla with such longing. She doesn't seem to have noticed them yet, which I think is a good thing.

"Yes. They were too scared to ever speak up, or to tell anyone in case he hurt them too. So when they found out he was found guilty they went straight to the police," she whispers, still on edge.

"That is really good Kayla, really good. I'm glad you finally got justice, and I know it doesn't change anything, but at least he can't hurt anyone anymore." Malik moves slowly as he speaks, back over to the other side of Harlow, not wanting to scare Kayla again.

"He did though, and that's because of me," she tells him, but doesn't look at him, instead keeps her eyes in her lap.

"No that isn't your fault, Kayla. Do you blame the little girl he raped first?" he asks.

Her head whips up at him. "What? No! Never," she asks completely taken back.

"So why would anyone blame you? The only one to blame is that sick son of a bitch. He doesn't deserve prison, he deserves to be hung."

Kayla winces and cowers back in her seat before turning to look at me. "I'm going to have to go, my dad is waiting outside, but I needed to come and see you. Charlie told me you lived here and that I'd find Harlow here too," she tells me, answering my silent question about how she knew where I lived now.

"You're always welcome here Kayla."

"Thank you," she tells me standing up at the same time Hope starts to cry for her bottle. She jumps at the sound before looking around the room for the cause.

"A baby? I thought you lived here," she says confused.

"I do. Hope is mine," I smile widely.

"Really?" she smiles genuinely and she looks so beautiful it knocks me back a step.

"Yes, want to see her?" I ask and she nods her head, walking slowly over to the moses basket, careful to walk wide around Malik.

"I'll get her," Max hollers from another room, rushing in with a bottle making everyone laugh. Kayla freezes at his sound and looks at me fearfully.

"You're safe," I assure her and she begins to relax a little. She turns a little and I notice a bruise forming at the top her neck and a few on her wrist. I frown looking at them and I know they are recent. My mind is whirling, do I say something? Or should I leave it alone? I don't want to embarrass her, or scare her by mentioning them.

She stares at Myles for a few more seconds before she shakes herself out of it and turns back to me and Hope. She walks closer and touches Hope's tiny fingers.

"She's beautiful," she murmurs, her voice low, and full of envy.

"She is," I agree, then scowl at Max who is standing next to us with a bottle, bib and a nappy tucked under his one arm, holding his arms out for Hope.

"Come on," he whines, looking lovingly at Hope.

"I need to go. Thank you for letting me in and letting me talk to you," she smiles. She turns to Harlow to say something similar and I take the chance to hand Hope over to Max, giving him a glare before grabbing Kayla's attention again.

I wrap her into a hug, mindful when she completely tenses in my embrace, but after a few seconds she relaxes and lifts her arms to hug me back.

"Please don't be a stranger. Call me sometime, or next time you're in town, pop in," I talk into her ear.

She pulls away smiling. "I'm back. I live with my dad now. After what my mom did-" she starts to explain, but then thinks better of it. "Anyway, he's opening another firm, so we're staying in the area. Plus, I need to re-do my exams so I'll be repeating the rest of year twelve at Grayson High," she tells us and I smile big.

"I'm so happy," I gush, squeezing her hands.

"Grayson high? This year?" Myles asks, speaking up for the first time since she walked through the door.

"Yes," Kayla blushes at Myles before looking away.

"So you're moving back . . . here?"

"That's what she said," I tell him, glaring at him from behind Kayla's back.

He looks to Kayla, back to me, then turns and walks out the door. All of us watch the door he walked out of wondering what the hell just happened.

"So you're back for good?" I grin, wondering how Myles is going to cope with her being in the same school as him again. Something tells me he isn't prepared to stay away from her.

"I am," she smiles.

The end
Myles and Kayla's story coming soon

MORE BOOKS FROM LISA HELEN GREY

STANDALONE NOVELS
If I could I'd wish it all away

FORGOTTEN SERIES
Better left forgotten Book One
Obsession Book Two
Forgiven Book Three

CARTER BROTHER SERIES
Malik (Book One) ~ Available
Mason (Book Two) NOW available.
Myles (Book three) coming soon
Max (Book Four) ~ coming 2016
Maverick (Book Five) coming 2016
Evan ~ (3.5 Novella) ~ coming soon. This book will be about Evan, Denny's brother.

ACKNOWLEDGEMENTS

Due to the time I have left to get Mason published, my acknowledgements will be short and sweet.

I'm hoping that everyone who has helped me during the Carter Brother series process knows how truly thankful I am for all their help.

I found parts of this book really hard to write, but with my good friends, Rachel Osbourne, Colette Goodchild and Charlotte Perry, I managed to get Mason typed out. It was a long process, but I got there in the end.

The reviews from Malik have been outstanding. I honestly never expected the responses I had when people read Malik. I had email after email asking for the next book, when it will be out and so on. I had people sending me pictures of their own Malik, writing reviews that had me in tears, and all sorts. I'm just praying that Mason does the series justice, and you'll keep reading the series. I'm excited for you all to meet Myles.

I will never be able to thank you readers enough for the courage you give me to keep on writing. You guys ROCK!!!

As usual, my beta's have been amazing and couldn't ask for a better team. My editor, Lori, thank you so much for helping me. You rock! And hope you feel better soon.

To Cassy Roop at Pink Ink designs, thank you again for the amazing covers. You really are a star.

Please, if you enjoyed Mason, think about leaving a review on Amazon, Nook, Kobo, or Goodreads, I love hearing from you guys.

All in all, thank you to everyone who has been one step behind me on this journey, whether you are mentioned or not, know that I will always be thankful to you.

Bloggers, readers, editors, friends, beta's, and family, I love you.

Printed in Poland
by Amazon Fulfillment
Poland Sp. z o.o., Wrocław